Simon & Schuster's

GUIDE TO
Herbs and Spices

Gualtiero Simonetti

Photography by Italo Pergher

Edited by Stanley Schuler

A FIRESIDE BOOK
PUBLISHED BY SIMON & SCHUSTER INC.
New York London Toronto Sydney Tokyo Singapore

ACKNOWLEDGMENTS

The Publisher wishes to thank the following for their invaluable assistance:
Bottega di Lunga Vita, Verona; Maria Pia and Patrizio Breseghello, Solesino,
Padova; P.C. EDA S.p.A., Verona; Luigi Signorato, Verona

FIRESIDE
Simon & Schuster Building
Rockefeller Center
1230 Avenue of the Americas
New York, New York 10020

© 1990 Arnoldo Mondadori Editore S.p.A., Milan
© 1990 in the English translation Arnoldo Mondadori Editore S.p.A., Milan

English translation by John Gilbert

Art Director: Giorgio Seppi
Symbols by Paolo Casti
Tables by Lino Simeoni

First published in Italian in 1990
by Arnoldo Mondadori Editore S.p.a.
under the title *Tutto Spezie, Aromi e Profumi*

Typeset by Rowland Phototypesetting Ltd, Bury St Edmunds, Suffolk, England
Printed and bound in Spain by
Artes Graficas, Toledo
D.L.TO:2158–1990

10 9 8 7 6 5 4 3 2 1

Library of Congress Cataloging in Publication Data
Simonetti, Walter.
    Simon & Schuster's guide to herbs and spices/Walter Simonetti:
edited by Stanley Schuler.
      p.   cm.
Translated from Italian.
"A Fireside book."
    Includes bibliographical reference and index.
    ISBN 0-671-73489-X
    1. Herbs.   2. Herb gardening.   3. Spice plants.   4. Herbs – utilization.
5. Spices.   6 Herbs – Pictorial works.   7. Spice plants – Pictorial works.
I. Schuler, Stanley.   II. Title.   III. Title: Simon and Schuster's Guide to
herbs and spices.
IV. Title: Guide to herbs and spices.
SB351.H5S573 1990
635'.7—dc20
                                              90-19615
                                              CIP

CONTENTS

KEY TO SYMBOLS

used fresh

used dried

cultivated

wild

cosmetics, perfumes

natural remedies

liquors and drinks

teas, infusions

Ever since I first became interested in plants, I have noticed how certain divisions have emerged in the investigation of the subject, depending on whether the emphasis is on botany, biology, forestry, agronomy, pharmacy or cultivation, while at the same time the specialist compartments have often overlapped in their information.

The spirit of enquiry and the urge to deepen our knowledge of the realm of plants makes it ever more necessary to acquire information on a worldwide scale so as to take into consideration all the elements that regulate the life of plants and that determine their possible uses. Study has reinforced my belief that we cannot ignore the repercussions exerted by plants upon human affairs, and not even in the sense of epoch-making developments such as man's transition from hunter–gatherer to farmer, but in the context of the everyday activities of individuals and peoples. Take, for example, the olive and Mediterranean civilization, the spices of the Orient and the voyages of exploration, the botanical origin of medicines, the food plants from America, the tulips of Holland, potato peronospora and emigration from Ireland, maize and pellagra, the vine and cryptogamic diseases, and, of course, coffee and tea.

There have always been close links between plants and food. From time immemorial man has learned to distinguish beneficial plants from those likely to cause problems; and in the former group, to separate those that are edible from those merely providing aromas and scents.

Most of the plants described in this book are known as officinal plants (meaning that they are utilized in the laboratory of apothecaries or herb and spice stores) or medicinal plants. And since we are concerned here only with plants used in the kitchen primarily as accessories, to improve the taste, the smell and even the appearance of main dishes, these have been grouped together as herbs and spices.

In former times herbs and spices and medicaments went hand-in-hand; and today the sale of all these products has been revived. Many of us, asked to name a medicinal plant, will automatically think of castor oil, harboring painful memories of an enforced cure based on swallowing spoonfuls of that unpleasantly viscous liquid, a task made all the more difficult by the slices of lemon stuffed into the mouth to allay the taste. Fortunately things have changed since then and even cod-liver oil (another bugbear for children earlier this century) is now served up as an appetizing orange syrup preparation.

A herb, on the other hand, is likely to be associated with the idea of food preparation, or with drink, such as a glass of herbal tea. When we mention spices, our thoughts turn to a product such as pepper, used for such a wide variety of culinary purposes. And finally there are the officinal plants used as a source of many important fragrant substances: the incense that has been offered for thousands of years in religious rituals and the more mundane deodorant stick for personal hygiene are both derived from the same plants that the ancient Egyptians gathered and imported from distant, mysterious lands.

This guide, which deals with aromatic plants, therefore has a very modern relevance, consonant with the rediscovery of a healthy lifestyle through the use of natural products; among these, an important role has always been played by those which in times gone by were called drugs, namely spices and herbs.

Although due mention is made in the text accompanying the plates of the medicinal properties of the various spices and herbs, emphasis is placed primarily on their uses in flavoring, improving, preserving, and diversifying everyday foods. A distinction is made between two principal groups: spices, which come mainly from tropical countries, and herbs, which grow in temperate regions and can therefore be easily cultivated. Among the plants selected as individual entries are some that are used in the preparation of food, not as the main ingredient but as an element giving the various dish a particular taste; thus a number of edible wild plants appear in the section on herbs. And the list is appropriately extended to include all those plants that provide infusions, among them stimulants such as coffee and tea.

There are descriptions, too, of plants (many of which also play a role in the kitchen) that are used as ingredients in the manufacture of perfumes.

One section provides practical information concerning the use, everyday or otherwise, of spices and herbs; and general recipes and suggestions as to the compatibility and particular applications of the principal essences are also given. Distinction is also made between the use of such substances for cooking or as ingredients for drinks because both the objectives and methods of preparation are often quite different. Finally, where liquors are concerned, reference is made to colorants of vegetable origin which, in some cases, coincide with the principal extracts of herbs.

The plates, which are arranged alphabetically by Latin names, are preceded by a systematic chart of families, genera and species which presents the taxonomic positions of the species discussed and illustrated.

The text for the plates gives the following information:

scientific name; family to which plant belongs; common name in English, German (G), French (F) and Italian (I); origin; botanical description; possible cultivation; the constituents and their uses.

The symbols accompanying the individual entries have been devised in accordance with criteria of use and environment: thus they indicate whether the herb is wild or cultivated, fragrant or unscented, used fresh or dried, intended for liquors or medicinal purposes and, finally, whether or not utilized for infusions.

A glossary lists and defines technical terms used in the text.

The bibliography indicates reference sources consulted in the compilation of this book and, where appropriate, works providing more detailed information on certain subjects.

The index which, like the plates, is arranged alphabetically by scientific name, contains synonyms and common names, thus linking the various entries and textual references.

The map shows the principal zones of the various spices. The numbers in parentheses indicate how the countries rank worldwide as producers/exporters of the spices.

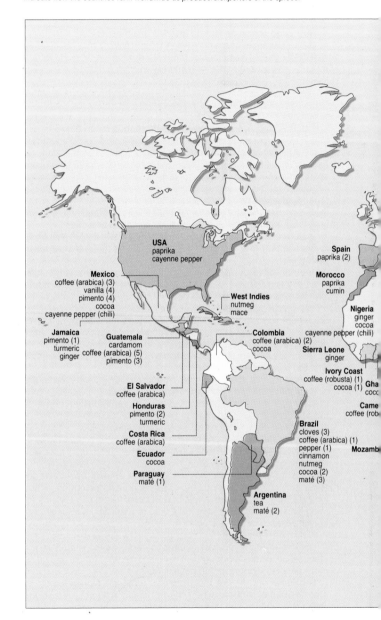

USA
paprika
cayenne pepper

Spain
paprika (2)

Morocco
paprika
cumin

Mexico
coffee (arabica) (3)
vanilla (4)
pimento (4)
cocoa
cayenne pepper (chili)

West Indies
nutmeg
mace

Nigeria
ginger
cocoa

Jamaica
pimento (1)
turmeric
ginger

Guatemala
cardamom
coffee (arabica) (5)
pimento (3)

Colombia
coffee (arabica) (2)
cocoa

cayenne pepper (chili)

Sierra Leone
ginger

El Salvador
coffee (arabica)

Ivory Coast
coffee (robusta) (1)
cocoa (1)

Gha
coco

Honduras
pimento (2)
turmeric

Came
coffee (rob

Costa Rica
coffee (arabica)

Brazil
cloves (3)
coffee (arabica) (1)
pepper (1)
cinnamon
nutmeg
cocoa (2)
maté (3)

Ecuador
cocoa

Mozamb

Paraguay
maté (1)

Argentina
tea
maté (2)

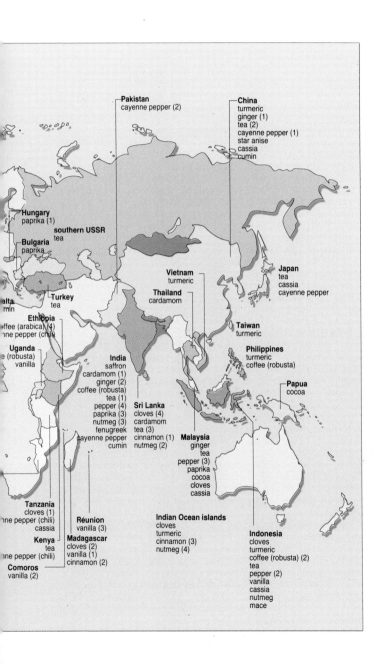

Pakistan
cayenne pepper (2)

China
turmeric
ginger (1)
tea (2)
cayenne pepper (1)
star anise
cassia
cumin

Hungary
paprika (1)

southern USSR
tea

Bulgaria
paprika

alta
min

Turkey
tea

Ethiopia
ffee (arabica) (4)
nne pepper (chili)

Uganda
e (robusta)
vanilla

Vietnam
turmeric

Thailand
cardamom

Japan
tea
cassia
cayenne pepper

Taiwan
turmeric

Philippines
turmeric
coffee (robusta)

Papua
cocoa

India
saffron
cardamom (1)
ginger (2)
coffee (robusta)
tea (1)
pepper (4)
paprika (3)
nutmeg (3)
fenugreek
cayenne pepper
cumin

Sri Lanka
cloves (4)
cardamom
tea (3)
cinnamon (1)
nutmeg (2)

Malaysia
ginger
tea
pepper (3)
paprika
cocoa
cloves
cassia

Tanzania
cloves (1)
nne pepper (chili)
cassia

Kenya
tea
nne pepper (chili)

Comoros
vanilla (2)

Réunion
vanilla (3)

Madagascar
cloves (2)
vanilla (1)
cinnamon (2)

Indian Ocean islands
cloves
turmeric
cinnamon (3)
nutmeg (4)

Indonesia
cloves
turmeric
coffee (robusta) (2)
tea
pepper (2)
vanilla
cassia
nutmeg
mace

ORIGIN AND HISTORY OF SPICES

The fact that certain plants give out pleasant aromas and that it is possible to extract their essences has been recognized since ancient times when, simply by distilling the parts of plants that were particularly rich in active principles, essential oils were obtained. And although it may seem that the use of aromas and perfumes is geared more to pleasure than necessity, the influential role that many of them play has to be emphasized.

The scent and taste of certain plants were surely associated by primitive man with magical and propitiatory effects; the presence of plants or of their toxic parts was a tangible sign that such species had links with demons, as against others which, with their medicinal properties, had obviously been provided by beneficent deities.

Man the hunter—gatherer was continually obliged to search for new sources of food; and although lacking botanical knowledge, primitive man collected plants of every kind, quickly learning to recognize, for example, the aromatic labiates which, although not true and proper food plants, give out a pleasant smell and can improve the taste of food substances. Nor was it just a question of taste: the mixing of certain foods with particular herbs proved an aid to digestion and very soon it became a common practice to accompany a meal with a few aromatic seeds or to chew these raw.

In the course of time the use of plants and particularly spices, herbs and perfumes came to be associated with the development of individual cultures. In China, some 5,000 years ago, the emperor Shen Nung assembled the first documentation on herbs. The Chinese were already eating cloves in the fourth century B.C., and a century later this spice, which among other things was prized in antiquity as an aphrodisiac, was being grown in the Moluccas.

In the Fertile Crescent those scrupulous bookkeepers, the Sumerians, handed down their testimony of hundreds of plants on clay tablets (3000–2000 B.C.). At Ur, in Mesopotamia, the people ate cereals and vegetables, flavoring them with watercress and mustard leaves, and washing everything down with beer, which they invented; this was not yet flavored with hops but probably with some local aromatic plant. The technique of brewing was then passed on to Egypt; here the basic food consisted of cereals prepared in liquid and often flavored.

The Babylonians grew bay, thyme, and coriander, and exported herbs, spices, and aromatic oils to Egypt, which also imported from the Orient star anise, cumin, fenugreek, opium, thyme, and saffron, used in food, medicine, cosmetics, and perfumery. Through their commerce with Asia, the Egyptians were also familiar with cinnamon and incense. Knowledge of aromatic plants was extremely important to them because production of oils and essences was not only vital to earthly existence but also in the attempt to conquer death through the process of embalming.

The regions of the Fertile Crescent therefore constituted an ideal bridge between the Orient and the Mediterranean basin, with a thriving trade in agricultural plants, herbs and spices.

On the Mediterranean island of Minoan Crete the plants of the families Labiatae and Umbelliferae, full of scent and flavor, were household items, then as now used for accompanying simple dishes that consisted mainly of vegetables including onions and garlic (the latter, however, being reserved by the Greeks for the lower classes). The Greeks also imported sesame and poppy, used in the form of aromatic seeds, from Asia Minor. The seeds of umbellifers (coriander, cumin) were utilized for flavoring a mixture of roasted barley meal; the basic food, in fact, was a kind of soup (*kikeon*), consisting of ordinary barley meal seasoned with cheese, wine, linseed, and aromatic labiates. Barley, still further diluted, was used in the preparation of a type of infusion (*ptisáne*), obtained by filtering with water and which was to provide the name (*tisane*) for all drinks so prepared. Aromatic herbs were also employed in a fish sauce (*gáron*) that was probably adopted later by the Romans for their *garum*.

The Etruscans (and in all likelihood the Latins) cultivated several species of cereals and also exploited woodland resources such as broad-leaved garlic (ramson), crow garlic, acorns, chestnuts, and beechnuts. Like other Mediterranean peoples, they associated such plants with woodland deities, giving pride of place to the myrtle and the laurel.

As the centuries passed, people devoted themselves more and more to non-essentials, seeking and demanding objects and products that would improve their daily lives. Tastes, smells and perfumes took on considerable significance at a time when direct relationship with others was the basic means of communication. Indeed, the improvement of food by adding spices, the search for products with stimulating qualities, the quest for perfumes designed to disguise natural body odors, were the motivating forces of the keen exchange between the zones of production and the consumers of such merchandise.

Among the earliest specialized traders in spices, herbs and perfumes were the Phoenicians. We have detailed information about the structure of their ships and the valuable goods they transported; but of the substances themselves, by definition far less durable, there are all too few traces.

The Bible tells how the Phoenician fleet returning from the lands of Ophir (probably modern Ethiopia) carried, in addition to metals and precious stones, ivory, rare animals, and sandalwood.

Together with polychrome glass, much in demand in the Mediterranean, the speedy ships were laden with fish sauce (*garum*) and probably balms, scented oils, and essences, packed in small glass vessels. To expand this traffic the Phoenicians renounced the idea of territorial conquest and, instead of establishing a kingdom or an empire, set up colonies and trading stations, far less difficult to maintain. This strategy was readopted almost two thousand years later by the European traders. In this manner they not only supplied their own countries with foreign products but also conducted a two-way trade with other countries. In the remains of the Punic ship of Motya, near Marsala, 22 centuries after the wreck, some myrtle branches were recovered, the berries of which had been used for flavoring meat. There were also residues in containers of *Cannabis indica* which, when infused or mixed with bread, may have been intended to stimulate the rowing endeavors of the slaves.

In the Carthaginian kitchen, in addition to honey, employed as a binder and sweetener, much use was made of garlic, which flavored the basic dish of the time, a soup (*puls punica*) containing flour, cheese, eggs, and honey.

With the expansion of Carthage, commercial fortunes derived from trade tended to be linked with the development of agriculture, a change underlined by the fact that the only Carthaginian text translated into Latin, according to the utilitarian notions characteristic of the Romans, was a treatise on agriculture in 28 books by Mago, as mentioned by Pliny and Varro.

From earliest times, the difficulty of preserving foodstuffs necessitated ample use of salt. It was this that probably originated the need to vary the taste of food with various flavors; salt itself was flavored with herbs and pungent seeds (*sal conditus*). Salt was also used for preserving condiments such as sauces. Soldiers were paid in salt (*salarium*) and aromatic herbs and pepper were added to make it taste more agreeable.

The Roman kitchen, especially under the Empire, was described by Apicius in the ten books of his work *De re coquinaria*. Bulbous vegetables such as onions, garlic, and leeks formed the basis of the Roman diet; in the modern kitchen these plants are treated mainly as flavorings but up to the present century they furnished an important supply of starch in the everyday diet. "Wild" vegetables such as burnet and cresses were sensibly used and brassicaceous plants like radish, horseradish and mustard were grown for their sharp taste, as well as mallow, eaten in salads. Instead of carrots, which were not yet known in the varieties with which we are familiar today, white-rooted parsnips were cultivated, and other umbellifers such as lovage and alexanders (*Smyrnium olusatrum*), a kind of wild celery, were also popular. Herbs were important because they helped to preserve vegetables, whether cultivated or wild, which were usually covered with brine or vinegar (*acetaria*). Olives preserved in brine were given extra flavor with myrtle, bay, fennel or even lentisk (a common constituent of mediterranean scrub vegetation). Coriander and cumin were used for conserving meat; and herbs served to improve the taste of such preserved foods.

Other ingredients included dill, aniseed, coriander and fennel; but far more important was lovage, nowadays confined to central European regions. Botanical identification of the *laser* or *laserpicium* (or *silphium*) is uncertain; this was a resinous product, obtained from a plant of the genus *Ferula* from Cyrenaica, the stems of which were lightly scraped; when it fell into disuse it was replaced by a Persian ferula or asafetida. An important part of the diet was made up of fish, regularly flavored with herbs, notably cumin, mint, and pepper. Fish, too, was preserved in salt and herbs. Milk, which was generally that of the goat, was flavored with lovage and other plants used in the preparation of cheese (thyme and other labiates).

Cane sugar was known, but only as a rare product, brought by caravan from the Orient; the universal sweetener was honey, particularly the type produced by aromatic plants such as lavender, rosemary, oregano, etc.

In the first century B.C., the cedar appeared in the Mediterranean, and its leaves and fruit were both used in medicine and cooking; in the late Empire lemons were already being grown in glasshouses, this fruit having long been imported from Africa and the Orient.

Among the seeds most frequently in demand for sauces and for direct consumption were pine seeds and pistachios. Poppy seeds were used for flavoring bread, sprinkled over honey or on simple desserts, cooked on bay leaves or made into sedative infusions ceremonially offered in the evening to young brides.

Wine, a drink preferred to beer by the Greeks and Egyptians, was kept in bottles lined on the inside with pine resin and also colored with saffron or scented with flowers of elder, bitter almonds, cinnamon or umbellifer seeds. Oil of myrtle helped to improve poor quality wines. Wine to which rue, reputedly an aphrodisiac, had been added was

family	genus and species	active principles
Aquifoliaceae	*Ilex paraguariensis* St. Hil.	caffeine in leaves
Illiciaceae	*Illicium verum* Hook f.	ethereal oils in fruits
Lauraceae	*Cinnamomum aromaticum* Nees	ethereal oils in bark
Lauraceae	*Cinnamomum zeylanicum* Bl.	ethereal oils in bark
Leguminosae	*Trigonella foenum-graecum* L.	plant with diverse principles
Malvaceae	*Hibiscus sabdariffa* L.	sepals with acidic principles
Myristicaceae	*Myristica fragrans* Hout.	ethereal oils in seeds (in aril)
Myrtaceae	*Eugenia caryophyllata* Thunb.	essential oils in flowers and inflorescences
Myrtaceae	*Pimenta dioica* (L.) Merr.	ethereal oils in fruits
Orchidaceae	*Vanilla planifolia* Andr.	ethereal oils in fruits
Papaveraceae	*Papaver somniferum* L.	fruits with alkaloids, aromatic seeds
Pedaliaceae	*Sesamum indicum* L.	aromatic seeds
Piperaceae	*Piper nigrum* L.	pungent principles in fruit
Rubiaceae	*Cinchona calysaya* Wedd.	plant with bitter principles
Rubiaceae	*Coffea arabica* L.	caffeine in seeds
Rubiaceae	*Coffea robusta* Lindl.	caffeine in seeds
Solanaceae	*Capsicum frutescens* L.	pungent principles in fruit
Sterculiaceae	*Cola acuminata* Schott. et Endl.	caffeine in seeds
Sterculiaceae	*Theobroma cacao* L.	theobromine in seeds
Theaceae	*Camellia sinensis* (L.) O. Kuntze	caffeine in leaves
Umbelliferae	*Cuminum cyminum* L.	ethereal oils in fruits
Umbelliferae	*Ferula assa-foetida* L.	root with aromatic resin
Zingiberaceae	*Alpinia officinarum* Hance	ethereal oils in rhizome
Zingiberaceae	*Elettaria cardamomum* (L.) Maton	ethereal oils in seeds
Zingiberaceae	*Zingiber officinale* Rosc.	ethereal oils in rhizome

Miniature of a fourteenth-century manuscript showing the departure of Niccolò, Matteo, and Marco Polo from Venice. The power and wealth of Venice depended on her fleet, and the swift galleys used for escorting the merchant ships that set sail twice a year for the ports of the eastern Mediterranean were built in the city's arsenal.

particularly popular, but in this form it could be an irritant and poisonous. Must was flavored with fenugreek, vinegar with mint. And special liquors were prepared with infusions of absinthe, myrtle, pepper, lentisk or the flowers of roses and violets.

The most famous sauce used by the Romans was *garum*: this was made with aromatic herbs (dill, savory, rue, mint, etc.), fish (particularly mackerel) and salt. Other sauces were obtained with aromatic wine. *Garum* was a product to be used sparingly, diluted with water or vinegar or even with exotic spices such as ginger or pepper. Pepper, which was extremely costly, reached Rome only after 100 B.C.; it was also used as a medicament. Evidence of its high value is provided by the fact that Alaric, when he sacked Rome, discovered 5,000 pounds of it stored in the state coffers. Ginger, spikenard, cinnamon, cloves, and nutmegs were all brought to the Mediterranean region by caravans from Samarkand.

The Romans also ate a sausage seasoned with myrtle berries (*murtatum*), a precursor of the modern mortadella; instead of very expensive pepper, fruits of the agnus castus or chaste tree were used, the only problem being that these have anaphrodisiac effects. Whereas all facts relating to commerce and use of foodstuffs were confined to oral traditions, the medicinal properties of plants were soon cataloged and handed down in treatises. Hippocrates (460–370 B.C.) described 400 species and their properties, while Theophrastus (370–285 B.C.), in his *On the History of Plants* and *On the Causes of Plants*, proposed the basis for an attempted classification. In the first century A.D. Dioscorides described, in what was to remain a groundwork for medieval herbals until 1600, the names and properties of 600 plants. Pliny the Elder, his contemporary, assembled legends and current practices in his massive *Natural History*.

Roman culture, which spread via the Empire as far as the misty regions of northern Europe, was of course more closely linked with the Mediterranean, but at least the Romans brought with them the tastes of the south, with seeds and seedlings of garlic, parsley, dill, savory, mint, thyme, and sage (this was a phenomenon of all the major migrations and settlements), and introduced to continental Europe the cultivation of fennel, borage, parsley, rosemary, and thyme.

Trade with the Orient, whence came cinnamon, cloves, ginger, cardamom, pepper, and indigo, was thrown into crisis with the decline of the Empire and, as a result, spices became very expensive. But there were always commercial links with Constantinople, through which trade in goods such as salt and salted meat could be carried out with the East.

When the Roman Empire fell, maritime traffic was restricted to small ships engaged in coastal navigation that carried limited quantities of costly merchandise.

During the eighth century trade in spices and perfumes revived. The Arabs, sailing from ports in Asia Minor, introduced saffron (*za'faran* = yellow) throughout the Mediterranean. It reached Spain by the ninth century. They refined chemical science and techniques: the Persian Avicenna (tenth century), in his *Canon of Medicine*, described the distillation of essential oils.

Spices and manufactured goods from the Orient were set fair to revive the flagging fortunes of bold entrepreneurs; and the first to profit from the European craving for foreign merchandise was Venice. In addition to silk from Damascus, Venetian ships carried spices which, at a time when tea and coffee were still unknown, helped to relieve the monotony and sparseness of the medieval kitchen; so, making their appearance on the dinner tables of the wealthy were luxuries such as ginger (cooked, raw or as seasoning), red-rooted galingale (wild ginger) from China, nutmeg, cloves, cinnamon, and pepper, regarded as black gold in the Mediterranean. Pepper was added to everything, from meat to wine and desserts. As in Roman times, it was universal currency. The Jews had to pay their taxes in pepper.

Alongside these products appeared others designed for use either as medicine or food, including sugar cane, saffron, aromatic substances such as incense, benzoin (sent by the Sultans of Egypt as a gift to the Doges), balsam, aloes, spikenard, and sandalwood. And still the list was not exhausted: madder for dyeing, shellac and gum tragacanth, alum (a mineral used for fixing dyes), pearls and precious stones. Such marvels were brought by the Arabs to their ports and transported by caravans to the outposts of the Christian world. At Trebizond, on the Black Sea, and at Antioch, Laodicea and

Alexandria, on the shores of the Moslem Mediterranean, the Byzantines loaded them and shipped them to Constantinople, the great transit center.

Access to the markets of the East spread the knowledge of other peoples, forms of government and, above all, different religions. Then, as now, money could open every door, and if cash was in short supply, craft products could be bartered. Venice engaged in this exchange of goods on a limited scale by offering what little she had, salt. Meanwhile invasions by warriors from Turkestan had closed the land routes to the traders in skins, amber, and honey who journeyed from the North Sea to the Black Sea. Venice was the collection point for the products of Flanders which crossed central Europe and the Alps to reach the Adriatic; and from there they went on to the Orient. After the Crusades Pisa and Genoa also shared in this commerce; as recompense for transporting soldiers, they obtained trading stations at Antioch and Laodicea, in the new Christian states of the East; and the spice route was thus opened to the various maritime republics.

The Serenissima was by this time steadily increasing her power, thanks in some measure to the development of events in Europe. She retained predominance in the pepper trade from Egypt, the country that was France's destination for a new Crusade in the twelfth century. Venice, in order not to lose her lucrative monopoly, shrewdly offered to furnish transport for troops in return for a considerable amount of money. The crusaders were delayed, however, trapped for the winter and unable to embark or pay. The Fourth Crusade eventually set sail but the crusaders, in order to pay for the voyage, agreed to assist Venice in the conquest of Zara, on the Dalmatian coast, which they captured not from the Moslems but from the Catholic king of Hungary; at Zara they also acceded to the request for aid by Isaac Angelus, son of the deposed *basileus* of Byzantium. In 1203 the Venetian fleet with the crusaders on board arrived in Constantinople to reinstate Isaac Angelus on the throne; a revolution provided the pretext for sacking the city, carried out by Doge Enrico Dandolo with merciless precision. Apart from saving Egypt and her own pepper trade, Venice had come away with a quantity of plunder unequalled in history!

The ships of Venice were trading galleasses with a single deck, 165 ft (50 m) long and 36 ft (11 m) wide, normally propelled by oars and put under sail only in the open sea (they could also be warships, when they were armed with bombards and gunners). The ships followed precise courses: in July they left the lagoon for Istria (N.W. Yugoslavia) to stock up and then headed down the Dalmatian coast to Corfu where the protecting troops were landed. Encircling Greece, the merchant ships split into groups for Constantinople, the Black Sea and Tana on the Sea of Azov, taking on furs, salted fish, caviar, and goods that had crossed Asia from China and India. In the fifteenth century Mohammed II blocked this route; so Venice headed instead for Syria and Egypt, bringing them choice goods from Flanders, Lombardy, and Florence, and returning with more than two tons of spices and a 100 percent profit on the sale. At the peak of her splendor, Venice boasted a fleet of hundreds of ships totaling 40,000 tons. The spices brought in by the Venetians were distributed through Europe by German merchants who had their own warehouse on the Grand Canal, the Fondaco dei Tedeschi.

The Normans, when they conquered England, introduced European customs including the use of pepper in the kitchen. In the twelfth century the London-based corporation of pepper suppliers did a roaring trade, and the term "peppercorn rent" subsequently entered the language to signify a nominal rent in perpetuity.

Spices, increasingly in demand, became a veritable status symbol and ever more costly. People less well off managed as best they could by using substitute wild species that provided similar flavors.

The fifteenth century saw the first great voyages of exploration, not in galleasses but in ships that were very different: the galleons, riding higher in the water, with three or four masts of square sails and a single lateen rigged sail behind. The Portuguese succeeded in dominating the oceans with these vessels, rounding Africa and reaching Calcutta in 1498. Thus they opened the way to direct trade in spices, which thereafter were mainly transported by sea.

Ginger, in the areas where it was produced, cost one third of the price charged in Alexandria; and a hundredweight of pepper cost only a few ducats, against 70 in Venice. Financed by Florentine bankers, Vasco da Gama in 1504 brought back to Europe 5,000 tons of pepper and 35,000 hundredweight of other spices; the profits from this venture were around 400 percent! The Portuguese blockaded the Venetian fleet in the Mediterranean. Dutch ships sailed south to Lisbon to sell goods from northern and central Europe, and then returned to Antwerp, which became the continent's trading center.

Venice did not give up the fight: in the pursuit of Mediterranean red coral, the Arabs opened gaps in the Portuguese blockade at Malabar, once again supplying Europe with identical quality merchandise at competitive prices; in fact, problems of conservation often arose on Portuguese galleons, with some goods becoming valueless. In 1509 Venice once more boasted the finest Indian spices.

Successive prolonged wars against the Turks, designed to limit the latter's expansion, resulted in the closure of Mediterranean ports and the gradual decline of Venice, which a century later was faced by the expansionist policies of Holland. The Dutch, in fact, were soon playing a major role; having defeated the Spaniards at Gibraltar (1607), they sailed to the Indies and proceeded methodically and relentlessly to buy up all the available pepper, none of which any longer came directly to Venice, and was imported there from western sources. Meanwhile the exhausting conflict with the Turks had wrenched away all Venice's trading bases, island after island and port after port. Nothing would ever be the same again: not even the alliance with Austria and the consequent victory of Lepanto (1571) would change things. Other powers were from now on to control the trade in spices.

In 1581, furthermore, England entered the fray, setting up the

Levant Company to sell tin and engage in direct traffic of goods. It snatched the trade in wine and raisins from Venice, which meanwhile developed her manufacturing potential by exporting to the Orient glass, lace and materials in exchange for spices.

Outside Europe there was fierce competition for control of the network of trade routes associated with the principal products of the Orient. In his first voyage to the East, Vasco da Gama found nutmeg trees in the Moluccas, thus breaking the Arab monopoly. The Dutch conquered these islands in the fifteenth century, and so total, in turn, was their monopoly that in the mid eighteenth century, in order to raise the price of nutmeg, excess supplies from the crop were burned in Amsterdam. In 1776 the French smuggled nutmeg and clove plants into Mauritius. The British East India Company did the same in the nineteenth century, sending many trees to Calcutta and Ceylon, and also, of course, to Kew Gardens.

In 1800 the Sultan of Zanzibar instituted the planting of clove trees, smuggled from their zones of origin, thus making the island the most important center for these spices in Africa.

Ceylon was the source of cinnamon, which was gathered from trees in the wild by native Tamils and Singalese; they sold it first to the Arabs and later to Portuguese and Dutch traders. It was De Koke, a Dutchman, who successfully initiated the first plantation in 1765; this activity continued even after the English conquest of 1796.

Vanilla, unknown prior to the sixteenth century, was already being cultivated in Mexico at the time of the Spanish conquest. This was the only country to grow it until 1846 when the Dutch plantations in Java and the French in Réunion went into production; in 1807, however, multiplication from cuttings of plants taken from botanical gardens had met with success.

Because of the periodic outbreak of pandemic disease which has scourged the world from medieval to modern times, the need for a more hygienic way of life within the home eventually came to be recognized. Aromatic plants were believed to have the power of warding off plague and disease; and to this end stacks of juniper were set afire in the streets. Oregano, cinnamon, camphor and garlic were widely used (and indeed we now know that these do possess germicidal properties).

In continental Europe study into the growing and preserving of plants was undertaken primarily by the monasteries, which emerged as veritable centers of medical practice. Most monasteries laid out gardens of "simples," containing the principal known medicinal plants, grown for pharmaceutical purposes; still there was, however, a prejudice against cultivated plants, wild species being regarded as more efficacious. As a result of this ferment of research, the Botanic Gardens of Padua and the Jardin des Plantes in Paris were founded.

Increasing importance was devoted to the applied sciences. The texts on the plants of the eleventh century had been based exclusively on Greek (Hippocrates and Dioscorides) and Roman (Galen) works. The need for more detailed knowledge of plants in accordance with modern criteria led to the publication of many books. In 1530 Otto von Brunfels brought out his *Herbarium vivae eicones*; and in 1551 William Turner published the *Newe Herball* in England, describing 238 species. The best known work on the subject, however, was John Gerard's *Herball* or *General Historie of Plantes* (1597), which even included American plants such as the potato and tomato, then called the love apple. In 1652 Nicholas Culpeper published *The English Physitian*, in which plants and astrology were intermingled. In America Nicolò Monardes, a Spanish doctor, collated information on the plants of the New World in 1569 (published in English in 1577). And in the eighteenth century the religious sect of Shakers in the United States set up a "utopian" community based on agriculture and in particular the collection and production of medicinal and aromatic plants.

In 1664 the *Kräuter Buch*, a three-volume work in German by the doctor Jakob Theodor Tabernaemontanus, was published in Basel. This contained 3,000 plants known or used in Europe, both wild and cultivated, of agricultural or ornamental interest; it described "many medicinal plants for external and internal diseases, of humans as well as of animals, with the use made of them, with drinks, syrups, preserves, waters, powders, extracts, ointments and poultices." The work was thus of interest both from the naturalistic and practical viewpoint, and the frontispiece described it as suitable for "doctors, pharmacists, barbers, smiths, gardeners, cooks, cellarmen, midwives, fathers of the family and all lovers of medicine." The book, which quoted many other previous works, represented a true summary of contemporary knowledge and was for a long time used in central Europe as a reference for all problems relating to plants.

In modern Europe, in addition to important tropical species, it later became possible and desirable to grow and sell herbs from temperate regions (coriander, fennel, mustard, cumin, etc.). As a rule these were cultivated on a small scale on family plots.

The use of aromatic plants decreased in towns and cities with the onset of the industrial revolution, but herbs and spices continued to play an important role in country kitchens. In countries that suffered most during the two World Wars, the collection of wild plants and the use of herbs helped to supplement the sparse diet, at least providing the vitamin content necessary for survival.

In the twentieth century the production of "natural" herbs and spices by chemical processes has made many principles readily available at low cost, mostly utilized by industry. It is not by chance that standards currently in force define as "natural aromatic substances" not only parts of edible plants and their derivatives but also aromatic substances produced by chemical synthesis, the commonest being vanilla.

HISTORY OF STIMULATING AND AROMATIC BEVERAGES

Man has always been fascinated by the inviting aroma of beverages produced by infusion; the ritual associated with their preparation as well as their stimulating properties help to account for the success of the principal drinks of this nature which are enjoyed today: tea, coffee and cocoa.

Tea.   The first mention of tea in Europe to be found is that of the Venetian Giovanni Ramusio in 1559, who drew attention to a drink called *sciài*; this was probably so-called green tea, which arrived in Europe via the caravan routes of Asia, extending to Russia. The Jesuit Matteo Ricci spoke of *cià* around 1600.

Tea first reached London in 1657, probably from Holland; this was black tea that had come to Europe by sea. In 1706 Thomas Twining first served tea in his London tearooms.

The introduction of a tax on tea in the American colonies proved a true disaster to Britain, helping to precipitate a revolution with all its consequences. In response to the levy imposed on tea imports, the Americans bought contraband tea from the Dutch who, moreover, sold it at a lower price. When the government of George III charged the East India Company to recover the taxes by exercising its monopoly to sell tea direct to the American colonies, there was no further hope of a settlement. The Five Laws decreed by London were pronounced "intolerable" by the Americans, and subsequent events culminated on 4 July 1776 with the Declaration of Independence.

The growing of tea nevertheless remained confined until the nineteenth century to China and Japan. Later the Dutch introduced it to Java, while the English, after the Opium War (1893–4), initiated it in India and Ceylon. Robert Fortune, sent to China by the Royal Horticultural Society to collect ornamental plants, shrewdly introduced tea plants to Assam, while in Ceylon, where tea had already been grown since 1828, the industry only began to flourish after the importation of species that grew wild in Assam.

Tea was carried to England by speedy tea clippers which, around 1820, covered the distance from Hong Kong to London in less than 100 days, the record being 60 days.

Coffee.   In Arabia the custom of drinking coffee dates back to the fifteenth century: from here it spread from Aden and Mocha eastward to Persia and westward to Egypt. The introduction of coffee to Aden is attributed to the Grand Mufti Gamaleddin, who in 1459 imported the usage from Persia. Coffee reached Constantinople by way of Damascus and Aleppo after the Turkish conquest. The Turks used to flavor their coffee, which was served strong and unsweetened, with star anise, cardamom, and amber essence. It was from Constantinople that the Venetians introduced it to the West in the early 1600s. The first coffee shops were opened in Venice around 1650; the Caffè Florian under the Procuratie Nuove was established in 1700. When the Turks were defeated outside Vienna (1683), part of the booty consisted of large quantities of coffee, and for the first time the bitter drink was sweetened. Soon afterwards the Dutch began to experiment with its cultivation in the East Indies (1690) and then in Surinam,

Stages in the flowering cycle of the coffee plant. The flowers, of very short duration, give out an extremely powerful scent that insects cannot resist.

Arab merchants grew wealthy on the trade in aromatic resins and the route followed by their caravans was called the spice road. When the spices reached the shores of the Mediterranean, they were loaded onto ships destined for the major ports of Europe.

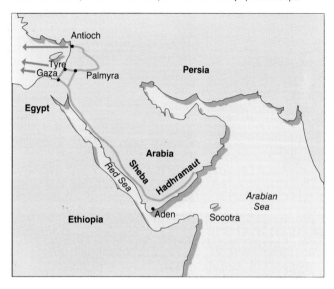

in South America (1718). From Surinam it was smuggled from Cayenne into Brazil. Several plants grown in the Paris botanical gardens (Jardin du Roi) were used in the early 1700s to introduce coffee cultivation to Martinique, and from here plants were taken to Jamaica.

Such was the popularity of coffee in Europe that the commodity had a strong influence on national balances of payments. At the beginning of the eighteenth century the royal gardener of Prussia's Frederick the Great, called Timme, discovered the properties of chicory as a coffee substitute; to save money, the king ordered him to grow chicory, the roasted and ground roots of which produced an aromatic powder, used to make a dark coffee-like infusion but with its own individual taste. Chicory was so successfully grown that it was widely used as a beverage until the Second World War. It also helped to popularize coffee with a somewhat milder taste, which accounts for the preference in Germany and other countries today for coffee rather less strong than the typically Italian espresso. In Europe, changing economic conditions dictated that the less affluent members of the population also resorted at various times to other substitutes for coffee, which was either too dear or simply unobtainable, such as barley or roasted soy beans.

Cocoa. In Aztec Mexico, at the time of the Spanish conquest, the cocoa plant had been grown for more than a thousand years; when Cortés arrived at Montezuma's court he found the cocoa beans, in

26

addition to furnishing an inimitable beverage, were also used as currency. For almost a century the Spaniards kept secret the recipe for preparing this popular drink. In 1606 the Italian Antonio Carlotti discovered it and helped to spread the use of cocoa but only around 1700 did it become a widely consumed beverage. From Central America the Spaniards took plants to the Philippines (1674), while the English brought them to Malaya in 1800; in West Africa the plant was introduced in the early 1900s (Ghana is today one of the leading world producers). Not until 1840 was the bar of eating chocolate invented. From then on cocoa was no longer just a drink.

PERFUMES FROM PLANTS

A passage from the Gospel of St Matthew (2:9–11) reads:

". . . they departed; and behold, the star which they had seen in the East moved on before them till it came to rest over the spot where was the child. And on seeing the star they rejoiced with exceeding great joy. And entering the house, they saw the child with Mary his mother, and falling down they worshiped him. And they opened their treasures and offered him gifts, gold and frankincense and myrrh."

The gifts of the Magi had clear significance: their symbolic and actual value were linked with the recognition of God on earth. Gold expressed Christ's sovereignty, incense His divinity (it was the perfume offered to God in the temples, the smoke of which rose to Heaven), and myrrh the Savior's humanity (balm was used for preserving bodies).

Aromatic and perfumed substances have been sought and used throughout history; such was their importance that they were regarded, as St Matthew indicates, as among the most precious of human possessions.

In the course of time myrrh fell into oblivion, so much so that it became difficult even to identify it botanically. But in antiquity it was one of the most desirable aromatic substances in western Asia and the Mediterranean area, being brought by caravan from its original sites in the Horn of Africa, through Arabia to Egypt.

The holy oil of the Jews was produced by mixing olive oil with myrrh, cinnamon, cassia, and aromatic reeds; the Jews also made use of incense, storax, and other spices.

The Egyptians used vast quantities of myrrh to embalm their dead and to produce perfumed smoke in their temples. Queen Hatshepsut (c. 1500 B.C.) sent a maritime expedition to the land of Punt (southern Arabia and the Horn of Africa) to procure gold, incense and myrrh, bringing back 31 trees in baskets to Egypt, as the bas reliefs of Deir el-Bahari, in western Thebes, testify.

Incense was much employed in religious ceremonies, and indeed the Phoenician name for the god Baal, Haamon, meant "Lord of the incense altars." It was burned together with saltpeter (soda and calcium carbonate), which was used with myrrh for embalming.

Plant perfumes. The table, arranged by families, lists the principal plants that furnish parts used for the extraction of perfumes, and zones of production.

family	genus and species	distribution	parts used
Amaryllidaceae	Polyanthes tuberosa L.	cult. France	flowers (simple)
Aristolochiaceae	Asarum canadense L.	USA, Canada	rhizomes
Burseraceae	Boswellia sacra Flückinger	Somalia, Arabia	"tears" (resin)
	Commiphora mirrha Holmes	Arabia	reddish brown "tears" (resin)
Compositae	Achillea millefolium L.	Europe, Siberia	entire plant
	Achillea moschata Wulf.	Alps	entire plant
	Anthemis nobilis L.	cultivated	flowers
	Artemisia dracunculus L.	central Europe	leaves
	Helichrysum italicum Don.	Mediterranean regions	flower heads, leaves
	Inula helenium L.	central Europe	roots
	Matricaria chamomilla L.	temperate regions	flower heads
Ericaceae	Gaultheria procumbens L.	Canada, USA	leaves (distilled)
Geraniaceae	Pelargonium suaveolens L'Hérit.	common cult. (Bulgaria)	leaves, branches (distilled)
Gramineae	Cymbopogon flexuosus (DC.) Stapf.	India, Central America, Caucasus	grass (distilled)
	Vetiveria zizanoides Stapf.	southern Asia, Central America	roots (distilled)
Hamamelidaceae	Hamamelis virginiana L.	North America	leaves and twigs (distilled)
	Liquidambar styraciflua L.	Asia, USA	resin, bark
Iridaceae	Crocus sativus L.	Italy	dry stigmas
	Iris florentina L.	Italy, France, Morocco	rhizomes
	Iris germanica L.	southern Europe	rhizomes
Juglandaceae	Juglans regia L.	common	hull, leaves
Labiatae	Hyssopus officinalis L.	Italy	leaves, flower heads
	Lavandula angustifolia Mill.	Mediterranean region	flower stems
	Lavandula hybrida	Mediterranean region	flower stems
	Melissa officinalis L.	Europe	leaves
	Monarda didyma L./ punctata L.	North America	fresh plants
	Ocimum basilicum L.	cultivated everywhere	leaves and green plant
	Origanum vulgare L.	Mediterranean region	leaves, flower heads
	Perilla frutescens Britt.	Japan	leaves, flower heads
	Pogostemon cablin (Blanco) Benth.	Indonesia, Malaysia	leaves (distilled)
	Salvia officinalis L.	Mediterranean region	leaves
Lauraceae	Cinnamomum camphora Nees	Southeast Asia	distilled wood
	Sassafras albidum (Nutt.) Nees	North America	bark of root
Leguminosae	Acacia dealbata Lk.	France	open scented flowers

family	genus and species	distribution	parts used
Leguminosae	*Copaifera* spp.	Amazon	oily resin in trunk cavity
	Melilotus officinalis (L.) Pall.	Eruasia	dried plant (distilled)
Liliaceae	*Convallaria majalis* L.	Europe	flowers with stalk
Malvaceae	*Hibiscus abelmoschus* L.	India, tropics	seeds (distilled)
Myrtaceae	*Myrtus communis* L.	Mediterranean region	leaves, flower heads
Oleaceae	*Jasminum grandiflorum* L./*officinale* L.	France, Morocco	flowers
Orchidaceae	*Vanilla planifolia* Andr.	Mexico	pods (fruits)
Pinaceae	*Abies alba* Mill.	Alps	leaves, twigs, buds
	Cedrus atlantica/*libani*/*deodara*	North Africa, Asia	resin
	Pinus mugo Turra	Alps	branches, buds, young cones
Ranunculaceae	*Nigella damascena* L.	India, Africa, s. Europe	seeds
	Nigella sativa L.	s. Europe, North Africa, w. Asia	seeds
Rosaceae	*Filipendula ulmaria* (L.) Maxim	Europe, Asia	leaves, flowers
	Geum urbanum L.	northern hemis.	rhizome, roots
	Prunus dulcis D. A. Webb	Mediterranean region	seeds
	Rosa spp. *damascena*/*centifolia*	Bulgaria	petals
Rutaceae	*Citrus aurantium* L. ssp. *aurantium*	Sicily	fruit rind
	Citrus bergamia Risso et Poit.	Italy	fruits (distilled)
	Citrus limon L.	warm temperate zones	fruit, juice
Santalaceae	*Santalum album* L.	India	wood, roots
Solanaceae	*Nicotiana tabacum* L.	cultivated	leaves
Styracaceae	*Styrax officinalis* L.	Turkey	balsam or resin
Umbelliferae	*Carum carvi* L.	temperate zones	fruits, young leaves
	Coriandrum sativum L.	temperate zones	fruits
	Daucus carota L.	temperate zones	fruits
	Ferula assa-foetida L.	Iran, Afghanistan	oil, gum resin of roots and stems
	Ferula galbaniflua Boiss. & Bulse	Mediterranean region	oil, gum resin of roots and stems
	Petroselinum crispum (Mill.) A. W. Hill	temperate zones	leaves, fruits
Violaceae	*Viola odorata* L.	Mediterranean regions	fresh flowers
Zingiberaceae	*Curcuma zeodaria* Rosc.	India	rhizome
	Zingiber officinale Rosc.	China, Japan, India	rhizome

Incense and myrrh possess, in addition to their distinctive perfume, stimulating, healing, and purifying properties.

The Greeks and Romans likewise burned incense for sacrificial rites; and fumigations of myrrh, also an ingredient in perfumery as a basic oil for all kinds of unguents, was used for propitiatory purposes and at funerals.

Perfuming of the body was common practice for marriage ceremonies (brides sprinkled themselves with stimulating scents) and for erotic purposes; and of course these substances continue to play a seductive role to this very day.

Arab merchants conducted a highly lucrative trade in fragrant resins, their caravans traveling regularly over the so-called incense road. They jealously guarded the method's of production and their commercial monopoly.

Other fragrant products had been closely associated with cosmetics since antiquity; but although widely used, they were very much the prerogative of the nobility or of women engaged in prostitution. This was why cosmetics and perfumes came to be associated with immorality, especially in the Dark Ages. The attitude of the Greeks was somewhat uncertain but eventually the vogue for cosmetics and perfumes was such that Solon, the Athenian statesman, was compelled to pass laws restraining their use (in the form of an obligatory tax on luxury goods).

The Romans set up local industries for the production of oils, unguents, perfumes and toilet preparations, and commercial centers for importing them from the producing areas such as Corinth in Greece, Alexandria in Egypt and Palmyra and Laodicea in Syria. The stalls selling these products were mostly concentrated in specialized streets (*Vicus unguentarius*) in Rome. Ovid has left us a treatise on cosmetics with exact recipes, which are often products for bodily hygiene, the ingredients including bleaches such as soda blended with flour to make them less abrasive and mixed with powdered iris to give them a delicate scent. Rose petals were also frequently used, as they are today for their multiple properties when applied to the skin.

After being neglected in medieval times, the fashion for perfumes was enthusiastically revived during the Renaissance; toward the end of the fifteenth century shops reopened and the commercial quest for raw materials was resumed. Leonardo da Vinci even anticipated chemical warfare by studying mixtures of foul-smelling products. In 1525 the *Experimenti* of Caterina Sforza were published; in addition to hints on medicine, hygiene and aphrodisiac recipes, subjects discussed included perfumes and poisons, seduction and death.

Venice was a leader in the perfumery field with its cosmetic shops, known as *muschiari*. In 1555 one of these establishments published a book on the *Notandissimi secreti de l'arte profumatoria* by Giovanni Ventura Roseto (or Rosetti); it described all the raw materials, both of animal and vegetable origin, their treatments (distillations and extractions) and, above all, the fragrant composition of bouquets, with their different nuances. The catalog includes: famous perfumes obtained from musk, cypress, sandalwood, benzoin, and amber; the use of rose, lavender, orange blossom, jasmine, elder, and violet waters; mention of fixatives such as civet and ambergris; and methods of preparing perfumed grains, musk-flavored pastilles, soaps, fumigants, and powders.

The primacy of Venice was soon being undermined by Florence. And with the marriage of Catherine de Médicis to Henry II (1533) and later of Marie de Médicis to Henry IV (1600), the secrets and techniques of extraction and distillation found their way to France at the end of the Renaissance period. From this point France was to predominate in the art of cosmetics to this day.

The famous perfume known as eau de Cologne merits a paragraph to itself. Its origins are mysterious and its formula is nowadays attributed variously to Giovanni Paolo Feminis and to Giovanni Maria Farina, both of whom emigrated around 1650 from northern Italy to Cologne. Initially extolled as "*aqua mirabilis, specificum miraculosum,*" and thus a remedy for an unlimited list of illnesses, this balanced mixture of the essences of citrus fruits and labiates was later sold commercially only as a perfume, after the Napoleonic decree of 1810 stipulated that the composition of all medicaments should be published. In order not to reveal the secret recipe, the manufacturers preferred to overlook its medicinal properties and to concentrate,

more profitably, on its qualities as a perfume. The first "waters" had been prepared by distillation of alcoholic infusions; subsequently, in the eighteenth century, the essences were dissolved in the alcohol (these products, in demand everywhere as perfumes, nevertheless have antiseptic properties, particularly in relation to the skin).

However, life in Europe at the dawn of the modern age, rather than being perfumed, was certainly full of odors that were far from pleasant. The French writer Louis-Sébastien Mercier, in his *Tableau de Paris*, spoke of walls soaked with urine and passages that had become filthy latrines; not to mention rubbish and sewage. Hygienic arrangements, in fact, were not exactly advanced; the first two lavatories were installed for Louis XVI and Marie Antoinette at Versailles. There was a general mistrust of water and cleanliness; baths were taken only, and very rarely, for therapeutic purposes (bearing in mind that contact with one's own body was considered to offend modesty). Doctors themselves encouraged the use of perfumes for concealing natural body odors; so scents followed fashion, amber and musk under the Sun King, rose water, lavender, and violet under Louis XV. Women carried little bags with fragrant herbs under their skirts, and all clothes and even accessories such as fans were sprinkled with perfume. A canon of odors was established: suitable scents for virgins, young women, and elderly ladies. Scent gardens and orangeries were all the rage. The discovery was made that the poor stank: social distinction determined by the nose! The stench of disease was regarded as contagious, so doctors went around wearing strange beak-shaped masks, smeared on the inside with herbs and vinegar, rather like modern gas masks.

Preference for a particular perfume or scent is a very personal matter. In the development of the senses, it is the human sense of smell, more than any other, which has lost its importance in relation to the outside world. We tend to use, or indeed to perceive, only those odors and perfumes that are strong and overwhelming, having wholly lost the capacity to distinguish anything in between. Familiarity with common fragrant plants, let alone the rarer species, may help to restore our use of this neglected sense, which is so essential for communicating with the world around us.

THE ACTIVE PRINCIPLES

Spices, perfumes, resins and gums belong to groups of substances that are derived from the metabolism of the plant as secondary products. This involves a very large number of different components, a principal role being played by the terpene derivatives. As an introduction to this complex subject and with a view to clarifying some of the references contained in the text accompanying the plates, the following section lists the main groups to which the active principles or ingredients belong.

Heterosides. The group of substances known as heterosides, also called glycosides, occurs widely in many families of plants; they are usually found in the vacuolar system and their precise function is still not completely understood. These are molecules derived from the synthesis of a sugar (glycone) and another molecule (aglycone), with the elimination of a water molecule; the link between glycone and aglycone can be effected by an oxygen bridge (−O−); this link is present in the most complex group of heterosides (there are also −S−, −N− and −C− bridges). If the sugar concerned is glucose these are known specifically as glucosides.

Among the various groups are the following:

Salicylic heterosides (aglycone → salicylates): present in families Salicaceae, Betulaceae, Rosaceae and Ericaceae.

Hydroquinonic heterosides (aglycone → hydroquinone): Ericaceae.

Cardiotonic heterosides (→ various aglycones): present in the genera *Nerium*, *Convallaria*, *Adonis*, *Digitalis*, *Urginea* and *Helleborus niger*.

Saponins or **saponisides** (→ various aglycones); present in the genera *Smilax*, *Ruscus*, *Digitalis*, *Dioscorea*, *Glycyrrhiza*, *Saponaria*, *Hedera*, *Aesculus*, *Polypodium*, *Polygala*, *Viola*, *Verbascum* and *Scrophularia*. They have an irritant action on the mucosae (diuretic and purgative effects) and, in the case of licorice, anti-inflammatory and scar-forming properties.

Cyanongenic heterosides (→ HCN); as in the case of amygdalin in the genus *Prunus*. The hydrolysis of the glucoside is associated with the presence of specific enzymes (emulsin); in *Prunus amygdalus* var. *amara* there is from 2 to 4 percent of amygdaloside from the hydrolysis of which are formed two glucose molecules, benzoic aldehyde and hydrocyanic acid. These compounds collect mainly in the leaves and seeds (leaves: cherry laurel and elder; seeds: bitter almond, apricot, peach, plum, and cherry).

HCN is toxic in very low doses, blocking the bulbar respiratory centers.

Cumarinic heterosides (→ cumarin or its derivatives): found in leaves, fruits, seeds, and rhizomes of Umbelliferae (rhizomes of *Peucedanum ostruthium*, achenes of *Heracleum sphondylium* and *Pastinaca sativa*, entire plants of Gramineae [or Poaceae] [*Anthoxanthum odoratum*] and Rubiaceae [*Galium odoratum*]).

Among the free cumarins are: umbelliferone (*Hieracium pilosella*, *Ferula assa-foetida*); bergaptene (in the essential oil of bergamot and in the achenes of *Amni majus*); melilotoside (in the flower head of *Melilotus officinalis*). By fermentation it is transformed into dicumarol, which explains the anti-coagulant action of anti-vitamin K; and aesculoside (in the seed tegument of *Aesculus hippocastanum*).

Anthraquinonic heterosides (→ derivatives of anthracene), with irritant or laxative properties (*Aloë ferox*, *Frangula*, *Rhamnus*

Wild herbs of the temperate regions. The table, arranged by families, lists various wild species, indicating their active principles and how they are used.

family	genus and species	uses	active principles
Boraginaceae	*Borago officinalis* L.	foodstuffs, bee, bee	ethereal oils in leaves
	Symphytum officinale L.	foodstuffs, bee	tonic principles in rhizome
Cannabaceae	*Humulus lupulus* L.	foodstuffs, spirits	bitter principles
Capparidaceae	*Capparis spinosa* L.	foodstuffs	mustard glucosides in leaves
Caprifoliaceae	*Sambucus nigra* L.	foodstuffs, spirits, infusions	aromatic principles in flowers
Compositae	*Achillea millefolium* L.	foodstuffs, spirits, perfumery	bitter principles
	Achillea moschata Wulf.	spirits, perfumery	bitter principles
	Artemisia absinthium L.	spirits	bitter principles in leaves
	Artemisia genipi Weber	spirits	bitter principles in leaves
	Carlina acaulis L.	foodstuffs	ethereal oils in root, bitter principles
	Cichorium intybus L.	foodstuffs, infusions, bee	bitter principles
	Cnicus benedictus L.	spirits	bitter principles
	Helichrysum italicum Don.	spirits, perfumery	ethereal oils in flower heads
	Matricaria chamomilla L.	foodstuffs, spirits, infusions, perfumery	ethereal oils in flower heads
	Taraxacum officinale Weber	foodstuffs, infusions, bee, bee	bitter principles
	Tussilago farfara L.	foodstuffs, bee	bitter, tonic principles
Cruciferae	*Alliaria petiolata* L.	foodstuffs	mustard glucosides in leaves
	Armoracia rusticana G., M. & Sch.	foodstuffs	mustard glucosides in tap-roots
	Brassica nigra (L.) Koch	foodstuffs	mustard glucosides in seeds
	Cardamine amara L.	foodstuffs	mustard glucosides
	Cochlearia officinalis L.	foodstuffs	mustard glucosides
	Nasturtium officinale R. Br.	foodstuffs	mustard glucosides
	Raphanus sativus L.	foodstuffs	mustard glucosides in roots
Cupressaceae	*Juniperus communis* L.	foodstuffs, spirits, perfumery	ethereal oils in fruits
Gentianaceae	*Gentiana lutea* L.	spirits	bitter principles in roots
Juglandaceae	*Juglans regia* L.	spirits, perfumery	tannic principles in fruits
Labiatae	*Melissa officinalis* L.	infusions, perfumery	ethereal oils in leaves
	Rosmarinus officinalis L.	foodstuffs, bee, bee	ethereal oils in leaves
	Salvia officinalis L.	foodstuffs, spirits, infusions, perfumery, bee, bee	ethereal oils in leaves

used in foodstuffs	used in perfumery
used in spirits	good bee-attracting species
used for infusions	excellent bee-attracting species

family	genus and species	uses	active principles
Labiatae	*Satureja montana* L.	🍴⚗⛰⛰	ethereal oils in leaves
Lauraceae	*Laurus nobilis* L.	🍴⛰⛰	ethereal oils in leaves
Liliaceae	*Allium ampeloprasum* L.	🍴	sulfurated principles in bulbs
	Allium schoenoprasum L.	🍴	sulfurated principles in leaves
	Allium ursinum L.	🍴	sulfurated principles in leaves
Malvaceae	*Malva sylvestris* L.	🍴 🛋	aromatic principles
Myrtaceae	*Myrtus communis* L.	🍴 🏺	ethereal oils in leaves and flowers
Oxalidaceae	*Oxalis acetosella* L.	🍴	acidic principles
Pinaceae	*Pinus pinea* L.	🍴	aromatic seeds
Polygonaceae	*Polygonum bistorta* L.	🍴	acidic principles in roots
	Rumex acetosa L.	🍴	acidic principles
Portulacaceae	*Portulaca oleracea* L.	🍴	ethereal oils in leaves
Rosaceae	*Filipendula ulmaria* (L.) Maxim.	🍴 ⚗	aromatic principles
	Geum urbanum L.	🍴 🏺	aromatic principles
	Rubus idaeus L.	🍴⚗⛰⛰	aromatic and dyeing principles
	Sanguisorba minor Scop.	🍴	cucumber-taste principles
Rubiaceae	*Galium odoratum* (L.) Scop.	⚗	coumarinic principles
Rutaceae	*Ruta graveolens* L.	⚗	ethereal oils in leaves
Tiliaceae	*Tilia cordata* Mill.	🛋 ⛰ ⛰	aromatic principles in flowers
Umbelliferae	*Carum carvi* L.	🍴⚗🏺⛰	ethereal oils in fruits
	Crithmum maritimum L.	🍴	ethereal oils
	Daucus carota L.	🍴⚗🏺⛰	ethereal oils
	Eryngium maritimum L.	🍴	ethereal oils in roots
	Foeniculum vulgare Mill.	🍴 ⚗ ⛰	ethereal oils in fruits
	Pastinaca sativa L.	🍴	ethereal oils in roots
	Peucedanum ostruthium (L.) Koch	⚗	ethereal oils in roots
	Smyrnium olusatrum L.	🍴	ethereal oils in roots
Violaceae	*Viola odorata* L.	🍴 🏺	aromatic flowers

catharticus, *Rheum officinale* and *Rumex alpinus*) inasmuch as they augment intestinal peristasis.

Flavonoidic heterosides (→ flavonoids, yellow-colored compounds), contained in flower heads of *Hyssopus* and *Spiraea ulmaria*, in the roots of *Ononis* and licorice and also in the Rutaceae (*Citrus*, *Ruta*).

Anthocyanic heterosides (→ anthocyanidin): these are compounds, the color of which is associated with the specific pH of the vacuolar content (amphoteric compounds: red in acid environment, violet–neutral, blue–basic). The compounds have to do with the vexillary function of the flowers and are thus directed toward reproduction or, according to some authors, to the filtration of ultraviolet rays. They are found abundantly in the fruits of myrtle (red and black), blackberry and raspberry, flowers of hibiscus (Java jute), mallow, and the leaves of wine grapes (*Vitis vinifera* var. *tinctoria*); they are also present in the peel of apples, pears, and cherries; other red colors are attributable to various chemical compounds known as betacyanins (beetroot, goosefoot, and *Bougainvillea*). The anthocyanosides influence the process of dim light and nocturnal vision, increasing the regenerative speed of visual purple (rhodopsin) in darkness.

Sulfurated heterosides (→ glucose + potassium sulfate + isosulfocyanates); a typical example is sinigroside (in *Brassica nigra*); this, through the action of the enzyme myrosin, liberates glucose, potassium sulfate, and allyl isosulfocyanate. Other species containing these compounds are *Armoracia rusticana*, *Sinapis alba*, *Cochlearia officinalis*, *Raphanus sativus*, *Nasturtium officinale*, and *Tropaeolum majus*. These principles act, among other things, on the stomach, stimulating gastro-intestinal secretions.

Gums. As a result of wounds, plants often produce exudations, consisting of colloidal suspensions of various polysaccharides, which serve for protection, especially in limiting water losses. They are commonly produced by leguminous plants such as *Acacia senegal* and *Astralagus gummifer*; in the former case gum arabic, collected in drops that are soluble, is obtained. In the latter instance gum tragacanth, partially soluble in water, is gathered in flakes and scales.

Bitters. Bitter principles are substances of very different kinds, but with a characteristic common taste. Thus they include heterosides: the root of *Gentiana lutea* contains a principle called gentianopicroside; esters of phenic acid; and the cardoon or wild artichoke; and alkaloids, such as the cinchona (*Cinchona*). Bitter principles are particularly abundant in plants of the family Compositae (wormwood, artichoke, cardoon, chicory, and dandelion), the Gentianaceae, and the hop. All bitter substances stimulate the production of gastric juices, helping digestion; for this reason many of them are used in the preparation of digestive liquors.

Tannins. Tannins, active principles with a typically astringent taste, are polyphenolic compounds. They are widely used for tanning hides, determining the precipitation of proteins in insoluble compounds. They are found in cellular vacuoles and in certain reserve cells (idioblasts), representing the final products of metabolism, with an antiseptic action. They accumulate principally in tree bark, in the cortex of stems, in roots, and in leaves. Gallic tannins (derived from gallic acid) are especially common and appear too in those conspicuous plant malformations known as galls, on the leaves of many species (notably oaks); they derive from the punctures made by the ovipositor of cynipid hymenopteran insects. Tannic principles have an astringent, antibiotic, anti-inflammatory, vaso-constrictive, anti-diarrhoeic and haemostatic function.

Essential oils. These comprise mixtures of natural compounds different from those already mentioned; they are extracted from certain plants and retain the characteristic smell and taste of these: their name is generally derived from the plant itself.

Spices and herbs are principally characterized by substances called terpenes. These are simple lipids (which do not contain fatty acids that are found in complex lipids), and are multiples of isoprene (so that they are referred to as mono-, di-, tri-, sesqui-terpenes, etc.). The molecules may be either linear or cyclic, or they may display structures of both types simultaneously.

Many terpenes produced by plants have a particular smell or aroma and thus constitute the principal element of essential oils; among these are camphor (in camphor oil), carvone (in cumin oil), geraniol (in geranium oil), limonene (in lemon oil), menthol (in peppermint oil) and pinene (in turpentine).

Among the higher terpenes (tetraterpenes) are the carotenoids, including beta-carotene, forerunner of vitamin A. Like vitamins E and K, they are water soluble and have essential biological properties.

The polyterpenes include natural rubber and gutta-percha, the hydrocarbonic chains of which contain hundreds of isoprene units arranged in a linear pattern.

It has been suggested that the accumulation of essential oils could have the task of furnishing an energy reserve in case of shortage of sugars or starch inside the plant tissues. Far more important and evident is the ecological significance of these aromas, as attractors or repellents, or simply as inhibitors in the germination and growth of concurrent plants. The polyterpenes, such as the gums present in latex, play no metabolic role but, like resins, have antiseptic, antibiotic, fungicidal and insecticidal properties.

The aroma of virtually any plant or spice is derived from a combination of active principles and by means of extraction it is possible to isolate the individual components, some of which are especially important or predominant. Vanillin, for example, is the principal constituent of the aroma of vanilla, which differs from that of synthetic vanillin by the presence in it of small quantities of other principles that

Wild herbs cultivated in temperate regions. The table lists plants that can be chosen as
ornamental garden subjects, indicating their main uses and active principles.

	family	genus and species	uses	active principles
[in garden]	Anacardiaceae	*Pistacia vera* L.	[foodstuffs]	colorative and aromatic seeds
[patio] [pots]	Boraginaceae	*Borago officinalis* L.	[foodstuffs] [good bee] [excellent bee]	ethereal oils in leaves
[patio]	Cannabaceae	*Humulus lupulus* L.	[foodstuffs] [spirits]	bitter principles
[patio]	Capparidaceae	*Capparis spinosa* L.	[foodstuffs]	mustard glucosides in seeds
[patio] [pots]	Compositae	*Anthemis nobilis* L.	[spirits] [infusions]	ethereal oils in flower heads
[patio]	Compositae	*Artemisia absinthium* L.	[spirits]	ethereal oils in leaves
[patio]	Compositae	*Artemisia dracunculus* L.	[foodstuffs] [spirits] [infusions]	ethereal oils in leaves
[patio] [pots]	Compositae	*Calendula officinalis* L.	[foodstuffs]	aromatic principles
[patio]	Compositae	*Cichorium intybus* L.	[foodstuffs] [good bee]	bitter principles
[patio] [pots]	Compositae	*Matricaria chamomilla* L.	[foodstuffs] [spirits] [infusions]	ethereal oils in flower heads
[patio] [pots]	Compositae	*Tanacetum parthenium* C. H. Schultz	[foodstuffs] [spirits]	ethereal oils in leaves
[patio] [pots]	Crassulaceae	*Sedum reflexum* L.	[foodstuffs]	acidic principles
[patio]	Cruciferae	*Armoracia rusticana* G., M. & Sch.	[foodstuffs]	mustard glucosides in tap-roots
[in garden]	Cruciferae	*Brassica nigra* (L.) Koch	[foodstuffs]	mustard glucosides in seeds
[patio]	Cruciferae	*Eruca sativa* Miller	[foodstuffs]	mustard glucosides
[patio]	Cruciferae	*Lepidium sativum* L.	[foodstuffs]	mustard glucosides
[in garden]	Cruciferae	*Nasturtium officinale* R. Br.	[foodstuffs]	mustard glucosides
[patio]	Cruciferae	*Raphanus sativus* L.	[foodstuffs]	mustard glucosides
[patio] [pots]	Iridaceae	*Crocus sativus* L.	[foodstuffs] [good bee]	ethereal oils in flowers
[in garden]	Juglandaceae	*Juglans regia* L.	[spirits] [perfumery]	ethereal oils in unripe fruits
[patio] [pots]	Labiatae	*Hyssopus officinalis* L.	[foodstuffs] [perfumery] [good bee] [excellent bee]	ethereal oils in leaves
[patio] [pots]	Labiatae	*Melissa officinalis* L.	[perfumery]	ethereal oils in leaves
[patio] [pots]	Labiatae	*Mentha x piperita* L.	[foodstuffs] [spirits]	ethereal oils in leaves
[patio] [pots]	Labiatae	*Ocimum basilicum* L.	[foodstuffs] [perfumery] [good bee]	ethereal oils in leaves
[patio] [pots]	Labiatae	*Origanum majorana* L.	[foodstuffs]	ethereal oils in leaves
[patio] [pots]	Labiatae	*Origanum vulgare* L.	[foodstuffs] [perfumery] [good bee]	ethereal oils in leaves
[patio]	Labiatae	*Rosmarinus officinalis* L.	[foodstuffs] [good bee] [excellent bee]	ethereal oils in leaves
[patio] [pots]	Labiatae	*Salvia officinalis* L.	[foodstuffs] [spirits] [perfumery] [good bee] [excellent bee]	ethereal oils in leaves
[patio]	Labiatae	*Salvia sclarea* L.	[spirits] [good bee]	ethereal oils in leaves
[patio] [pots]	Labiatae	*Satureja hortensis* L.	[foodstuffs] [spirits]	ethereal oils in leaves
[patio]	Lauraceae	*Laurus nobilis* L.	[foodstuffs]	ethereal oils in leaves

[in garden] in garden	[foodstuffs] used in foodstuffs	[good bee] good bee-attracting species
[patio] on patio, window boxes	[spirits] used in spirits	[excellent bee] excellent bee-attracting species
[pots] in pots	[perfumery] used in perfumery	[infusions] used for infusions

	family	genus and species	uses	active principles
	Leguminosae	*Glycyrrhiza glabra* L.		sweet principles
	Leguminosae	*Trigonella caerulea* (L.) Ser.		aromatic principles
	Liliaceae	*Allium ascalonicum* L.		sulfurated principles in bulbs
	Liliaceae	*Allium sativum* L.		sulfurated principles in bulbs
	Liliaceae	*Allium schoenoprasum* L.		sulfurated principles in leaves
	Myrtaceae	*Eucalyptus globulus* Labill.		ethereal oils in leaves
	Papaveraceae	*Papaver somniferum* L.		fruits with alkaloids, aromatic seeds
	Pinaceae	*Pinus pinea* L.		aromatic seeds
	Polygonaceae	*Rheum spp.*		acidic principles
	Portulacaceae	*Portulaca oleracea* L.		ethereal oils in leaves
	Ranunculaceae	*Nigella damascena* L.		aromatic seeds
	Rosaceae	*Prunus dulcis* D. A. Webb		aromatic seeds
	Rosaceae	*Rubus idaeus* L.		aromatic and colorative fruits
	Rutaceae	*Citrus limon* L.		acidic principles and oils in fruits
	Rutaceae	*Ruta graveolens* L.		ethereal oils in leaves
	Solanaceae	*Capsicum annuum* L. var. *annum*		pungent principles in fruits
	Tropaeolaceae	*Tropaeolum majus* L.		mustard oils in fruits
	Umbelliferae	*Anethum graveolens* L.		ethereal oils
	Umbelliferae	*Angelica archangelica* L.		ethereal oils in tap-root and stem
	Umbelliferae	*Anthriscus cerefolium* (L.) Hoffm.		ethereal oils in leaves
	Umbelliferae	*Apium graveolens* L.		ethereal oils
	Umbelliferae	*Carum carvi* L.		ethereal oils in fruits
	Umbelliferae	*Coriandrum sativum* L.		ethereal oils in fruits
	Umbelliferae	*Foeniculum vulgare* Mill.		ethereal oils in fruits
	Umbelliferae	*Levisticum officinale* Koch		ethereal oils in leaves
	Umbelliferae	*Pastinaca sativa* L.		ethereal oils in root
	Umbelliferae	*Petroselinum crispum* (Mill.) A. W. Hill		ethereal oils in leaves
	Umbelliferae	*Pimpinella anisum* L.		ethereal oils in fruits
	Umbelliferae	*Smyrnium olusatrum* L.		ethereal oils
	Verbenaceae	*Lippia citriodora* Kunth		ethereal oils in leaves

are not produced by synthesis. In some instances the identity of an aroma is attributable to one or several principles (as in the mandarin), while in others there may be a hundred or so different principles (as in cocoa for chocolate).

Balsams and resins. These are mixtures of compounds that are solid or only partially fluid, soluble in organic compounds such as alcohol, turpentine, etc. Balsams contain a higher quantity of essential oils than resins or oleoresins, secreted by conifers.

Other compounds. Various parts of plants also contain organic compounds belonging to the groups of acids (e.g. citric, malic and oxalic acid) and enzymes. The latter are fundamental to the plant's metabolic activity and control the catalystic activities of specific biochemical reactions. Among those with a special bearing on the subject in hand are the enzymes found in the Cruciferae and lilies of the genus *Allium* which liberate sulfurous compounds (allyl isosulfocyanate). Fresh aromatic plants are also a source of important groups of vitamins.

Alkaloids. These particular compounds, produced only by plants, have a molecule with an electrocyclic ring in which there is as a rule a nitrogen atom; they generally possess a basic reaction, hence their name, which means "similar to alkali." Among the first alkaloids to be isolated, in the early nineteenth century, were morphine, caffeine, and quinine. Today more than 3,000 are known. They often have important pharmaceutical properties or are responsible for the toxicity of many poisonous plants.

CULTIVATING AROMATIC PLANTS

Because of the wide variety of special needs and possible uses of individual aromatic plants, there is a mass of literature about growing methods and techniques. Since this is not an agricultural manual, no information will be found in these pages concerning large-scale cultivation for specialized and industrial purposes. Our aim is to concentrate on fairly straightforward practices devoted to what is, after all, the predominant use of aromatic herbs, namely in cooking. With this in mind, emphasis will be placed on methods of growing that, without use of substances which damage the environment, will provide a reasonable supply of natural products for household use. It is always worth experimenting, however modestly, to see what species and varieties grow best in the general environmental conditions of your garden (climate, soil, position); even if you have only a simple patio or balcony, the results, whatever your degree of success, are bound to be interesting.

Obtaining seedlings. A very simple method is to obtain a few seedlings from a nursery or friend's herb garden and plant them directly in the soil or in pots. Check the needs of the different species and take special precautions depending on whether it is a herbaceous or woody plant.

One problem may be the precise botanical identification of the plant concerned, which is important if it is intended for edible purposes. There are many books that help you to identify vascular plants, based on detailed description of morphological features; read these carefully as it is as well not to rely solely on illustrations, which may sometimes lead to mistakes.

Remember that the quantity of essential oils contained in aromatic plants can vary according to the altitude where they are grown, the density of culture, the choice of variety and the ecotypes of individual species. If production of essential oils is not the primary purpose, these elements may be of secondary consideration compared with the pleasure of simply having a herb garden tucked away among your flowers and vegetables.

If it is impossible to start with seedlings or if the species you want are herbaceous, you can resort to seeds. Although it may not always be easy to obtain a complete and varied range, there is as a rule little difficulty in buying all the most common herbs, not only from garden centers and specialist shops, but nowadays often from supermarkets.

Seeds may be sown either in open ground, or indoors or under glass in beds or trays, thinning out and transplanting in the usual manner. This will provide you with early seedlings which, given adequate protection, will be ready for transplanting in spring.

Vegetative multiplication as an alternative to seed-sowing is feasible for a number of plants, particularly many labiates, by transplanting rhizomes that are split and provided with at least two buds (mint); many composites can be propagated by dividing the clumps (tarragon), separating parts of the root system; in the case of lavender, since it is a hybrid, multiplication is done by cuttings, and this can also be done for perennial woody species. To encourage rooting, insert the cuttings in appropriate hormonal preparations.

Feeding. It is extremely important to know the characteristics of the species you want to grow: often it is sufficient to apply fertilizers sparingly, partly because the active principles may be compromised by an excessive supply of nutritive elements. It is also important to be familiar with the parts of the plant that will be utilized: in fact, the development of flowers and inflorescences requires a good supply of phosphate, while the fruits or roots need potassium feeds.

If you want to apply organic fertilizers, such as manure, you should use it only when it is fully aged. Since it is not always easy to get hold of manure, an alternative is to obtain organic fertilizers from nurseries. In the average garden it may be useful to reserve a corner for the maintenance of a compost heap with plant and domestic vegetable residues; if an eventual addition of minerals is necessary, you can use

The most common diseases afflicting herbs. The table lists the principal effects with suggestions as to how they can be countered.

family	genus and species	parts used	diseases
Compositae	Achillea millefolium L.	whole plant	rust (*Puccinia millefolii*)
	Anthemis nobilis L.	flowers	brown leaf spots (*Alternaria*); white rust (*Albugo tragopogonis*)
	Artemisia dracunculus L.	leaves	rust (*Puccinia absinthii*)
Iridaceae	Crocus sativus L.	dry stigmas	cankers (*Rhizoctonia violacea*); rot (*Phoma crocophila*); bulb rot (*Penicillum cyclopium*); fusarium wilt
Labiatae	Hyssopus officinalis L.	leaves and flower heads	rust (*Puccinia glechomae*); mildew (*Oidium erysiphoides*)
	Lavandula angustifolia Mill.	flower stems	dodder; root rot (*Rosellina necatrix*); mycoplasms transmitted by cicadas; *Septoria lavandulae*; *Phoma lavandulae*
	Melissa officinalis L.	leaves	scab (*Phleospora melissae*)
	Mentha x piperita L.	whole plant	rust (*Puccinia menthae*); *Ramularia menthicola* (white spots)
	Ocimum basilicum L.	leaves and green plant	seedling rot; root rot
	Origanum majorana L. (and O. vulgare L.)	leaves and flower heads	seedling rot
	Rosmarinus officinalis L.	leaves	yellowing leaves
	Salvia officinalis L.	leaves	rust (*Puccinia salviae*); mildew (*Oldium erysiphoides*)
	Salvia sclarea L.	leaves, flower heads	seedling rot; labiate peronospores (*Peronospora lamii*)
	Satureja montana L. (and S. hortensis L.)	leafy branches, flowering branches	*Puccinia menthae, Rhizoctonia* (collar rot)
	Thymus vulgaris L.	flowering herb	rust (*Aecidium thymi*)
Malvaceae	Althaea officinalis L.	rhizomes, leaves in salad, fresh fruits	root rot (too much water) rust
Rutaceae	Ruta graveolens L.	leaves and flowering branches, fruits	rust (*Aecidium rutae*); mildew (*Oidium erysiphoides*)
Umbelliferae	Anethum graveolens L.	leaves, flowers, fruits	seedling rot
	Angelica archangelica L.	fresh leaves, stalks, stems, roots, fruits	rust (*Puccinia bullata*); *Fusicladium dendriticum*
	Apium graveolens L.	fruits, roots, green parts	seedling rot; *Septoria apiicola*
	Coriandrum sativum L.	fruits	mildew (*Oidium erysiphoides*)
	Foeniculum vulgare Mill.	leaves, fruits for essence	seedling rot; *Cercospora apii* (yellowing of stems)
	Levisticum officinale Koch Petroselinum crispum (Mill.) A. W. Hill	leaves, stems, rhizomes leaves, fruits	root rot; *Septoria* fusaria
Verbenaceae	Lippia citriodora Kunth	leaves (tea) chopped in sauces	root rot; rust; leaf drop

control	pests	control
	Galeruca tanaceti; Rhopalomya millefolii	Rotenone
no treatment	*Agriotes* sp.; moths; aphids	disinfect soil;
rotation	leaf miners	no treatment of plant; chromotropic traps
Bordeaux mixture	nematodes (yellowing leaves)	rotation; Rotenone
	leaf curl (caterpillars?)	
disinfect soil and bulbs when planting	nematodes	disinfect soil
	nematodes, cicadas	rotation
weedkiller; better surroundings; Bordeaux mixture	*Thomasiniana lavandulae* (gall midge) stem necrosis; *Alucita tetradactyla* (butterfly)	repellents, pyrethrum
decoction of horsetail wettable sulfur powder	slugs among seedlings; leaf-eating beetles; green aphids; cicadas; flea beetles; nematodes (*Meloidogyne hapla, Pratylencoides* sp.); *Chrysomela manthastri*; mite (*Phytopitus magacerus*)	no treatment possible against nematodes except to sterilize soil; pyrethrum and Rotenone
disinfect seeds avoid too much water	cicadas; aphids	chromotropic traps
disinfect seeds	cicadas	Rotenone, pyrethrum
protect the plant from low temperatures	*Chrisolina americana* (stem and leaf beetle)	
sulfur-based products, but apply with care	cicadas (froghoppers) (*Lapyronia coleoptrata*); defoliant fly (*Phytomyza atricornis*)	
disinfect seedlings; Bordeaux mixture		
Bordeaux mixture		
	nematodes (yellowing leaves) (*Meloidogyne hapla*); leaf-roller moth (*Tortrix pronubana*)	disinfect soil eliminate nests
improve drainage	aphids; flea beetles; cicadas	tobacco extract, repellents chromotropic traps
	swallowtail butterfly (*Papilio machaon*)	tobacco extract
disinfect seedlings	slugs	metaldehyde
	mites (yellowing of leaves); celery miner fly (*Acidia heraclei*)	normally no treatment
disinfect seeds; Mancozeb	celery fly (*Phylophylla heraclei*)	Rotenone
	aphids (rarely); in fruits; *Setomorpha insectella*	chromotropic traps
disinfect seeds	aphids and moths (*Depressaria nervosa*)	gardening insecticides; tobacco extract, Rotenone
improve drainage Maneb	aphids	chromotropic traps
improve drainage insufficient water		

natural mineral compounds, following the instructions for use on the package.

On small plots you can resort to green manuring, which involves digging in herbaceous plants growing on the site (legumes such as trefoil or crucifers such as white mustard); in this way you can provide against a possible lack of manure by means of rotation.

One of the most frequent and serious problems encountered after transplanting is the spread of weeds; in the kitchen garden or on the balcony they can be kept under control quite simply by hoeing or removing by hand. One piece of advice, however: before proceeding, try to find out the name and characteristics of the offending plant, which will gradually increase your botanical knowledge: it is possible that these species may have some aromatic property or that they are wild vegetables. This is not the place, however, to discuss the various agricultural methods of preventive or selective weed killing, the province of specialized publications.

Two further techniques may be recommended for the larger kitchen garden: turning the soil between the rows up to a safe distance from the foot of the plant, and mulching, which entails covering the soil surface around the seedlings or between the rows with suitable material (straw, sawdust, wood shavings). As a rule the problem of weeds decreases as the plant grows and in the case of labiates can virtually be discounted once the clumps spread to cover all the available space.

Pests and diseases.   As a rule little provision has to be made to protect herbs from parasites: almost all the principles secreted by these plants tend to repel insects and fungi and only occasionally, as a result of errors in feeding (too much nitrogen), are there likely to be attacks, and those seldom serious. In the case of labiates, the presence of ethereal oils serves as a natural defense, preventing the germination of weeds or of parasitic fungi. But should an attack be verified, it is always advisable not to apply products of high persistence and in any event to remember that if applied during a period when oils are scarce the principles used will not persist in the plant afterwards. There are also biological products, such as infusions of camomile against mallow mildew, and concoctions of *Equisetum* and pulp of stinging nettle that are effective against mildews and rusts. Insecticides of vegetable origin (pyrethrum, rotenone and nicotine) or adhesive chromotropic traps or electric traps can be used against insects. In cases of absolute necessity, the protection of new plantings and seed beds may be provided by products on the market that have cytotropic action (in which the active principle is absorbed by the tissues of the plant dosed with the product) or systemic action (whereby the active principle is absorbed by all the organs); once the problem is solved, no further measures are needed. The final treatment should be given well before harvesting or use of the parts of the plant being cultivated, in accordance with times of low concentration of aromatic/essential oils. In all situations both on open ground and in the herb garden, biological weapons are always to be preferred.

Harvesting.   When harvesting the plants or parts of them with a view to storage and deferred use or extraction of active principles, you must bear in mind that the concentration and presence of oils and principles are never constant in time and that they are at their maximum during a period which varies from species to species.

The harvesting of the leaves and green parts is usually carried out in the peak period of vegetative development, before flowering (laurel, sweet basil, lemon balm, mint, and sage); the inflorescences and flowers at the beginning of the flowering period (milfoil, lavender, oregano); seeds and fruits when mature (anise, fennel, rose, mustard); underground organs (tubers, rhizomes, bulbs, roots) when the plant enters the rest period and thus before the next vegetative cycle (chicory, gentian, iris).

Storage.   When a herb garden furnishes a fairly large range of different products, you can prepare a good reserve of them to last their entire rest period. Due provision must therefore be made to pick at the right moment and then to preserve the parts in which you are interested by drying. The commonest method in the home is to hang the bunches in an airy, shady place until they are completely dried. This process should be sufficiently rapid to ensure that the useful substances do not alter as a result of fermentation, which may come about if the surroundings are too humid. This technique provides dried herbs which retain their characteristics only for a short time, usually about a year. When you have a large quantity of herbs to harvest, you can use racks, with the plants in layers one above the other; regularly turn and shift them to dry them out; the better the ventilation, the quicker they will dry.

Drying at a high temperature of 95°–104°F (35°–40°C) is likely to produce alterations; for large quantities, therefore, it is preferable to dry them in an air current by dehumidification, using an electric fan, whereby the products will be unaltered either in color or quality. The dried herbs may be kept in containers that are airtight or at any rate made of non-hygroscopic materials. Be sure to label them individually; in the end, with so many closed containers that look alike, there is no other way to distinguish them.

CALENDAR OF WORK IN THE HERB GARDEN

January.   In warm climates, this is the time to start preparing the beds for planting. Plan for covering tender herbs with leaves or straw to protect the buds from frost. You can still harvest the roots of tarragon and comfrey. Rocket and mustard can be sown in a spot that is not too much exposed.

February.   In warm climates, harvest the flowers of butterbur, transplant garlic bulbils and sow onions in open ground. Sow sweet basil and garden cress in a protected spot. Propagate rhubarb by root cuttings. Prune woody labiates. Dig up rhizomes of mint for propagation by division. If you have not already done so, make time to harvest roots and rhizomes (dandelion, horseradish, marsh mallow), also usable for multiplying the plants themselves.

March. In temperate climates you can start to prepare the garden for planting but in the coldest climates you must still wait another month and maybe two. In the south you can work the ground thoroughly, tidying up, feeding and, if need be, planting. Transplant garlic and onions and sow red pepper and celery in protected seed beds: sow parsley, rocket, mustard and cress in ground. Divide and replant clumps of tarragon and discard outworn chive plants. Take cuttings of the more common labiates.

April. Propagate sage, rosemary, and lavender by cutting and burying the prostrate side branches that have produced roots; thyme, winter savory, oregano, and majoram by dividing clumps. In temperate areas sow annual cold hardy plants such as the umbellifers dill, chervil, and coriander. It will probably be necessary to hoe in order to rid the ground of weeds. If necessary, apply organic feeds.

May. It is still possible to multiply labiates, tarragon, and chives by clump division. This is the end of the useful season for sowing annual or biennial umbellifers (dill, cumin, and coriander); seeds should be sown thinly and then lightly hoed over. Sow borage and harvest mustard, separating the seeds. Pick rhubarb stalks and thyme, prior to flowering, for drying. Remove the inflorescences of sweet basil so as not to wear out the seedlings. You can pick thyme, borage, rocket cress, and marigold flowers. Apply some fertilizer to restrengthen the plants.

June. You can still sow rocket, parsley, sweet basil, and, in seed beds, leek. Thyme has finished flowering, so you can harvest it by cutting it drastically and then drying it. Water and feed to encourage new shoots. Pick the leaves of rosemary and lemon balm, laying them out in the shade in a thin layer to keep them from turning dark. Cut sage and mint and dry them in the shade. Elder is now in flower; harvest the inflorescences to use immediately or after drying. Angelica concludes its biennial cycle; harvest the fruits as they ripen. Remove the leaves of mallow affected by rust, burning them after picking.

July. Water lemon balm, mint, and rhubarb. Harvest the inflorescences of lavender and oregano, the heads of thyme, lemon balm, and tarragon. Virtually all herbs, especially the labiates, can be propagated by cuttings this month. Sow angelica in sandy propagating mixture. Propagate iris and also harvest the rhizomes for drying so as to obtain the delicate fragrance, which resembles that of violets.

August. Continue, until harvesting, to water lemon balm, mint, mallow, and rhubarb; harvest their stalks; the flowers of the hollyhock (*Althaea rosa*), once picked, are set out to dry in shade after making a necklace of them with needle and thread. Pick oregano and marjoram (now in full bloom) and dry them in bundles, separating the leaves and flowers into paper bags. Pick tarragon and put the leaves in the freezer. Clumps of sage, thyme, rosemary, lavender, and hyssop can be pruned back.

September. Transplant leeks. Winter savory comes into flower; harvest it when in full bloom, cutting it off within an inch of the ground. Hyssop may again be cut back. Later the two labiates can also be propagated by division of clumps. Fruits of the wild fennel are now maturing; remove the umbels and leave them to dry upside down so that all the achenes are harvested. Sow feverfew, crumbling a few old flower heads over the place where it is to grow. Do the same for camomile, lightly pressing down the soil.

October. You can still go over the beds and take woody root cuttings such as rosemary, lavender, hyssop, thyme, savory, oregano, marjoram, and tarragon. Transplant garlic bulbils. Begin harvesting the underground parts of marsh mallow, comfrey, horseradish, elecampane, and angelica. Perennial plants, with the exception of angelica which reproduces by seed, can be propagated by dividing the upper parts of the roots (neck area). Proceed with drying of the roots: brushed and cleaned, cut them into slices and put them in the oven at 120°F (50°C). Horseradish is picked and chopped up immediately; given the weed-like character of the plant, it is best to give it a corner in the garden where it can grow for several years; harvesting of the roots is never ending and even a small piece will develop new vegetative parts.

November. Protect delicate plants, by covering the base or better still, in northern regions, by shielding the entire plant.

December. Package some of your harvest as Christmas gifts.

HERBS IN POTS

You do not need a large area to grow herbs. People who live in flats, for instance, will probably not have a private garden, and it is therefore a matter of making the best of what space is available, whether it be a terrace, patio, balcony or even just a windowsill.

If the terrace is sufficiently big, you can grow herbs in pots of suitable size; and broadly speaking, anything that is cultivated in the herb garden can be grown indoors, though in lesser quantities.

Above all, bear in mind two very important factors: position and ventilation. The position cannot always be easily chosen or changed, depending on chance or on the layout of the home. But if some thought has been given in the design to local climatic conditions, the terrace may face southeast to southwest, sheltered from the winds; if not, there are likely to be problems of light, extremely important for many herbs. But it is always worth trying to grow them, provided you have enough indirect light.

This brings us to ventilation. Terraces open on two sides are often buffeted by wind and heavy rain: this situation can be improved by putting up side walls of wood or glass, in which case it may be a matter of getting planning permission or approval from neighbors. Remember, too, that walls bring their own problems related to microclimate; reflection can cause notable temperature fluctuations during the day, bringing about serious dehydration.

Of all plants grown on a terrace, herbs are undoubtedly the least difficult, much simpler, say, than cultivating a geranium. Broadly speaking, the woody perennials (thyme, sage, lavender, etc.) can put up with average changes of temperature and irregularities in watering, but everything depends on the size of the pot or container holding the soil. In this respect pay special heed to the drainage; water must never be allowed to stagnate in the pot, for this can lead to root rot and leaf loss, symptoms that may prove lethal to annual plants such as sweet basil.

The plants need special attention during the long winter months: if you give them protection with a sheet of plastic film, remember to water them every now and then. Protect the more delicate plants with a little straw and spread some , too, around the pots to limit the radiant surface.

On small terraces, and also on windowsills, you can grow a few seedlings in pots: given the more restricted possibilities, you will need to think carefully about which species to grow, probably going for plants that are attractive rather than useful. Make certain they do not get too hot in the sun, especially if the seedlings are behind glass. If need be, get a screen or shade.

Avoid plastic containers, even large ones, at all costs. Earthenware and wood are the materials to use, but if necessary you can put plastic dishes underneath to collect excess water. If you go on holiday do not forget your seedlings: you could install an automatic watering system outdoors (available at garden centers and hardware stores) and on a windowsill you can use the method of turning a bottle upside down resting against the bottom of a dish.

HERBS AS ORNAMENTAL SUBJECTS

This section may seem superfluous to those who already know the aesthetic qualities of many of the plants listed in this book. But it is worth underlining the variety of roles that they can assume, providing a range of appeals not only to the palate but also of delightful sensations, appealing, as circumstances dictate, to the nose and the eye.

In the garden, of course, the arrangement of plants is very much a matter of personal taste and choice. Many herbs, particularly the small-sized labiates, are very suitable for forming borders to paths and flower beds; others, like lavender, can be successfully used for low flowering hedges. Having planned their position, it is a good idea, before actually planting them out, to do some tests, because nurseries offer many varieties and not all give the same result. In the case of lavender, for example, plants may have inflorescences that are erect and not too long or, vice versa, elongate and drooping; their aesthetic effect is quite different.

In organizing the garden there are two fundamental schemes, depending on personal circumstances; one is applicable to those who have a lot of time to spend on tending the garden, including pruning and other basic jobs; the other is for those with little time to devote to garden tasks.

In the former case the choice will probably be for a garden of paths and beds, reminiscent of the seventeenth-century Italian style; but even here there is a risk of overdoing things; if the garden is small, too much emphasis on geometry will be hard on the eye, if it is big, you risk becoming a slave to it.

The famous monastery gardens of "simples" were based on geometric principles: inside a cloister, the geometric beds accommodated clumps of medicinal and aromatic plants, and as a rule there was a fountain in the center. By reproducing this you create an atmosphere of other-worldness in which only the tinkling of the fountain marks the passage of time. But the environment may not cater to such a rarified atmosphere. More informally, you can soften hard lines of the garden by using plants to frame the benches, the table, the house door, and you can provide an original note by planting thyme, mint, and camomile between the paving stones. In the flower beds themselves the plants that tend to grow tallest (umbellifers, rosemary, and damask roses) should go at the back; in the center you can put the plants with showy flowers (borage, marigold, and oregano); and at the front you can have borders of wild thyme, chives, hyssop, wall germander, and wall pepper. Separating hedges can be of lavender, laurel or angelica.

For the gardener with little time, however, the preference will probably be for a natural garden on the English pattern. Here too, you will need to take care. There is a risk of your spending the day fighting weeds or trying to contain the growth of a tree guaranteed on purchase to have a dwarf habit! After making your visual choice, trying out a number of species and using as many locally-grown specimens as you can (the thinking is, if it grows wild in your neighborhood, a plant will certainly not be too demanding in your garden), the real work begins. You will need to provide the substrate with suitable drainage so that pools of water do not form and stagnate. Create an area of shade to offset one in full sun, and reserve a "Mediterranean" corner (sage, thyme, rosemary) as near as possible to the kitchen door. A dry wall will provide a suitable surface for many rock plants, which can also be tucked into the cracks (as is often found in nature); in south-facing gardens typical of the southern regions of the Mediterranean a caper plant will grow in the cracks.

Another interesting feature that we have not so far mentioned is that almost all the wild and cultivated aromatic plants of temperate regions are melliferous, i.e. they are visited by bees (and also bumblebees and butterflies) which gather nectar and, sometimes, pollen. The scents given out by the flower show the insects the way; try to follow the movements of bees among rosemary flowers or lavender inflorescences and watch how carefully each insect collects the nectar.

USES OF HERBS

Plants or their parts can be used fresh and it is also possible with appropriate treatment, to preserve them or, by special techniques, to concentrate the aromatic contents in liquid form. Mention has already been made of harvesting and drying them.

The following section briefly describes the methods for preparing juices, infusions, decoctions, and alcoholic extracts, and for distillation.

Juices. In the higher plants the greater part of the vegetal cell, enclosed by the cell wall, is constituted by the vacuole, a special organ that contains a solution of various salts, together with numerous substances made by the cell itself. In addition to having an important function in the exchange of liquids circulating in the cell by osmosis, the vacuole allows distension of the herbaceous organs as a result of hydrostatic pressure, which determines the cell's turgor. Among the materials of which the vacuole is composed are reserve substances and products of secondary metabolism such as various active principles (glucosides, alkaloids, tannins, etc.).

The preparation of a juice involves extracting all the components of the living plant, without altering them; in a slightly acidic watery solution (the variations of pH depend on the species and the parts utilized) we find both mineral salts in an ionic form, with macroelements (N, P, K, S) and microelements (Fe, Mn, B, Cu, Zn, etc.), some of which are normally rare in nature.

Apart from these there are other organic substances, varying from species to species, such as alcohols, phenols, aldehydes, ketones, organic acids, oxygenated heterocyclic compounds, glucosides and heterosides; and, more rarely, lipids such as lecithin (glycerophosphates) and alkaloids. No less important are the vitamin groups (A, E, K, group B, C, etc.) and molecules with an enzymic function. Substances present in the cytoplasm, including cartenoid pigments and chlorophyll, also find their way into the juices.

Because of the very complexity of the components of the vacuole, extraction of juice is no simple process, inasmuch as the components themselves are subject to alteration. A vegetable juice, as a rule, has a slightly cloudy consistency, since the afore-mentioned substances are not completely transparent; subsequent clarification may remove

Aromatic plants used for the preparation of infusions and decoctions.

plant	parts used	presoaked	infusion	decoction
Althaea	root	•		
Anise	fruits		•	
Balm	leaves		•	
Burdock	root	•	•	
Camomile	flowers		•	
Chicory	root	•	•	•
Dandelion	root			•
Eucalyptus	leaves		•	
Fennel	fruits		•	
Gentian	root	•	•	•
Lavender	flowers		•	
Linden/Lime	inflorescence		•	
Licorice	root	•		•
Mint	leaves		•	
Orange	dry flowers	•	•	
Orange	dried peel	•	•	

the quality of the finished product. A reliable indication of the freshness of the extraction is its green color, due to the presence of chlorophyll; slight oxidations that tend to turn the liquid brown do not adversely affect its naturalness. A juice possesses a high degree of activity (e.g. tonic, stimulant, medicinal) thanks to the procedure of mechanical extraction, which does not cause significant alterations. It is easy to assimilate and wholesome by reason of the presence of various complex molecules, and brings out the essences contained in the plant, which are beneficial to the sense organs.

Infusions. Juices should be used almost immediately, because the components can easily undergo degradation or oxidization, thus altering their original composition. The use of infusions, on the other hand, makes it possible to utilize parts of the plant not only in a fresh state but also after being harvested and dried. These parts can be cut into pieces and chopped up so as to increase the surface in contact with the water: in some cases, where woody and extremely dry parts are used it may be necessary to macerate them beforehand. Meanwhile the water is prepared and once it has come to the boil this is poured over the material already chopped up. Keeping the container covered, let the infusion stand for a period of time that will vary according to the plant or mixture used. Eventually it is filtered and drunk. The infusion cannot be kept because here too, as it cools, there is a chance of fermentation and alteration of its components (at the most you can keep it for a day in the refrigerator).

Not all the compounds find their way easily into the solution obtained: the apolar substances, as for example the essential oils, have difficulty in becoming soluble; only if the oil is made up of partially polar molecules is it possible to extract it, moistening it with alcohol, as can be done, for instance, with terpenic esters. Hot water will also detach the partly dissolved droplets of oil. It must be remembered that the thermolabile molecules can undergo modifications as a result of high temperature and that the subsequent maceration must be of short duration, to avoid alterations. And it is a good idea to prepare the chopped or ground parts of the plant at the time of use and not beforehand, so that there is no risk of this greater surface area altering the product if and when it is subsequently stored.

The time of infusion may be extended for half an hour at the most, but this often depends on the product being used and the intended application.

Decoctions. Whereas in the preparation of an infusion boiling water is poured over the herb, in the case of a decoction the water and the plant parts are left to boil together in the same container. Here too prior maceration may be necessary. The herb is mixed in a suitable proportion with the water, brought to the boil and kept on a low flame as long as necessary (as usual, variable according to the plant, the plant material or the mixture). The whole decoction is then left to cool in the same receptacle and then strained through a sieve or thick gauze.

This technique makes it possible to extract substances from the particularly tough parts of the plant (roots, rhizomes, etc.). It is unsuitable for aromatic plants containing essential oils, most of which pass distilled into the steam.

Alcoholic extracts. The process of fermentation has been used since ancient times to extract certain aromatic elements of plants and to make alcoholic beverages.

Alcohol, unlike water, is not a polar solvent, but easily penetrates the tissues, thus rendering soluble molecules that are insoluble in water. In this way it is possible to obtain simple extracts of the fresh plant (spirit solution: ratio of plant and alcohol 1:1) or of the dried plant. Extracts with more complex treatments involve concentration of the macerate (hydroalcoholic extracts) or distillation in ethanol (spirit solutions).

It is important, in all cases, that maceration be carried out at room temperature and subsequently in a vacuum to avoid oxidization. The temperature can be raised above 104°F (40°C) only in the case of components that are not altered by heat. Maceration is followed by percolation, when the liquid extract, possibly filtered, is passed repeatedly through the herb, which has been put into an apparatus with a tap at the bottom. A subsequent concentration concludes the treatment. To make sure the product keeps, it is often a good idea to add a small quantity of an anti-oxidant such as ascorbic acid. Extracts of this type are called tinctures or mother tinctures

Picking times. The table indicates the months for harvesting certain aromatic plants and the parts used.

species \ months	1	2	3	4	5	6	7	8	9	10	11	12
Althaea officinalis L.	root	root	root		flowers	flowers	leaves	leaves		root	root	root
Angelica archangelica L.			stems	stems	stems				fruits	root	root	
Artemisia absinthium L.					leaves	leaves	flowers	flowers	flowers			
Artemisia vulgaris L.					leaves	leaves	flowers	flowers		root	root	
Cichorium intybus L.	root	root	leaves	leaves						root	root	
Gentiana lutea L.			root	root						root	root	
Hyssopus officinalis L.						leaves	leaves / flowers	flowers				
Juniperus communis L.									fruits	fruits		
Laurus nobilis L.						leaves	leaves					
Lavandula angustifolia L.								flowers	flowers	flowers		
Matricaria chamomilla L.						flowers						
Melissa officinalis L.				leaves	leaves	flowers	flowers					
Mentha spp.						leaves / flowers	leaves / flowers	leaves / flowers	leaves / flowers			
Ocimum basilicum L.					leaves / flowers	leaves / flowers	leaves / flowers	leaves / flowers	leaves / flowers			
Origanum vulgare L.							flowers	flowers				
Pimpinella anisum L.							fruits	fruits				
Rosmarinus officinalis L.					leaves	leaves						
Salvia officinalis L.				leaves								

root   fruits ●

flowers or inflorescences   leaves

stems

53

Species from the temperate regions of Europe used for the preparation of liquors, bitters, and digestive and tonic drinks, with an indication of the parts used and the months for harvesting.

genus and species \ months	1	2	3	4	5	6	7	8	9	10	11	12
Achillea millefolium L.						FH	FH	FH	FH			
Achillea moschata Wulf.							FH	FH				
Acorus calamus L.			R	R					R	R	R	
Allium ursinum L.				L	L							
Anethum graveolens L.								FR	FR			
Angelica archangelica L.			R	R					R S	R S		
Anthemis nobilis L.							FL	FL				
Apium graveolens L.			L	L	L			S	S R	R		
Artemisia absinthium L.							L	L	L			
Artemisia dracunculus L.					L	L						
Artemisia genipi Weber							EP					
Artemisia pontica L.					L	L						
Artemisia vulgaris L.								FH	FH			
Carum carvi L.							S	S				
Citrus aurantium L.	FR								FR	FR	FR	FR
Citrus limon L.	FR	FR	FR	FR	FR	FR					FR	FR
Cnicus benedictus L.							FH	FH				
Coriandrum sativum L.							S	S				
Crocus sativus L.								FL	FL	FL		
Cuminum cyminum L.							FR	FR				
Filipendula ulmaria (L.) Maxim.					L	FH						
Foeniculum vulgare Mill.									S	S		
Galium odoratum (L.) Scop.						FH	FH					
Gentiana lutea L.			R	R							R	R
Geum urbanum L.			R	R	FH	FH	FH	FH	FH	R	R	
Glycyrrhiza glabra L.	R	R									R	R	R
Humulus lupulus L.							FL	FL				

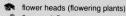

🌿 leaves   ● fruits   ☌ buds
🌺 flower heads (flowering plants)   ↑ entire plant   ⚘ roots
⚘ flowers, inflorescences   ●● seeds or achenes

genus and species	1	2	3	4	5	6	7	8	9	10	11	12
Hyssopus officinalis L.					●	●	●					
Inula helenium L.							●			●	●	
Iris germanica L. var. *florentina*							●	●				
Juglans regia L.									●	●	●	
Juniperus communis L.									●	●		
Lippia citriodora Kunth						●				●		
Matricaria chamomilla L.						●	●	●				
Melissa officinalis L.				●	●		●	●	●			
Mentha x piperita L.							●	●	●	●		
Myrrhis odorata (L.) Scop.						●	●		●	●	●	
Ocimum basilicum L.					●	●	●	●	●			
Origanum majorana L.							●	●	●			
Origanum vulgare L.							●	●				
Pimpinella anisum L.							●	●				
Pinus mugo Turra					●	●						
Prunus dulcis D. A. Webb								●	●			
Rheum spp.									●	●		
Rubus fruticosus L.							●	●	●	●		
Rubus idaeus L.							●	●	●			
Ruta graveolens L.					●	●	●	●				
Salvia officinalis L.				●	●							
Salvia sclarea L.					●	●	●	●				
Sambucus nigra L.						●	●					
Satureja hortensis L.							●	●	●			
Satureja montana L.								●	●	●		
Thymus vulgaris L.				●	●	●						
Viola odorata L.			●	●			●	●				

Above: diagram of an alembic for steam distillation.
Below: diagram of plant for vacuum distillation.

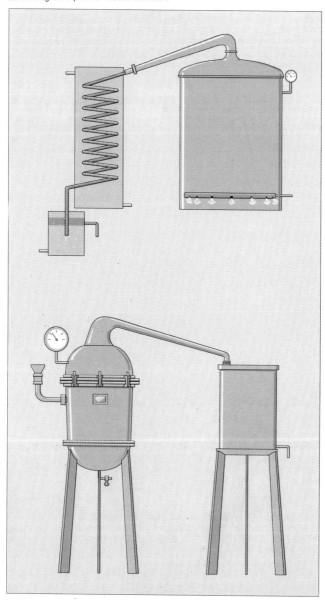

according to the concentration (tincture: ratio of plant to alcohol 1:5).

Essential oils may be extracted from either the fresh plants or dried herbs that are previously macerated with ethyl alcohol and then distilled.

Essences and distillations. Distillation is based on extraction through evaporation and then condensation of the principles sought, in a suitable coolant, normally water. In the ancient alchemists' shops and pharmacies the alembic, an old type of distillation equipment, reigned supreme, often giving excellent results.

The hot steam from the material being treated travels from the receptacle through a coiled tube, out of which flows the condensate, where the water and oil are separated.

Oils that are not sensitive to high temperatures can be obtained by direct distillation. This is of two types: distillation by immersion (to avoid direct contact of the parts of the plant with the walls of the boiler) and distillation in a current of steam, obtained by placing the plants in a distillation chamber. The latter is more reliable because the material for treatment is not in direct contact with the flame but is separated from it by a heater containing water which, in the form of steam, passes through the material itself. This procedure eventually improves both the quantity and quality of the distillation. The current of steam carries the various oils to the condenser (usually a coiled tube cooled with water); the oil, in liquid form, unable to mix with water, forms a layer above it. Actually, small quantities of odorous principles also remain in the water, which then takes on the individual scent; this is referred to as distillate or distilled water. By distillation with water only a few compounds pass into the condensate; consequently this method is not suitable for all herbs or, more precisely, for the extraction of all the compounds. On the other hand, alcoholic extracts can be handled by distillation in a bain-marie and this produces a solution (and therefore not a separation in two phases, as is the case with distillation in a watery solution) containing a number of compounds and principles.

The essences are stored in dark or opaque, well-stoppered containers, in cool surroundings; like this they can last for several years. They should be used sparingly, bearing in mind their composition and yield: these are highly concentrated substances of which only a tiny amount, often just a few drops, is sufficient.

Particularly important, moreover, is the need to adhere to optimum picking times; in fact, if the plant is harvested at the right moment the yield of essence may be much higher (i.e. somewhere between 0.1 and 4 percent of the dry weight).

Plant perfumes. The extraction of odorous principles is a very ancient art; certainly the earliest experiments were done by impregnating oil-bearing seeds, perhaps sesame, with the aromas. This is the technique of extraction with fatty solvents, nowadays known as enfleurage, whereby the parts of the plant are placed on a thin layer of animal fat, spread on an absolutely flat surface (glass or metal); after various procedures, when the greasy material has been fully absorbed, there remains a pomade rich in odorous principles. This is then treated with a solvent, such as hexane, which makes the essential oil soluble; the subsequent evaporation of the solvent contains compounds such as waxes and other substances. This, dissolved in high-strength ethyl alcohol and distilled, produces the so-called "absolute" liquid. This is the finished product or alternatively the raw material from which various perfumes are made by means of mixtures or other treatments.

Among the natural substances that bear a pleasant scent are the essences and natural products; the latter are gums, resins, and balsams, in a fluid or semi-solid state.

Essences are for the most part extracted from modest plants, either wild or cultivated, and when combined they can produce prized and costly perfumes. According to their effect, they are separated into distinct groups of odors:

extractive odors: herbaceous, weak, and short-lived
fleeting oily odors: of the jasmine or tuberose type, soluble in oil
volatile oily odors: of the lavender type, soluble in alcohol
acidic aromatic odors: of the vanilla or benzoin type
hydrosulfurous odors (obviously not used in perfumes); of the horseradish or onion type

The following is a brief list of odors or scents forming the basis of a range of perfumes, with indications of the plants possessing them:

anise	dill, coriander, fennel
bitter almond	laurel, cherry laurel
camphor	rosemary
cinnamon	cinnamon, mace, nutmeg
citrus	orange, bergamot, lemon
clove	cloves, herb bennet
fruity	strawberries, apples, pears
jasmine	jasmine, lily of the valley
juniper	junipers
lavender	marjoram, thyme
mint	sweet basil, mint, savory
orange flower	orange leaves, acacia
rose	geranium, rose
sandalwood	cedar
tuberose	jonquil, hyacinth, lilies
vanilla	heliotrope, storax
violet	iris

Although the technique of distillation makes it possible to obtain

Exotic species used as spices for the preparation of liquors, bitters, and digestive and tonic drinks.

family	genus and species	parts used
Araliaceae	*Panax pseudoginseng* Wall.	root
Araliaceae	*Panax quinquefolius* L.	root
Illiciaceae	*Illicium verum* Hook f.	fruits with seeds
Lauraceae	*Cinnamomum aromaticum* Nees	bark, unripe fruits (cassia buds)
Lauraceae	*Cinnamomum zeylanicum* Bl.	bark
Leguminosae	*Tamarindus indica* L.	flesh of legume
Myristicaceae	*Myristica fragrans* Hout.	seeds, aril (mace)
Myrtaceae	*Eugenia caryophyllata* Thunb.	flower buds
Orchidaceae	*Vanilla planifolia* Andr.	pods (fruits)
Ranunculaceae	*Nigella sativa* L.	seeds
Rubiaceae	*Cinchona calysaya* Wedd.	bark
Rutaceae	*Cusparia trifoliata* Engl.	bark
Sterculiaceae	*Cola acuminata* Schott. et Endl.	nuts, seeds
Sterculiaceae	*Theobroma cacao* L.	seeds
Zingiberaceae	*Alpinia galanga* Swartz	powdered rhizomes
Zingiberaceae	*Alpinia officinarum* Hance	rhizomes
Zingiberaceae	*Curcuma longa* L.	powdered rhizomes
Zingiberaceae	*Elettaria cardamomum* (L.) Maton	fruit seeds for oil
Zingiberaceae	*Zingiber officinalis* Rosc.	rhizomes

extremely concentrated qualities of active principles, it must be emphasized that this treatment cannot be carried out on all plants or their parts, since not all essences can sufficiently withstand heat.

Other techniques. It is possible to extract the active principles of herbs using an oily substance, usually olive oil; still more simply, squeeze out the desired part (for example from citrus-fruit skins); finally for dried herbs a particular preparation is the powdered form, obtained by finely crushing the herb.

As well as distillation, the cold-maceration method can be used to extract the perfume from delicate ingredients such as jasmine and tuberose flowers. The petals are laid on a coating of inodorous oil or fat and replaced with new ones each day. The perfume is extracted from the impregnated oil or fat by immersion in alcohol.

The dissolution technique requires the harvested petals to be placed directly into a glass jar with lid, containing either ether or a solvent that will be impregnated by the scent. The solvent is then separated by low-temperature distillation. Finally, as already mentioned, citrus-fruit skins and iris rhyzomes can be pressurized; afterwards, simply filter off the liquid, rich in essential oil.

Not everybody reacts to perfumes in the same way; some people cannot stand the strong perfume of roses, tuberoses or jasmine. It is something to bear in mind when choosing the plants for your own garden: what mixtures of smells will you have in the various seasons of the year?

Alphabetical list of mentioned families and species

The numbers without parentheses refer to the species illustrated and described in the plates; the numbers in parentheses indicate species mentioned in the text accompanying the plates; asterisks indicate species listed in the Table on pp 64–65 which are not mentioned in the text to the plates.

Arizoaceae
  Mesembrianthemum crystallinum L. (116)
Amaryllidaceae
  Polyanthes tuberosa L.   115
Anacardiaceae
  Pistacia lentiscus L.   (113)
  Pistacia vera L.   113
  Schinus molle L.   (112)
Aquifoliaceae
  Ilex paraguariensis St. Hil.   76
Araceae
  Acorus calamus L.   5
Araliaceae
  Panax pseudoginseng Wall.   104
  Panax quinquefolius L.   (104)
Aristolochiaceae
  Asarum canadense L.   *
Betulaceae
  Betula pendula Roth   22
Boletaceae
  Boletus edulis Bull. ex Fr.   21
Boraginaceae
  Borago officinalis L.   24
  Symphytum officinale L.   (24)
Burseraceae
  Boswellia sacra Flückinger   23
  Commiphora mirrha Holmes   45
  Commiphora opobalsamum (L.) Engl. (23)
Cannabaceae
  Humulus lupulus L.   74
Capparidaceae
  Capparis spinosa L.   27
Caprifoliaceae
  Sambucus nigra L.   124
Compositae
  Achillea millefolium L.   3
  Achillea moschata Wulf.   4
  Anthemis nobilis L.   13
  Arctium lappa L.   *
  Artemisia abrotanum L.   (18)
  Artemisia absinthium L.   18
  Artemisia dracunculus L.   17
  Artemisia genipi Weber   19
  Artemisia pontica L.   (18)

  Artemisia vulgaris L.   20
  Calendula officinalis L.   26
  Carlina acaulis L.   31
  Cichorium intybus L.   33
  Cnicus benedictus L.   41
  Cynara scolymus L.   (31)
  Helichrysum italicum Don.   71
  Inula helenium L.   78
  Matricaria chamomilla L.   89
  Petasites sp. pl.   (143)
  Santolina chamaecyparissus L.   *
  Silybum marianum Gaertn.   (41)
  Tanacetum balsamita L.   (134)
  Tanacetum parthenium C.H. Schultz   134
  Tanacetum vulgare L.   135
  Taraxacum officinale Weber   136 (33)
  Tussilago farfara L.   143
Crassulaceae
  Sedum acre L.   (130)
  Sedum reflexum L.   130
  Sedum telephium L.   (130)
Cruciferae
  Alliaria petiolata L.   6
  Armoracia rusticana G., M. & Sch.   16
  Barbarea vulgaris R. Br.   (85)
  Brassica juncea Czern.   (25)
  Brassica nigra (L.) Koch   25
  Capsella bursa-pastoris (L.) Med.   (57)
  Cardamine amara L.   (42)
  Cochlearia officinalis L.   42
  Diplotaxis muralis (L.) DC.   (57)
  Eruca sativa Miller   57
  Lepidium sativum L.   85
  Nasturtium officinale R. Br.   96
  Raphanus sativus L.   (57)
  Sinapis alba L.   (25)
Cupressaceae
  Juniperus communis L.   82
Cyperaceae
  Cyperus longus L.   (9)
Ericaceae
  Gaultheria fragrantissima Wall.   (65)
  Gaultheria procumbens L.   65
  Gaultheria punctata Blume.   (65)

Gentianaceae
Centaurium erythraea Rafn *
Gentiana asclepiadea L. (66)
Gentiana kochiana Perr. & Song. (66)
Gentiana lutea L. 66
Gentiana punctata L. (66)
Gentiana purpurea L. (66)
Gentianella amarella (L.) Borner (66)
Geraniaceae
Geranium macrorrhizum L. 67
Pelargonium graveolens L'Hérit. (107)
Pelargonium odoratissimum L'Hérit.
(107)
Pelargonium radens H. E. Moore (107)
Pelargonium suaveolens L'Hérit. 107
Pelargonium x fragrans (Poir.) Willd.
(107)
Graminaceae
Cymbopogon citratus (DC.) Stapf. (54)
Cymbopogon flexuosus (DC.) Stapf. 54
Cymbopogon nardus L. Rendle (54)
Cymbopogon winterianus Jowitt (54)
Hordeum volgare L. (33)
Vetiveria zizanioides Stapf. 146
Hamamelidaceae
Hamamelis virginiana L. 70
Liquidambar styraciflua L. (133)
Illiciaceae
Illicium anisatum L. (23, 77)
Illicium verum Hook. f. 77
Iridaceae
Crocus sativus L. 50
Iris germanica L. var. florentina Dykes
79
Juglandaceae
Juglans regia L. 81
Labiatae
Agastache anethiodora (Nutt.) Britton
(114)
Glechoma hederacea L. *
Hyssopus officinalis L. 75
Lavandula angustifolia Mill. 84
Lavandula hybrida (84)
Lavandula latifolia Med. (84)
Lavandula multifida L. (84)
Marrubium vulgare L. (129)
Melissa officinalis L. 91
Melittis melissophyllum L. *
Mentha aquatica L. (92)
mentha longifolia (L.) Huds. (92)
Mentha pulegium L. *
Mentha spicata L. (92)

Mentha suaveolens Ehrh. *
Mentha x piperita L. 92
Micromeria thymifolia Fritsch *
Monarda didyma L. (114)
Nepeta cataria L. (102)
Ocimum basilicum L. 99
Origanum heracleoticum L. (102)
Origanum majorana L. 101
Origanum onites L. (102)
Origanum vulgare L. 102
Perilla frutescens Britt. *
Pogostemon cablin (Blanco) Benth. 114
Rosmarinus officinalis L. 120
Salvia officinalis L. 123
Salvia sclarea L. (123)
Satureja hortensis L. 128
Satureja montana L. 129
Thymus serpyllum L. (138)
Thymus vulgaris L. 138
Thymus x citriodorus Schreb. (138)
Lauraceae
Cinnamomum aromaticum Nees 35
Cinnamomum camphora Nees (36)
Cinnamomum zeylanicum Bl. 36
Laurus nobilis L. 83
Sassafrass albidum (Nutt.) Nees 127
Leguminosae
Acacia dealbata Lk. 2
Acacia farnesiana Willd. *
Copaifera sp. pl. 47
Copaifera guyanensis Benth. (47)
Copaifera multijuga Hayne (47)
Copaifera officinalis L. (47)
Copaifera reticulata Ducke (47)
Glycyrrhiza glabra L. 69
Melilotus officinalis (L.) Pall. 90
Myroxylon balsamum (L.) Harms (2)
Tamarindus indica L. (69)
Trigonella caerulea (L.) Ser. (140)
Trigonella foenum-graecum L. 140
Liliaceae
Allium ampeloprasum L. (7)
Allium cepa L. (7)
Allium fistulosum L. (8)
Allium porrum L. (7)
Allium sativum L. 7
Allium schoenoprasum L. 8
Allium ursinum L. (8)
Convallaria majalis L. 46
Malvaceae
Althaea officinalis L. 10
Althaea rosea (L.) Cav. (10)

This table contains a series of plants that are not included in the entries but which nevertheless have useful aromatic properties.

family	genus and species	common name	
Aristolochiaceae	*Asarum canadense* L.	wild ginger	
Compositae	*Arctium lappa* L.	burdock	
	Santolina chamaecyparissus L.	cotton lavender	
Gentianaceae	*Centaurium erythraea* Rafn.	common centaury	
Labiatae	*Glechoma hederacea* L.	ground ivy	
	Melittis melissophyllum L.	bastard balm	
	Mentha pulegium L.	penny royal	
	Mentha suaveolens Ehrh.	mint	
	Micromeria thymifolia Fritsch	micromeria	
	Perilla frutescens Britt.	perilla	
Leguminosae	*Acacia farnesiana* Willd.	cassie	
Papaveraceae	*Papaver rhoeas* L.	corn poppy	
Rosaceae	*Fragaria vesca* L.	strawberry	
	Rosa canina L.	dog rose	
Umbelliferae	*Aegopodium podagraria* L.	goutweed	
	Bunium bulbocastanum L.	black sira	
	Ligusticum mutellina L.	mountain lovage	

parts used	food	spir.	perf.	medic.	distribution
rhizomes	🍴		🍶	●	temperate USA, Canada
first year roots, rhizomes	🍴	🍷	🍶		temperate Eurasia
flower heads			🍶		Mediterranean Europe
flowering plant		🍷		●	northern hemisphere
leaves		🍷			northern hemisphere
leaves	🍴			●	central-southern Europe
leaves	🍴		🍶		Mediterranean Europe
leaves		🍷			Mediterranean Europe
fresh leaves	🍴				southeastern Europe
leaves and flower heads	🍴		🍶		eastern Asia
inflorescences			🍶		Central America
seeds, leaves	🍴				Alps
leaves, fruits	🍴		🍶		northern hemisphere
hips, petals	🍴	🍷	🍶		northern hemisphere
young leaves (salad)	🍴				Europe, Siberia
root, fruits	🍴				western Europe
leaves and stems	🍴				southern Europe

1 ABIES ALBA Mill.

Abies pectinata DC.
Pinaceae
Silver fir, (G) Tanne, (F) sapin, (I) abete bianco

This handsome conifer, widely found in mountain zones mingled with beech, seldom forms woods on its own. The name *alba* is derived from the characteristic light bark. The leaves are blunt-tipped, flat, and arranged brush-like on the branch. A resinous essential oil, smelling strongly of pine, is extracted from the twigs, leaves, buds, and seeds or from the immature cones; it is used for preparing perfumes, salts, and bath foams. The oil has notable soothing properties (it is among the constituents of medicaments taken by inhalation or in aerosol forms). The resins and balms of the Pinaceae species are products of their metabolism, accumulating in resin canals or glands, with the function of closing any wounds caused by physical or biological agents. The balms, which contain more ethereal components, solidify very slowly; this accentuates the scent and gives them a prolonged soothing action.

A. balsamea Mill. (balsam fir) grows in Canada and the north-eastern U.S. and furnishes a yellowish, pleasantly fragrant oleoresin. As it dries it becomes solid and transparent (Canada balsam). This is used in perfumery to produce soaps, in medicine as a balsamic tropical, in microscopy for the preparation of microscopic specimens, and in optics for cementing lenses. An essential oil used for scenting soaps is obtained by steam distillation from the wood of *Cedrus atlantica* Man. (Atlas cedar), which is native to the Atlas range of North Africa. The oil from *C. deodara* G. Don (deodar) is used in India for the preparation of particular perfumes.

2 ACACIA DEALBATA Lk.

Acacia decurrens var. *dealbata*
Leguminosae
Mimosa, silver wattle, (G) Akazie, (F) mimosa, (I) mimosa

Originally from Australia, this plant is widely cultivated for ornamental purposes. It can be grown in mild climates but has to be protected in cold winters because it cannot withstand prolonged sub-zero temperatures. Botanically the name *Mimosa* belongs to a different genus; the name acacia is derived from Greek, the prefix -*ak* signifying sharp or thorny.

This is an evergreen, inermous (lacking spines) tree. The leaves are pinnatisect with numerous leaflets (1⁄6 in [4 mm]); the small yellow pompon flower heads are in pendant clusters; the fruits are berries. The tree should be grown in a sunny spot protected from the wind. Propagation is by seed in spring or by woody cuttings. The plant produces a gum, used like that of other acacias, and known as wattle gum. The yellow flower heads that form the herb furnish an essence, highly valued in perfumery, called cassie or apopanax. The leaves are used in India for the preparation of sugary and acid sauces (chutney).

To give the gums a particular scent for chewing, use is made of a resin extracted from the leguminous *Myroxylon balsamum* (L.) Harms var. *pereirae*, a tall tree growing in San Salvador that furnishes the so-called balsam of Peru, thus named because the resin used to be shipped from that country; it is used in the production of cosmetics and soaps, being a good fixative with a delicate fragrance.

3 ACHILLEA MILLEFOLIUM L.

Compositae

Milfoil, yarrow, (G) Schafgarbe, (F) millefeuille, (I) achillea, millefoglie

The name of the genus refers to Achilles, Homer's hero who is credited for having discovered the vulnerary properties of the plant. It is a composite which grows widely in the northern hemisphere, in fields and on roadsides both at low and high altitude. A rhizomatous perennial plant, with a flower stem sometimes in excess of 3 ft (1 m), its leaves, often quite big, are completely divided into primary and secondary leaflets (bipinnatisect), which are in turn subdivided into thin laciniae, hence the name ''milfoil.'' The small flower heads, in terminal corymbs, are made up of white, cream or pink flowers, those of the central disk being tubular and the outer ones ligulate; the fruits are small achenes.

It is grown in gardens to form grassy carpets that are resistant to trampling, and in the herb garden for medicinal use. It is multiplied by clump division and can be harvested in the first year after planting. The flower heads in full bloom are cut and then dried in the shade.

The plant gives off a strong aroma that is something like that of chrysanthemums. The active principles consist of a mixture of compounds, particularly azulene, pinene, limonene, borneol, tannins and various organic acids. The leaves and flower heads are used for making liquors and in mixture with other herbs for producing bitters. It has been known as a medicinal plant since ancient times, for its digestive, astringent, spasmolytic, emmenagogic and vulnerary actions.

4 ACHILLEA MOSCHATA Wulf.

Compositae

Iva, musk yarrow, (G) Moschus-Schafgarbe, (F) iva, (I) iva

This yarrow gets its specific name from its particularly persistent aromatic, musky scent. A small composite of mountain regions, it is found among siliceous rocks through much of the Alps, especially western and central zones, at heights of over 10,000 ft (3,000 m). A perennial herbaceous plant, its leaves form rosettes at the base of the flower stems; each leaf is pinnatisect, divided into laciniae, gray from the down that covers them. The flowering stems bear a small inflorescence of flower heads in a corymb, each of which has showy, white ligulate flowers enclosing a few central tubular flowers; the fruits are achenes. The receptacle bears characteristic black-bordered green bracts.

Although wild plants can be harvested, they may then have problems of survival; and cultivation is not easy because, as these are alpine plants, associated with particular types of terrain, they have difficulty in adapting. Seeds should be sown in a seed bed with a substratum of sand and gravel, peat and loam, and then transplanted into a place that reproduces the natural habitat. The plants can be distilled to obtain an essence that contains a specific oil, cineole, valerianic aldehyde, camphor and other principles. Both the flower heads and aerial parts are harvested; the young leaves can be used for flavoring mixed salads, and the flower heads in the manufacture of aperitifs, bitters, herbal liquors and iva liquor. The properties are digestive, aromatic, spasmolytic and diaphoretic.

5 ACORUS CALAMUS L.

Araceae
Sweet flag, (G) Kalamus, (F) acore vrai, (I) calamo aromatico

The specific name is derived from the Latin, signifying a cane, and this meaning is echoed in the generic name, from the Greek. The plant reached Europe from Arabia and India and is cultivated both in tropical and temperate zones. Growing widely in the northern hemisphere, the sweet flag is found in shallow water, in ditches and marshlands of continental Europe. Resembling a reed, the plant has a stem that is triangular in section with many rough, sword-shaped leaves up to 3 ft (1 m) long; the spadix-like inflorescence is laterally attached. The sturdy perennial rhizome is the only part of the plant utilized. In temperate regions the plant is sterile and is propagated only by vegetative methods, the underground rhizome being divided and the portions provided with a bud transplanted.

The rhizome is fleshy and contains ethereal oils (principally asarone and eugenol) which give it a sweet, spicy, camphor-like scent, with a bitter aftertaste. The rhizomes are harvested in autumn, quickly cleaned and then dried.

Essence of sweet flag is used in perfumery for amber and oriental preparations and also for flavoring pipe tobacco. In the liquor industry the essences are used for making bitters. It can be eaten in crystallized form (when it is known as German ginger) and to flavor fruit salads. It has diuretic, laxative, carminative, sedative and analgesic properties.

---

6 ALLIARIA PETIOLATA L.

Alliaria officinalis Andrz.
Cruciferae
Garlic mustard, hedge garlic, (G) Lauchkraut, (F) alliaire, (I) alliaria

The penetrating odor of garlic given off by this plant is reflected in the generic name; *petiolata* refers to the long leaf stalk. The species is widespread in temperate regions, in hedges and wet woodland, among rubble and in waste matter where there are plenty of nutritive substances; it tends to spread in shady built-up areas. A biennial herbaceous plant, it grows up to 3 ft (1 m) when in flower, with the stems erect and slightly hairy; the large long-stalked basal leaves are oval with a heart-shaped base and dentate-crenate margins; the upper leaves are smaller, becoming progressively sessile and lanceolate. The white flowers measure about ½ in (1 cm) across and are arranged in long, erect terminal racemes; the fruits are cylindrical siliquae, about 2 in (5 cm) long.

The plant contains a glycoside, sinigrin, which by enzymic action is transformed into sulfurated compounds found in crucifers and mustard, which are similar to garlic. The young leaves, finely chopped, are used, in moderation, for flavoring salads, possessing an agreeable odor and taste with a hint of bitterness, though not as long-lasting as garlic, since the principles are not the same. They can also be used in pungent sauces. In France the seeds are used directly for seasoning foods. The medicinal properties are diuretic, cicatrizing and disinfectant.

7 ALLIUM SATIVUM L.

Liliaceae

Garlic, (G) Knoblauch, (F) ail, (I) aglio

The name *Allium* is derived from Celtic and Persian words used as a general indication of edible bulbs. The origin and provenance of this plant are uncertain, but it was cultivated, as its specific name also suggests, in antiquity. There is documentary evidence that the ancient Egyptians regarded it as an important food plant, but nowadays it does not exist in its wild state.

A perennial bulbous plant that grows to 20 in (50 cm) when in flower, the "head" of the garlic is a compound bulb, in which the single bulbils are separated into compact segments, covered by a stiff white skin. The flower stem is hollow, covered at the base by the sheath of the smooth, straight leaves; both stem and leaves are bare and waxy. The small flowers, with six whitish tepals, form a spherical umbel, protected by a transparent spathe, at the top of the scape. The entire plant, but especially the bulbs, when slightly bruised, give out a penetrating and persistent odor; this is due to the enzymic transformation of the alliin into allylsulfenic acid, from which allicine, responsible for the typical aroma, is derived. In its turn this may be transformed into allyl sulfide, which produces the unpleasant and lingering odor after it has been taken with food.

Garlic is grown by separating the bulbils that constitute the heads, discarding the drooping parts, and planting them out in rows in autumn, leaving 6 in (15 cm) between the bulbils and the rows. The ground should be well dug and drained, rich in humus but with no fresh manure, and hoed periodically. The flower stems are often tied, although this procedure has no special advantages. Garlic is used for seasoning and flavoring meat, sausages, sauces, salads, soups, and vegetables. The plant possesses hypotensive, hypoglycemic and anthelminthic properties and is also a disinfectant by reason of its bacteriostatic and bactericidal action. The essential oil may be utilized for the same purposes and also serves as an insectifuge and biological insecticide. The major world producers are China, Korea, Spain, and India. California is the leading source of garlic in the U.S.

Many species of the genus *Allium*, with large bulbs and a strong flavor, have been harvested and used since antiquity. Only a few of them remain important today, notably in the Mediterranean regions. Among these is *A. ampeloprasum* L., the vine leek, originally from southern Europe, similar in appearance to the common leek; it has a rounded bulb with a yellowish skin, the leaves are flat, and the spherical umbels of pink flowers are covered by a spathe that soon drops off. The leek (*A. porrum* L.), is a cultivated species, probably derived from the previous species, and is to be found, outside gardens, by roadsides or on wasteland; the plant has a cylindrical bulb, covered at the base with white tunics, producing straight, broad leaves, folded in the center; the whitish flowers form a dense umbel. Apart from serving as a vegetable, the leek is used for flavoring soups, rice dishes, salads, and sauces. The common onion (*A. cepa* L.), has been an important food plant since time immemorial; it is also used for seasoning because of its aromatic principles, penetrating but less persistent than those of garlic. Onion extracts are used in the food industry for flavoring many kinds of foods. It has antiseptic, cholagogic and diuretic properties. The shallot (*A. ascalonium* var. *ascalonium* Backer), has a pungent flavor and in recent years especially has been widely used in cooking.

8 ALLIUM SCHOENOPRASUM L.

Liliaceae
Chives, (G) Schnittlauch, (F) civette, (I) erba cipollina

The rush-like shape of the leaves is reflected in the name; the plant is widely found in the north of the northern hemisphere, particularly in wet, swampy mountain zones; farther south it is cultivated as a herb. This plant has a slender bulb covered by a reddish brown skin; the leaves and scape are cylindrical and fairly soft. The violet flowers, with short stalks, are arranged in a globular dense umbel, protected by a scarious bract. Sow in a seed bed in March, transplanting into rows, with 6 in (15 cm) between plants. Harvest the entire leaves, cutting them at the base, thus stimulating the plant to produce new ones. The fairly pungent taste and very agreeable scent are reminiscent of the onion but are less persistent. The finely chopped leaves are used raw to flavor soups, salads, and sauces. The properties are stimulant, diuretic, and antiseptic, and there is a high vitamin C content.

The Welsh onion (*A. fistulosum* L.), with similar uses and properties, is exclusively cultivated but is susceptible to frost. Ramsons (*A. ursinum* L.), has a simple, soft white bulb. It is common in lowland and upland woods, where it forms dense clumps, with flat, stalked, elliptical-lanceolate leaves similar to those of the lily of the valley. The scapes bear loose umbels of white stellate flowers. Both the leaves and the bulbs are used for flavoring.

9 ALPINIA OFFICINARUM Hance

Zingiberaceae
Galingale, (G) Siam Ingwer, (F) grand galanga, (I) galanga

The generic name commemorates Prospero Alpini (1553–1617), the Italian botanist, who described exotic plants. The vernacular name comes from the Chinese *Liang-tiang* (*Alpinia galanga* Swarz), the essence of which was at one time extracted; today only *A. officinarum* is used. The galingale originated in China and is cultivated in Hainan and Thailand. It is a herbaceous plant with lanceolate leaves and stems up to 10 ft (3 m) tall, with spikes of white, red-streaked flowers. Like ginger, the plant produces rhizomes more than 3 ft (1 m) long that possess aromatic and bitter principles, with a spicy flavor.

The galingale is cultivated for the rhizomes, brown on the outside, orange inside. They are harvested in autumn, washed and dried before use. The commercial center is Hong Kong. The plant was known at the time of the Crusades and known for its pungent taste and scent of roses. It is used in powder form and, mixed with other spices, as an ingredient for curry; it is employed for flavoring sausages and exotic dishes, for making soft drinks and in puddings and jellies. The rhizomes also possess stimulant and digestive properties. The essence, yellow-brown, has a fresh and spicy scent of camphor; its constituents are pinene, cineole and eugenol.

The sedge-like *Cyperus longus* L., family Cyperaceae, also known as the galingale, has similar uses. Its rhizomes are swollen into tubers and contain a lot of starch. They have a spicy taste and can be used for cooking.

10 ALTHAEA OFFICINALIS L.

Malvaceae

Marsh mallow, (G) Stockmalve, (F) guimauve, (I) bismalva

The generic name comes from the Greek *altháinein*, meaning to heal, referring to the medicinal properties of the plant. The marsh mallow is widely distributed, though not commonly cultivated, growing mainly in wet places. It is a perennial herbaceous plant, up to 6½ ft (2 m) tall, with an erect stem and lobed, pointed, downy leaves with dentate edges. The large flowers, with pink-violet petals, are sparse or arranged in groups on the stem; the dried fruits are schizocarps that separate when mature into button-shaped achenes. The plant may be propagated by dividing the root clumps or growing from seed, the seedlings later being planted out some 16 in (40 cm) apart. Occasional hoeing and feeding will be necessary.

Parts used are the roots, leaves and flowers, chiefly for their secretion of mucilage, which furnish emollient properties. The roots are harvested in autumn of the second or third year, and the leaves and flowers during the vegetative period. Leaves, buds and immature fruits can also be used for edible purposes and the root extracts for flavoring drinks, desserts, and various dishes.

The hollyhock (*Althaea rosea* [L.] Cav.), originally from the Orient, often grown as an ornamental subject, produces edible young leaves and buds; the flowers of the variety *nigra* contain a large amount of anthocyanin and are harvested because they furnish a natural pigment in various bluish shades, used principally in wines and foodstuffs.

---

11 ANETHUM GRAVEOLENS L.

Umbelliferae

Dill, (G) Dill, Gurkenkraut, (F) aneth odorant, (I) aneto

The specific name describes the heavy scent given out by the plant, the generic name being that already used by the Romans. Mentioned since antiquity, dill was also used by the Egyptians and Jews. It probably came originally from the eastern Mediterranean area and once had a much wider distribution. It is cultivated in the herb garden and is occasionally found growing wild in built-up zones and wasteland.

The species is an annual umbellifer, with large compound, tripinnatisect leaves and delicately laciniate leaflets that clasp the grooved stem. The flower stems are up to 3 ft (1 m) tall and bear dense umbels made up of modest yellow flowers. The fruits are formed of two ovoid mericarps, attached to the smooth lower surface and compressed by a pale wing. Dill may be sown directly out in the spring and early summer in sunny spots; the feathery foliage can be picked at any time; the seeds are harvested when ripe.

The leaves contain essential oils rich in limonene and carvone, the latter ingredient found principally in the fruits. The green parts can be used for flavoring salads, sauces, and cooked foods, the seeds also in preserves, pickles, cheeses, mushrooms, and fish. The flowers are sometimes utilized as ingredients for soups and cooked meat dishes. The essential oil is used for flavoring drinks. Properties are spasmolytic, carminative and emmenagogic.

12 ANGELICA ARCHANGELICA L.

Angelica officinalis Hoffm.
Umbelliferae
Angelica, (G) Engelwurtz, (F) angélique, (I) angelica

The exceptional medicinal properties of this plant are reflected in its name. An umbellifer distributed around the Arctic, angelica has a robust tap-root extremely rich in ethereal oils; the tripinnate leaves are attached by sturdy sheathed stalks to a stem uncommonly large for a herbaceous plant; growing to more than 6½ ft (2 m), it is smooth, hollow and reddish, bearing a large hemispherical umbel of whitish flowers. Growing wild in cool, wet places, in hedgerows and thickets, the fruits are disseminated by flowing water. It is often found together with the related wild angelica (*A. sylvestris* L.), which is smaller with a fluted stem. In southern France the var. *sativa* (Mull.) is cultivated for edible and medicinal purposes.

The hollow flower stems and leaf stalks are harvested in the summer or autumn of the second year, shredded and crystallized for use in flavoring confectionery and biscuits. The fruits in the form of mericarps (incorrectly called seeds), picked in summer, are used for the preparation of bitter and digestive beverages. Angelica is cultivated only by sowing the mericarps first in a seed bed and then transplanted into open ground.

The plant, with bitter, tonic, eupeptic, and carminative properties, is stocked by herbalists, the leaves and roots being harvested, the latter in the second year prior to flowering.

---

13 ANTHEMIS NOBILIS L.

Chamaemelum nobile (L.) All.
Compositae
Perennial camomile, (G) römische Kamille, (F) camomille romaine,
(I) camomilla romana

This plant came originally from western Europe and is grown in northern and central Europe as a medicinal herb. A composite with a strikingly pleasant scent, it is a perennial growing to 20 in (50 cm) . The compound, bipinnatisect leaves are similar to those of *Achillea millefolium* L., but altogether smaller; the flower heads, 1 in (2 cm) across, are of two types; the disks are yellow and tubular, the rays white and ligulate, and the ligule ½ in (1 cm) long. The double-flowered varieties have no tubular blooms. The flower heads display membranous bracts and white paleae on the conical receptacle. The fruits are small, very light achenes.

Camomile is propagated quite easily by division of the clumps in spring, setting out the plants in rows about 20 in (50 cm) apart; they need hoeing and watering. From May onward the flower heads may be picked so as to get a quality product. They should be laid out in the shade and dried rapidly. Entire plants, cut at intervals, are used for distillation. One planting will be productive for about three years. Although sometimes employed for flavoring, camomile is principally used for tisanes and for making cosmetics. In perfumery it is used in flowery scents. It has bittertonic, spasmolytic, anthelminthic and sudorific properties.

14 ANTHRISCUS CEREFOLIUM (L.) Hoffm.

Umbelliferae
Chervil, (G) Gartenkerbel, (F) cerefeuil, (I) cerfoglio

The plant, originally from western regions of Asia, the Caucasus and eastern Europe, is cultivated as a herb. The scientific name is derived from Latin and Greek words for wild, aromatic umbellifers.

Chervil is an annual plant, 20 in (50 cm) or more in height; the erect, downy stem bears compound bipinnatisect or tripinnatisect leaves, delicate as lace. The white flowers are arranged in compound umbels, with characteristic bracts at the base; the dark brown fruit is formed of two elongated mericarps attached on the inner side, thicker at the base and thinner at the top. Chervil can be sown outside in spring, in cool, fertile soil, and sown again in late summer for harvesting the leaves. Weeds may cause problems, so hoeing is necessary.

The leaves, which winter quickly, or the youung plants can both be used; they contain essential oils (isoanethole), glycosides, vitamins and mineral salts. The young leaves, constituting a very delicate herb with a scent similar to aniseed, are popular for seasoning; they are chopped up and used in soups and for flavoring sauces, cheese, salads, fried dishes, and meats, and for producing aromatic vinegar. The plant has digestive, depurative and stimulant properties.

15 APIUM GRAVEOLENS L.

Umbelliferae
Wild celery, (G) Sellerie, (F) céleri, ache, (I) sedano

Among the many forms of cultivated celery, the variety *secalinum* Alef. is important as a herb. The specific name of the plant refers to its heavy, penetrating odor. The species, of uncertain origin but perhaps from the Mediterranean region, is to be found growing wild on wet and flooded ground. In ancient times it was regarded as magical and associated with rites and celebrations of death; the town of Selinunte in Sicily derived its name from the Greek word for the plant, *sélinon*.

A biennial species, up to 3 ft (1 m) tall, the plant has an erect, hollow, grooved stem and pinnatisect leaves with oval, lobate leaflets. The small white flowers are arranged in compound umbels. The fruits are oval mericarps, paired on the lower side, with five conspicuous dorsal ribs.

The variety *rapaceum* (Mill.) Gaud. is grown for the turnip formed by the swelling of the hypocotyl and the upper section of the root, which furnishes a delicately fragrant pulp, to be eaten raw or cooked; the variety *dulce* (Mill.) Pers. is cultivated for its leaves with swollen stalks, pleasantly flavored, which turn white when the base is covered with opaque materials. The leaves of good-sized plants are harvested for their essential oils, which stay active after drying and are used for flavoring sauces, soups, sausages, and also for preparing aromatic salts. An essence used in perfumery for flowery effects is extracted from the fruits.

16 ARMORACIA RUSTICANA G., M. & Sch.
Armoracia lapathifolia Gilib.
Cruciferae
Horseradish, (G) Meerettich, (F) raifort, (I) barbaforte, cren

The ancient name of Britain was Armorica, from which the generic name of this species is derived; the specific name underlines that the plant was grown mainly in the country. This crucifer came originally from eastern Europe and was widely distributed after the thirteenth century as an aromatic and medicinal plant. Horseradish is often grown in the kitchen garden for seasoning, given its strong, penetrating and stimulating flavor. A perennial, glabrous, dark green plant, it has long-stalked basal leaves that are lanceolate, 24 in (60 cm) long, with crenate margins; the stem leaves, however, are pinnatifid. The flower stem consists of a large panicle of white flowers. The fruits are roundish siliculas.

The part used is the cream-colored, branched root which, when broken, gives out a penetrating smell that induces tears. Horseradish is not difficult to cultivate and is done by dividing the rootstock, if possible in good, well fertilized soil. Harvesting is in the autumn when only the roots required for consumption should be taken up, because they do not keep. They contain the glucoside sinigrin which, when the root is crushed, together with the enzyme myrosin, is split into glucose and isosulfocyanate of allyl, this being responsible for the characteristic pungent taste. The young leaves can also be used for flavoring. The properties are antiscorbutic, diuretic, digestive, revulsive and rubefacient.

17 ARTEMISIA DRACUNCULUS L.
Compositae
French tarragon, (G) Estragon, (F) estragon, (I) dragoncello, estragone

The specific name of the plant may refer to the sinuous shape of the roots or, more precisely, the rhizomes, which perhaps resemble a snake or dragon; and in Roman times the plant was attributed with the power of healing snakebites. The species is native to Asia and eastern Europe, nowadays cultivated as a seasoning and seldom found outside the herb garden. It has a bushy habit, with upright branches, growing to the height of 3 ft (1 m). Much ramified and glabrous, it has lower leaves divided into three segments, and upper leaves which are lanceolate-linear. The small, cylindrical heads of yellowish flowers form dense panicles. Cultivation is by division of clumps, because the species is sterile; plant them directly outside in late spring, in rows 20 in (50 cm) apart. They need fertile, well drained soil, and hoeing is necessary to keep down weeds.

All the aerial parts are harvested when flowering starts; these give out a strong, characteristic scent and contain ethereal oils, tannins, and bitter principles. They are mostly used for distillation. The extract serves in small quantities to flavor sauces, preserves, pickles, and aromatized vinegar. It is used in the manufacture of spicy oriental perfumes and is an ingredient in herbal liquors. The fresh parts help to flavor omelets, soups, roasts, fish, mayonnaise, and mustard. It has aperient, digestive, stimulant, and carminative properties.

18 ARTEMISIA ABSINTHIUM L.

Compositae

Wormwood, (G) Wermuth, (F) absinthe, (I) assenzio romano

The generic name refers to Artemis, goddess of maternity, because wormwood was used in regulating women's menstrual disorders. Originally from southern Europe, the plant now grows everywhere, notably in sunny places and on dry wasteland. A perennial species, covered in down which makes it look gray, it has tripinnatisect leaves and erect stems bearing small panicles of yellow-brown flowers. The plant is easily cultivated by direct sowing or clump division; hoeing and moderate feeding are necessary.

The leaves are picked from the woody stems and around the flowers, and are quick to dry. They have a sharp, bitter, and persistent taste that is derived from an ethereal oil that contains thujone and a bitter principle (absinthin). Kitchen use is virtually restricted to the flavoring of meats; the flower heads are utilized in the drinks industry to make vermouth and aperitifs.

Wormwood (also known as absinthe) gained wide popularity in the latter half of the nineteenth century as a drink, especially in France, where it was the favorite of many artists and intellectuals. Sales were subsequently prohibited when it was found that the drink provoked serious nervous and psychological disorders. The first recipes were developed in Switzerland in the late 1700s, but later Pernod used wormwood for his drink when he opened a factory in France. His liquor consisted of alcohol and aromatic herbs that determined its distinctive green color, as well as its characteristic taste and smell. The main ingredients were aniseed, fennel, hyssop, and lemon balm; minor ingredients were angelica, star anise, dittany, juniper, nutmeg, and veronica; these were all macerated together with wormwood plants dried in alcohol. After being left to stand, water was added and distillation proceeded. Other dried and powdered herbs were added to the distillate, including Roman wormwood. The liquid was then diluted to give a concentration of 74% alcohol by volume. The liquor appeared green because of the solution of chlorophyll, extracted from the plant. The custom was to drink it with water which was poured over a lump of sugar in a strainer. The drink turned cloudy and slightly yellow, due to the suspension of essential oils, predominantly thujone, separated by the dilution. Thujone is contained in numerous other plants, in conifers of the genus *Thuja* but also in *Tanacetum vulgare*, *Salvia officinalis* and other species of *Artemisia*. To improve the look of the drink, some producers would add trichloride of antimony, a poisonous salt; but already the effects of the thujone were poisonous, provoking symptoms similar to epilepsy, without further additions. In 1913 the French drank 40 million liters of absinthe, and its sale was prohibited after 1915. As a substitute for this popular drink, Pernod was soon sold everywhere, which excluded wormwood from its formula and increased the amount of aniseed.

Along with Roman wormwood (*A. pontica* L.), cultivated in eastern Europe, wormwood is used as an aromatic bitters. Wormwoods were already known to the ancient Egyptians for their anthelminthic properties (*A. caerulescens* L.). Sea wormwood (*A. maritima* L.), was used for making an aromatic beer in 1700. Southernwood (*A. abrotanum* L.), has a graceful habit, with compound leaves and narrowly laciniate leaflets; it is an old medicinal plant, also used for flavoring beers and herbal liquors, with a scent of lemon.

19 ARTEMISIA GENIPI Weber

Artemisia spicata Wulf.
Compositae
Black wormwood, (G) schwarze Edelraute, (F) génepi, (I) genepi nero

The various wormwoods of the genus *Artemisia* all grow at high altitude and furnish a drug for the extraction of bitter principles used in the manufacture of liquors. Black wormwood is found exclusively in alpine regions, growing in siliceous rocky regions at over 10,000 ft (3,000 m). It is a small shrub, not much more than 4 in (10 cm) high, and completely covered in down, which gives it a silky white appearance. Compound, three-lobed, deeply divided leaves sprout from the base of the creeping, unbranched stems. The small heads of yellowish flowers are covered by dark bracts, forming spikes.

 White wormwood (*A. umbelliformis* Lam. = *A. mutellina* Vil.), is a similar species but with even more deeply divided leaves; and it also grows in zones of limestone. Greater wormwood (*A. glacialis* L.), very rare, has a flowering stem with terminal groups of flower heads and grows only in rocky and stony areas of the western Alps. Indiscriminate harvesting has endangered the species and for that reason attempts are being made to cultivate it, multiplying it by division of clumps. Harvesting of the flower heads only can thus be started in the second year of planting. The whole plant contains bitter aromatic principles used in the manufacture of herbal liquors.

 Black wormwood has tonic, digestive, expectorant and balsamic properties. The much more common and less expensive white milfoil (*Achillea clavenae* L.), growing throughout the Alps, is used for the same purposes.

---

20 ARTEMISIA VULGARIS L.

Compositae
Mugwort, (G) Belfuss, (F) armoise, (I) artemisia, assenzio

This species, found throughout the northern hemisphere, grows typically in built-up areas, tending to form dense clumps along roadsides and in hedges, on banks and escarpments and on waste ground. A perennial plant, up to 6½ ft (2 m) tall, the stem is grooved and strongly branched, with pinnate-parted, dentate leaves that are very dark green above and silvery white below. Along the stem the leaves are lanceolate-linear. The small oval heads of tiny reddish brown flowers, covered by gray bracts, are in terminal panicles. The species is not cultivated but grows wild in the places already mentioned, spreading as a weed into vineyards and orchards.

 Together with the similar *A. verlotiorum* Lamotte, originally from northeast Asia, the leaves of which differ in that the lower ones also have linear segments, mugwort is used as a spice by reason of the inflorescences which contain an essential oil (cineole) with bitter and aperient properties; it was used for seasoning many dishes at a time when parsley was mistrusted because of its allegedly poisonous properties. Moreover, prior to the introduction of hops, it was used for flavoring and stabilizing beer. Roman wormwood (*A. pontica* L.), has deeply divided, gray, downy leaves and panicles of flower heads; in ancient times it was grown for its stomachic, stimulant, and disinfectant properties, and nowadays is used in liquor-distilling for its bitter principles.

21 **BOLETUS EDULIS** Bull. ex Fr.
Boletaceae
Cep, (G) Steinpliz, (F) cèpe, (I) porcino

Edible fungi, especially those that can be preserved in dried form, are very commonly used for flavoring foods. One of the most popular and widely available of these edible mushrooms is the cep, one of the many species of *Boletus*. The generic name is uncertain but may be derived from the Greek *bolites* or fungus.

It grows in deciduous and coniferous woods, especially of fir, from lowlands to mountains, forming a root symbiosis with other forest species.

The cep belongs to that group (Basidiomycetes) known as club fungi which bear spores (basidiospores) inside tubules positioned in the lower part of the cap, where they form a spongy yellowish or creamy white mass. The cap is at first hemispherical, sturdy and lumpy, much smaller than the stalk; it then broadens, becoming flat and convex, until it measures about 6 in (15 cm) in diameter; the color ranges through various shades of brown while the stalk is paler, yellowish. Both cap and stalk have white flesh, firm in young specimens but less compact in older ones. The characteristic smell is very strong when the mushroom is dried, and the flavor is sweet. The most common method of preserving it is by drying; the mushrooms are cleaned and cut into thin strips and may be dried in various ways, the most usual being to string the pieces up in a dry, airy place; and mats can be used for drying them in the sun. In very rainy areas the mushrooms can be put in a moderate oven at 86°–104°F (30°–40°C) for a few hours, removing them from time to time to get rid of the moisture, and repeating these procedures alternately, gradually raising the temperature to 140°F (60°C). When dried, the slices become leathery and fragile and should be kept in paper bags in a dry place; it is not a good idea to put them in glass containers because mold may easily form. Before use, the strips should be plunged into water to soften up. A different method of preserving, after drying the mushrooms, is to crush them to powder in a mortar. In this form they can be stored in sealed glass jars and used for flavoring foods.

Cultivated mushrooms also play an important part in providing flavors; the most common is the field mushroom (*Agaricus hortensis* Pilat. syn. *A. bisporus*) of the family Agaricaceae. The mushroom spawn is grown in a suitable substratum, ideally horse manure, and this compost eventually changes color, appearing moldy. In fact this mold or mycelium develops into a mushroom plant. It is divided into pieces roughly 2 in (5 cm) long and scattered over the substratum in rows. After 40 days or so the first mushrooms appear, and will be produced for two or three months, to be harvested in the required size and quantity. World production amounts to some 1.5 million tons (1987).

Other species that can be cultivated on wood are *Pleurotus ostreatus*, *Kuehneromyces mutabilis*, *Lentinus edodes* and *Flammulina velutipes*; in Germany *Stropharia annulata* is cultivated, with straw as the substratum.

22 BETULA PENDULA Roth

Betula alba L.
Betulaceae
Silver birch, European white birch, (G) Birke, (F) bouleau, (I) betulla

The original areas of this birch are northern regions of Europe and Siberia, but it is also widely distributed over central and southern Europe and grows well in North America. The name is derived from the Celtic root *betù*, perhaps meaning resin, a reference to the tar which is one of the tree's products. The birch grows in wet woodland, mixing with conifers, and in shrubby zones up to an altitude of 6,500 ft (2,000 m), spreading to clearings and un-wooded areas. It prefers acid soil but adapts to poor terrain. The tree has an erect trunk that grows to 65 ft (20 m), with silvery white bark that comes off in transverse strips and tends to turn cracked and blackish with the passage of years. The oval-rhomboid leaves, with double dentate margin, are pointed, with short stalks when young. Male and female flowers are borne on inflorescences with separate catkins; the fruits are winged achenes, commonly called seeds. Use is made of the leaves, bark, and shoots. The leaves, bitter in taste, have a slightly aromatic odor and contain tannins, resin, and saponin.

An essential oil is distilled from the bark and is used for flavoring confectionery, toothpastes, shampoos, hair tonics, and skin preparations; tar essence, used in perfumery, gives the nuance of "Russian leather," so called because it evokes the smell of hides dressed with the tannin extracted from the bark and wood. The birch also features in folk medicine, with properties reputed to be diuretic and capable of curing kidney disorders.

23 BOSWELLIA SACRA Flückinger

Boswellia carterii Birdw.
Burseraceae
Frankincense, olibanum, (G) Weihrauch, (F) oliban, encens, (I) incenso, olibano

The generic name refers to the Scottish botanist John Boswell (1710–80) and the specific name to the sacred and ritual use of this plant. Together with other species of the genus, it grows wild in the Horn of Africa and southern Arabia.

The oleoresin resin that collects in small hollows of the tree trunk is extracted by making incisions in the bark; the resinous droplets ooze out in the form of tears along the trunk and round its base, and are scraped off. Harvesting is suspended only in the rainy season. The incense is made up of different varieties of resin; the white tears, of top quality, are used for religious rituals, for when burned the resin gives out a strong perfume. The tears with pieces of bark, because impure, are ground, along with pieces of no commercial value, into powder. The waste matter is distilled to produce a balsamic oil, used in perfumery, giving particular nuances to scented soaps. Dissolution of the resin in alcohol, and subsequent filtration and concentration, yields a resinoid with fixative properties, employed for making cosmetics.

For religious ceremonies, in addition to frankincense proper, a species of myrrh from Arabia is also used, *Commiphora opobalsamum* (L.) Engl.; the resin burned in Japanese temples, however, comes from the bark of *Illicium anisatum* L. (= *I. religiosum* Sieb. & Zucc.).

24 BORAGO OFFICINALIS L.

Boraginaceae
Borage, (G) Boretsch, (F) bourrache, (I) borragine

Borage grows widely through Mediterranean Europe, though not wild in all regions; it was in fact introduced and cultivated in ancient times, then turning wild. It is found on waste ground near human habitations, around gardens and in arable fields. The name of the genus is derived from the Arabic *abu araq*, father of sweat, with reference to the plant's diaphoretic properties. It is an annual species, covered with sharp bristles, with a branching stem up to 20 in (50 cm) high. The leaves are slightly differentiated: the basal leaves are clearly petiolate, oval, rather pimply, with an irregular margin; the stem leaves are lanceolate and smaller near the top. The flower branches terminate in scorpioid (scorpion-like) cymes, with reclinate flowers on the peduncle. The calyx is sharply lobed; the corolla consists of a short tube and has five large triangular lobes, bright blue, in striking contrast to the black stamens. The fruit separates into four nutlets or mericarps.

The plant is quite easy to cultivate, with seeds sown in spring, in rows on open ground. The distance between the rows depends on the part of the plant to be harvested; in fact, both leaves and flowers can be used. Adequate feeding is necessary plus regular hoeing to keep down weeds. Harvesting of the leaves or heads should be carried out before the flowers are fully out.

The leaves and flowers contain large quantities of mucilage and mineral salts, with emollient, diaphoretic, diuretic and depurative properties, and can be used in summer drinks to give them a refreshing flavor; the leaves are utilized in perfumery for bath oils and salts. The young leaves and flower heads, tasting vaguely of cucumber, can be eaten cooked in salads or fried; they are also used in stuffings, omelets, and pancakes. The flowers can be crystallized and used for decoration of sweets and pastries. An infusion can be prepared from them and they give a characteristic scent and color to vinegar or wine.

Comfrey (*Symphytum officinale* L.), is another species of the Boraginaceae from Europe and the Caucasus, found in fields, ditches, wet woodlands, embankments, and on stream and river banks, where it forms dense cover. The common name suggests its medicinal properties, notably the healing of wounds. It is a perennial plant covered with fairly thick hairs, the stem growing to 3 ft (1 m), with pointed lanceolate, petiolate basal leaves, becoming sessile near the top. The rather large flowers, arranged in scorpioid cymes, have a calyx with a short tube and sharp teeth, while the corolla is tubular, initially narrow and then broadening at the tip, where the style protrudes. As a rule the color is violet but often creamy white. The plant contains vitamins, mucilages, tannins and other principles. The root is full of starch, sugars, and essential oil. The young leaves, in moderation, can be eaten raw in salads (with time they become rough and hairy). The root, harvested in late autumn, was formerly dried and used, sparingly, in liquors. The properties are astringent, emollient and cicatrizant, for which reason it was mainly used externally to cure skin inflammations and to put into bath water (at one time it was believed that immersion in water containing comfrey would enable women to regain their virginity). The rhizome also has dyeing properties, furnishing a brown pigment.

25 BRASSICA NIGRA (L.) Koch

Cruciferae

Black mustard, (G) schwarzer Senf, (F) moutarde noire, (I) senape nera

The generic name, used by the Romans, may have been derived from the Celtic *bresic*, horse, inasmuch as some species and varieties are used as forage. The common name is explained by the fact that the seeds of black mustard are dark brown whereas those of white mustard are yellowish. The species may have come originally from the Mediterranean area, where it is found as a weed among cereals, growing on untilled land.

Once it was widely cultivated for its herbal properties, used for seasoning food and for medicinal purposes.

An annual plant of bristly appearance, it grows to some 3 ft (1 m) and has an erect, branching stem that bears differentiated leaves; the basal leaves, up to 6 in (15 cm) in length, are bright green, pinnatisect and lyrate; the stem leaves gradually decrease in size and are lanceolate. The flowers, approximately ½ in (1 cm) in diameter, have bright yellow petals and form upright, rather contracted racemes. The fruit is a bare, tapering siliqua, about 1 in (2 cm) long; when ripe, the pod contains finely reticulated, blackish or reddish brown seeds.

The seed contains the glycoside sinigrin and the enzyme myrosin, which after lesions of the tissues make contact and produce glucose and isosulfocyanate of allyl; it also contains the bitter principle sinapine and a fatty oil that reduces its keeping qualities. The principles give out a penetrating odor and have an irritating effect on the skin and mucous membranes; and even in small quantities they provoke tears. The dark yellow powder obtained by grinding, with the addition of vinegar and other flavorings, including particularly seeds of white mustard, are used to produce the table mustard, widely used with foods.

The plant was once used medicinally for "senapisms" i.e. to make mustard plasters with a revulsive action, mixing flax seeds and mustard flour with hot water (the high temperature inactivating the principles of mustard).

Indian mustard (*Brassica juncea* Czern.), is a hybrid of *B. oleracea* and *B. nigra* and is cultivated in central and eastern Europe for purposes similar to those of black mustard. It is a slightly smaller plant but the siliquae are up to 2 in (5 cm) long, with a beak of ½ in (1 cm).

White mustard (*Sinapis alba* L.), cultivated since antiquity, is thought to have originated in the eastern Mediterranean regions and was commonly grown for forage. This annual plant has an erect, striated downy, much branched stem of up to 3 ft (1 m), bearing large, pinnate-parted or lyrate leaves up to 10 in (25 cm) long. The divaricate racemes of yellow flowers produce hairy siliquae of about 1¼ in (3 cm), with a long beak of 1–1¼ in (2–3 cm). The rough, greenish brown seeds contain, in addition to fatty oils, the glycoside sinalbin which, by means of enzymic action in the course of grinding, liberates the active principle which, although almost odorless, has a more markedly pungent taste than black mustard. The whole seeds, together with tarragon and other herbs, are used for preparing pickled vegetables.

The two plants may be grown by the same methods, seeds being sown in spring in rows 20 in (50 cm) apart. The siliquae should be harvested before they are fully ripe, with the husks still on.

26 CALENDULA OFFICINALIS L.

Compositae

Calendula, pot marigold, (G) Ringelblume, (F) souci, (I) calendula

The name of the genus comes from the Latin *calendae*, pertaining to the calendar as an indicator of time, because the flower heads open when the sun rises; another interpretation refers to the duration of flowering, inasmuch as flowers are present every month of the year. This is an annual plant but if it is suitably protected from frost it can be biennial. In places cultivated specimens have reverted to the wild on untilled ground. It is a leafy species, with a stem up to 20 in (50 cm) tall, the stems more or less branching, the leaves spathulate and elongated. The central flowers are tubular, the outer ones ligulate, but all the same color, either deep orange or, depending on the variety, bright yellow, measuring up to 2 in (5 cm) across. The fruits are characteristic half-moon achenes, brown and wrinkled, without a pappus. Seeds are sown in spring, in rows, preferably in the open, because the seedlings dislike being transplanted: the soil, of average consistency, should be enriched with a good organic fertilizer. Plants half way through the growth cycle should be strengthened by being cut back. They need a sunny position sheltered from wind, and regular watering.

The flower heads of the double-flowered varieties are harvested just as they come into bloom and at intervals during the summer. They contain carotenoid and flavonoid pigments, essential oils, mucilages and resins, with a heavy, not too pleasant scent. They are used in cosmetics to make creams and soaps; medicinally, the plant has calmative, sudoriferous, and vulnerary properties and is useful against insect stings and bites.

27 CAPPARIS SPINOSA L.

Capparidaceae

Caper, (G) Kapernstaude, (F) câprier épineux, (I) cappero

The derivation is probably from the Greek *kápparis*, from which also comes the Arab name *kabar*. The plant has a wide distribution throughout Eurasia, growing in warm climates. It is a perennial shrub with erect, smooth branches, divided at the top. The glaucous green leaves are deciduous, round-ovate, with a blunt tip; at the stalk's point of insertion in the stem there are two spines, which soon drop off. The flowers are borne at the leaf axils and appear in May–June, with characteristic ovoid buds. The calyx is formed of four pink sepals, the corolla of four large pinkish white petals, with purple veins. The many long stamens with their violet tips form a conspicuous tuft and give the flower a feathery appearance. The fruit is an oval berry, violet, with a large number of seeds. The plant may be cultivated in suitably warm zones, even out in the open, where it grows in bushes. Cuttings of the young shoots are used for propagation and, should be rooted in barely moist sand. When the wood forms, the cuttings are transplanted into sunny, well-drained soil. The caper grows wild on slopes and old walls in southern parts of Mediterranean Europe and the root system goes deep into the ground.

Only the flower buds, the capers, are used for seasoning; they are left to wither and then pickled in salt and vinegar. The buds contain glucosides (rutin and glucocapparidin) which break up during the drying process through enzymic action into glucose and a characteristic sulfurous compound that gives them their spicy flavor.

28 CAMELLIA SINENSIS (L.) O. Kuntze
Thea sinensis L.
Theaceae
Tea, (G) Teestrauch, (F) théler, (I) tè

The tea plant grows wild in Tibet and Assam and is cultivated in many tropical or subtropical lands; the major tea producers are, in order, India, China, Sri Lanka, USSR, Kenya, Turkey, Indonesia, Japan, Argentina, and Iran. World production of tea is over two million tons annually. The name of the genus commemorates the German Jesuit G. Kamel (Camellus), a seventeenth-century botanist and zoologist; the specific name, *sinensis*, is an appropriate reminder that the plant was used to prepare a ritual beverage in China known as *ch'a*. The history of the plant is very ancient and complex, its uses and details of cultivation go back to early times. There is no certainty even as to where it was first grown, but since the Chinese were the first to utilize it as a drink, they may well have initiated its cultivation. In Europe tea-drinking had been introduced to Holland by the seventeenth century and soon became the rage throughout the continent, but particularly in England. It was Thomas Twining who in the early eighteenth century opened the first establishment to serve cups of tea.

The plant is a small evergreen tree, though cultivated as a shrub to facilitate harvesting. The oval leaves, alternate, leathery and dentate, with a short stalk, are dark green, 2–5 in (5–13 cm) long. The single five-petaled flowers at the leaf axils, with feathery stamens, are white or pink. The fruit is a rounded woody capsule. Tea cultivation requires a warm, humid climate – temperatures between 64° and 83°F (18° and 28°C) and 80 in (2,000 mm) of rainfall annually – at altitudes of up to 6,500 ft (2,000 m). The plant is propagated by seed or cuttings and pruned to shrub size. The leaves are harvested in summer and autumn, from the fourth year onward.

The immature leaves and terminal shoots are plucked and immediately taken to the factory where they are subjected to various stages of processing according to the quality of tea to be obtained. The leaves are placed in airy surroundings where they lose much of their moisture. Then they are prepared for fermentation in special machines that break up their internal tissues. This brings about enzymic action, which is responsible for the aroma and dark color of the leaves through oxidization of the catechins. The leaves are then dried at around 212°F (100°C). Basically there are two types of tea, black and green. The preparation of green tea entails inactivating the enzymes with steam so that they retain their green color. In the course of harvesting, the large leaves are separated from the shoots and the small leaves, which have special names (Flowery Orange Pekoe, etc.) and determine the quality. For commercial reasons tea is often flavored by adding plant drugs such as flowers of jasmine or lemon, orange and bergamot essence. Tea flowers are often sold in dried form to make a highly aromatic infusion rich in mineral salts.

Tea contains alkaloids such as caffeine (2–3 percent), theobromine (0.17 percent), theophylline, mineral salts and many tannins, which give the drink its color. The caffeine speeds up respiration and stimulates the superior nerve centers and cardiac activity; this stimulant action combines with digestive, astringent, remineralizing, sudorific, and diuretic properties. Excessive consumption provokes anxiety, palpitations and may be habit-forming.

29 CAPSICUM ANNUUM L. var. annuum

Solanaceae
Red pepper, (G) Gewürzpaprika, (F) piment, (I) peperoncino

The etymology of the generic name may perhaps be associated with the shape of the fruit, container-like, from the Latin *capsa*. The genus contains a number of important agricultural species and varieties that are cultivated in vegetable gardens. The plant comes from tropical America and reached Europe around 1500. Growing to a height of 3 ft (1 m), it is glabrous, with a stem swollen at the nodes and pointed oval leaves with an irregular margin and a long stalk. The flowers are borne singly at the leaf axils; the short tubular corolla opens into a bright yellow lobate disk. The fruit is a glossy, hollow berry, varying in color from shades of green to yellow and red.

There are numerous cultivars that differ in the shape and consistency of the fruit, destined for various uses. Those with a large, fleshy fruit, like *C. annuum* var. *grossum*, are used as a vegetable, to be eaten cooked or raw; the cultivars *C. annuum* var. *annuum*, with their conical, waxy red fruit, long and pointed at the tip, and thin pericarp full of pungent seeds, are used for seasoning. Seeds should be sown in a warm bed and the plants subsequently transplanted into deep, fertile soil, in rows about 20 in (30 cm) apart.

The fruits contain, in addition to the bitter and pungent alkaloid capsaicin, carotenoids, vitamins A and C, mineral salts and the antibiotic capsidicin. The dried fruits are ground into powder that is used as a flavoring and stimulant in sauces, sausages and other foods.

30 CAPSICUM FRUTESCENS L.

Solanaceae
Chili, chili pepper, cayenne pepper, (G) Cayennapfeffer, (F) cayenne, piment, (I) pepe di Cayenna

The plant, which originated in Central and South America, is today cultivated in virtually all tropical parts of the world. It is a perennial species, forming a shrub about 6½ ft (2 m) high, with lanceolate leaves smaller than those of *C. annuum*, and it produces, at the tips of the branches, numerous slender bright red berries, up to 1¼ in (3 cm) long. These so-called chili or cayenne peppers contain almost twice as much capsaicin as red peppers and thus have a much stronger, burning flavor. They are usually prepared in dried or powdered forms, serving as a base for sauces (such as Tabasco) or as ingredients for vegetable preserves and curries; the powder is often mixed with that of garlic, marjoram or caraway for a variety of spicy food products. The fruits of the chili pepper have stimulant, digestive, and bacteriostatic properties but taken in excess may do harm to the mucous tissues, forming ulcers and causing digestive or renal disorders. They may also be used externally as rubefacients or, biologically, as insectifuges.

Selection and cross-breeding in cultivation, notably with the species *C. baccatum* L., known as sambal and nowadays found widely in South America and Africa, has produced innumerable varieties that differ in the shape and color of fruit (which may even be subspherical) and have a more or less pungent taste.

31 CARLINA ACAULIS L.
Compositae
Carline thistle, (G) Silberdistel, (F) carline, (I) carlina

The name may come from *cardelina* or *cardina*, in the sense of small thistle, or it may go back to the reign of the Emperor Charlemagne whose soldiers were cured of the plague with such plants. It grows in fields and meadows, from the low plains to an altitude of 6,500 ft (2,000 m). A perennial wild herbaceous plant, very common in mountain pastures, it has basal rosettes of stiff, spiny, gray-green leaves, deeply dentate and virtually pinnatifid; a short, inconspicuous flower stem emerges from the rosette. The flower head, 2½ in (6 cm) in diameter, is covered in spiny silver scales, arranged like a halo and made up of tubular violet-red flowers. The fruits are achenes with a pappus which remain for some time in the receptacles. The fleshy, aromatic receptacle, before flowering, may be harvested and eaten as a vegetable, having a pleasant artichoke flavor. The root, containing inulin, essential oils and resin, has tonic, digestive diuretic, diaphoretic and antibiotic principles, and was used to combat the Spanish influenza epidemic of 1918.

The artichoke (*Cynara scolymus* L.), is grown in the Mediterranean region, in southern England, and in the Monterey, San Mateo and Santa Cruz areas in California. The heads, enclosed in fleshy bracts, may grow to 6 in (15 cm) across, borne on scapes of up to 3 ft (1 m). This vegetable was grown by the Etruscans and its distinctive taste is due to the presence of cinarin, a bitter principle, which stimulates the liver. Aromatic extracts are used in aperient and digestive liquors.

---

32 CARUM CARVI L.
Umbelliferae
Caraway, (G) Kümmel, (F) carvi, (I) carvi

The plant's common name is derived from the Greek *káron*, an umbelliferous herb. Originating in the temperate areas of the Old World, it grows in alpine and mountain fields and meadows, beside paths and in clearings. A shortish herb, it has a delicate, grooved, hollow stem with numerous compound leaves, the basal ones bi- or tripinnatisect and finely laciniate, the upper ones smaller. The five-lobed pink flowers are arranged in sparse umbels. The fruit is a mericarp ²⁄₁₀ in (½ cm) long, tapered and curved, with shallow, paler ridges. Seeds should be sown, not too thickly, in moist, fertile open ground, in spring; the umbels should be cut before they are fully mature, in the cooler part of the day.

The achenes constitute the principal source of the essence but the leaves and roots can also be used for medicinal and culinary purposes; the roots in particular are edible, like parsnips. The fruits contain essential oils, mainly carvone and limonene. Caraway is used as an ingredient for alcoholic drinks and for garnishing and flavoring bread and cheeses. It is utilized, too, for mixed spices in the preparation of curries, in feeds for poultry and as seasoning for meat. It has stimulant, carminative and galactagogue properties.

33 CICHORIUM INTYBUS L.

Compositae

Chicory, succory, (G) Kaffeezichorie, (F) chicorée à café, (I) cicoria

The scientific name was used by the Romans for this particular plant while *intybus*, endive, referred to the salad as a whole. The Egyptians mentioned the species in documents back in the fifth millennium B.C., when it enjoyed considerable reputation as a medicinal and food plant, known for its bitter properties, stimulating digestion and also with laxative, depurative and diuretic actions.

Chicory is found all over the world, on roadsides and embankments, and in fields, pastures, and gardens where it grows like a weed. It is an annual or biennial plant, hairy, with a sturdy tap-root and a stiff stem of zigzag habit, up to more than 3 ft (1 m) tall. The lower leaves are lanceolate, deeply divided, and sharply toothed, the upper ones elongate, whole or lobate, sessile, clasping the stem. The flowers, deep blue, more rarely white or pinkish, have a long ligule and the heads are 1¼ in (3 cm) across. The fruits are very small achenes with barely evident ridges. The long leaves, with veining that is often red, are very bitter and are eaten raw or cooked with plenty of water. Chicory is not difficult to grow, being sown May–June in trenches abundantly watered to stimulate germination and subsequently thinned out to encourage the roots to swell. The roots should be harvested in November and thoroughly dried. There are techniques of forcing and bleaching to produce quality products.

The root has a bitter taste and the aroma of the roasted roots is somewhat like that of coffee. In the nineteenth century, in Germany, roasted and finely ground chicory root became popular as a substitute for expensive coffee. It was widely planted in central Europe and the Balkans, and even today chicory finds favor among those who prefer a lighter drink than coffee. It is popular in the U.S. among Louisianians.

Since being introduced into Europe as an alternative to coffee, the seeds of the chicory plant are used to produce a beverage that is similar, at least, in appearance. Roasting liberates the aromatic compounds and the carbohydrates are caramelized (though care must be taken to control the temperature of the raw material). In fact, experiments were carried out with various plants, of which chicory proved the most reliable and successful.

The roots of other plants that have been employed to produce coffee substitutes are the dandelion (*Taraxacum officinale* Weber), viper's-grass (*Scorzonera hispanica* L.) and beet (*Beta vulgaris* L.), which makes an infusion without a bitter taste, with a caramel flavor. The seeds of certain cereals can also be used, notably barley (*Hordeum vulgare* L.), which after roasting is full of dextrin, bitter substances, and even malt; and among a number of legumes with seeds that can be roasted and ground are lupins, chickpeas, French beans, soy beans, and groundnuts. In times of particular shortage coffee has also been made from acorns and from horse-chestnuts (the bitter taste disappears with roasting). Even the roots of carrots have been used. Finally, sugary fruit substitutes have been obtained from dates, figs and carob beans.

34 CINCHONA CALYSAYA Wedd.

Cinchona officinalis L.
Rubiaceae
Cinchona, (G) Chinarindenbaum, (F) quinquing, (I) china

The generic name is in memory of the countess de Chinchon, consort of the Viceroy of Peru, who was cured of malaria in 1638 with the bark of this tree; the specific name is from "quechua," used by the native Indians when it was first discovered. Originally from the Andes, growing widely from Peru to Bolivia, the species was also known as *Quina quina*.

The tree, growing to 100 ft (30 m), has a smooth trunk with yellowish bark, and is an evergreen, with alternate, oval-lanceolate, leathery leaves. The flowers, in terminal panicles, are small, with a yellow-pink corolla, and they come in two forms, with short or long stamens. The fruit is an ovoid capsule with numerous flattened, long-winged seeds. The genus comprises some 15 tropical species, including *C. pubescens* Vahl, with red bark, all growing in the rainforests between altitudes of 3,330–10,000 ft (1,000–3,000 m). At one time the trees were cut down, leaving large zones of forest bare; today they are cultivated and cut down every 15 years not only in South America but also in India, Africa and Java, where 90 per cent of the world production of cinchona, from *C. pubescens*, is obtained.

The bark (which contains more than 30 different alkaloids) is the source of quinine, the only known remedy against malaria, until the arrival of modern compounds plasmoquine and atebrin. Quinine is used as an antidolorific and febrifuge. The bitter principles are also used in the manufacture of tonic drinks.

---

35 CINNAMOMUM AROMATICUM Nees

Cinnamomum cassia Bl.
Lauraceae
Cassia, Chinese cinnamon, (G) Zimtcassie, (F) cannelle de Chine, (I) cassia

The species is a native of subtropical lands where it grows wild and is cultivated, as in China (Kwangsi) and Burma. An evergreen tree, it has long, glossy, pointed leaves with three characteristic veins parallel to the margins, small greenish flowers and bark that peels off in strips. The young shoots of the cassia furnish the drug, with a pungent and penetrating aroma, often used instead of cinnamon proper. For this purpose the bark of ten-year old trees is collected; this peels off, but not in such compact form as that of the Ceylon cinnamon. The fruits and flower calyces are used for flavoring drinks and sweets and for potpourris; the unripe fruits, known as cassia buds or Flores Cassiae, are used to make the dried spice. Cassia is used commercially in the U.S. as "cinnamon" but in the U.K. this name is only applicable to *C. zeylanicum* Bl. Cassia oil is extracted from the leaves and bark.

Cassia has a stronger taste than that of cinnamon, although it lacks eugenol, while cinnamic aldehyde is present in both drugs, (up to 75 percent in cassia), and is used for flavoring spicy sweets, puddings, chocolate, tobacco, liquors, and perfumes. It should not be confused with *Cassia angustifolia, C. acutifolia, C. obovata*, etc. (Leguminosae), which are known as senna, medicinal plants with a purgative action.

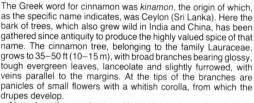

36 CINNAMOMUM ZEYLANICUM Bl.

Cinnamomum verum J. S. Presl
Lauraceae
Cinnamon, Ceylon cinnamon, (G) Ceylon-Zimt, (F) cannelle, zimet, (I) cannella

The Greek word for cinnamon was *kinamon*, the origin of which, as the specific name indicates, was Ceylon (Sri Lanka). Here the bark of trees, which also grew wild in India and China, has been gathered since antiquity to produce the highly valued spice of that name. The cinnamon tree, belonging to the family Lauraceae, grows to 35–50 ft (10–15 m), with broad branches bearing glossy, tough evergreen leaves, lanceolate and slightly furrowed, with veins parallel to the margins. At the tips of the branches are panicles of small flowers with a whitish corolla, from which the drupes develop.

Nowadays the species is cultivated in the form of a shrub to facilitate the harvesting of the branches. The plants are grown on sandy soil beside rivers in warm, wet zones not only in Sri Lanka but also in India, southern China, Japan, Madagascar, the West Indies, and Brazil.

The branches are cut in the rainy season, when the bark is easily stripped off from the woody part. Since the cambium is active, the branches, particularly the straight ones, are cut longitudinally; then the bark is detached in single strips from the stem. The material is left to dry for 24 hours, then scraped so that the external upper part is removed, leaving the inside. The strips of bark are rolled up tightly in layers and left to dry, first in the shade and then in the sun. This dried bark, originally white, takes on the characteristic cinnamon color. The twigs and pieces of bark from other branches are also collected. When ground, cinnamon quickly loses its typical aromas and must therefore be consumed immediately.

The ethereal oil present in the spice contains mainly cinnamic aldehyde (70 percent) and eugenol (10–20 percent).

Cinnamon is used for flavoring in confectionery, in pickles and for giving a special flavor to preserved fruit. It is very much used in pipe tobaccos and in various liquors. The fruits serve as ingredients for potpourris and the oil obtained from the seeds is utilized in perfumery.

From the medicinal point of view, cinnamon has diverse properties, principally stimulating the gastric and digestive juices, and carminative; it also displays marked antiseptic and antimycotic properties.

Camphor is extracted from the tree *Cinnamomum camphora* Nees, grown in central Asia. Forty-year old trees are felled and the white camphor crystals separated by distillation of the wood. This is produced primarily in Taiwan under the name of Chinese camphor. The essential oil has antiseptic and disinfectant properties, being much used for the manufacture of deodorants and soaps.

37 CITRUS AURANTIUM L. ssp. aurantium

Rutaceae

Seville orange, sour orange, (G) Bitterorange, (F) bigarade, (I) arancio amaro

The name orange is derived from the Persian *naranga* and that of the genus from the Greek word *kitron*, the lemon. The plant appears to have originated in southeastern Asia, from where it was introduced to Europe, and cultivated in the Iberian peninsula, France and Italy. It was grown in Sicily from the fifteenth century, probably having been brought there by the Arabs, and as it was more adaptable than the sweet orange to local climatic conditions, it was used for grafting. It is a rounded shrub between 20–25 ft (6–7 m) tall. Its tough, persistent leaves have a broad-winged stalk and visible glands containing ethereal oils. The flowers are white with a gamosepalous calyx and free petals. The fruit is a special kind of berry called a hesperidium, bright orange in color, with a leathery rind and an acidic, bitter pulp.

The leaves, flowers, and small fruits are distilled to obtain the essence called "petit-grain"; the rind is utilized to produce liquors and aperitifs such as bitters and Curaçao, because of its strong scent and stimulating action on the digestive system; the fruits are used to make orange marmalade. The fresh flowers are used in perfumery, the plants are shaken and the flowers are collected in large sheets. The distilled flowers give the essence of "neroli" or orange flower water; this was discovered by and named after a French duchess who was married to Prince Orsini di Nerola. The orange as a fruit is derived from *C. sinensis* (L.) Pers., similar to the preceding but with a narrow-winged leaf stalk and a smooth rind to the fruit.

38 CITRUS BERGAMIA Risso et Poit.

Citrus aurantium ssp. *bergamia* Engl.

Rutaceae

Bergamot, (G) Bergamotte, (F) bergamotte, (I) bergamotto

Introduced to Italy in 1600 as an ornamental plant and nowadays cultivated for its essence, this is a small tree up to 13 ft (4 m) high, with persistent leaves and a barely winged stalk. The round fruits, similar to oranges, are light yellow, with an acidic pulp. The specific name alludes to Pergamum, the city in Asia Minor. In Italy the area of cultivation in Calabria along a narrow coastal belt is where 90 percent of the world's crop is produced. The plant is rare elsewhere, but is cultivated in Morocco, Tunisia and Algeria. Essential oil is extracted from the aromatic rind and used in perfumery and for scenting Earl Grey tea. It contains limonene, neroli, and numerous specific principles. It is mainly used as an ingredient to lend freshness to eau de Cologne. The myrtle-leaved orange (*C. aurantium* L. var. *myrtifolia* Ker-Gawl.) is grown along the Mediterranean coast and has a scented rind, from which are extracted essences used for liquors and syrups, in conjunction with bitter principles of other origins; the partly ripe fruits can be crystallized. From *C. limetta* Risso, which has unwinged leaves and a round, light yellow fruit, bulging at the tip, an essence is obtained which is used for flavoring food and also in perfumery. The hardy orange (*Poncirus trifoliata* Raf.), with deciduous leaves, branches with flattened spines and a round, non-edible fruit of 1½ in (4 cm) with a velvety rind, is used to produce hybrids with special characteristics.

39 CITRUS LIMON L.

Citrus mediva var. *limon* L.
Rutaceae
Lemon, (G) Zitrone, (F) citron, (I) limone

The species, originally from northeast India, derives its specific name from the Persian word *limun*. It is a small rounded tree, up to 16 ft (5 m) high, with dark green foliage and branches bearing a few spines; the leaves are oval-elliptical, pointed and slightly toothed, sufficiently transparent to show the glands with essential oils, and the stalk is unwinged, the flowers are solitary or in small racemes, white or slightly pink. The yellow fruits are oval with a typical knob at the tip known as the umbo. More hardy than the orange, the lemon was introduced to Europe by the crusaders and is today widely cultivated in the Mediterranean regions. However, southern California produces more lemons than all of Europe combined. The juice contains vitamins, especially vitamin C, and organic acids, particularly citric acid; the rind contains limonene, camphene and pinene. The juice can be used in food in place of vinegar and as a flavoring for many types of drink. It has an astringent, refreshing, antiscorbutic, and disinfectant action.

The highly fragrant essential oil extracted from the rind is used in perfumery, especially for making eau de Cologne, soaps, and toothpastes; and the fresh or dried peel is used in the liquor industry. Lemon provides a flavoring for confectionery and lozenges; it has a pharmaceutical use in improving the taste and odor of various products; and is widely used to scent housecleaning products. The mandarin (*C. deliciosa* Ten.) is one of the last citrus fruits to have reached Europe, in the nineteenth century, and is grown for its sweet, fragrant fruit; the oil extracted from its peel is used in similar ways to that of the lemon.

40 CITRUS MEDICA L. var. vulgaris Risso

Rutaceae
Citron, (G) Zitronatzitrone, (F) cédrat, (I) cedro frutti

The citron is a species originally from the East Indies and may have reached Europe as early as Roman times; its medicinal properties have determined its specific name. This is a small tree of graceful habit, with thorny branches that bear narrow, slightly dentate leaves and an unwinged stalk. The fruits, 3–6 in (8–15 cm) in diameter, have an umbo at the tip and a thick rind, most of which consists of spongy white albedo. This is used for making candied fruit, for the extraction of essential oil and the preparation of syrups. The citron is most widely grown in the Mediterranean region and exported mainly to northern Europe. The fruit, before being candied, is kept in brine until it has a shiny appearance. It is distilled for the extraction of essence, which is used mainly in perfumery together with lemon and bergamot.

The juice provides the basis of cooling citrus drinks, and the fruit is used in pickles and pungent sauces. An essential oil extracted from the leaves and twigs is an ingredient of eau de Cologne and perfumes with a touch of freshness. In folk medicine it is used against insect bites, for skin trouble and muscular aches in general.

Kumquats, about the size of small plums, with a soft, fragrant rind, are cultivated from several species of the genus *Fortunella*. They are grown in the Orient and in the United States throughout the deep South, but primarily in California and Florida, as ornamentals and for their tasty fruits. They are often used in preserves.

41 CNICUS BENEDICTUS L.

Compositae

Blessed thistle, (G) Bitterdistel, (F) chardon bénit, (I) cardo santo

This plant, as its specific name suggests, has long been famed for its medicinal properties. *Cnicus* is derived from the Greek *knicos*, meaning thistle. The region of origin is uncertain but is thought to have been somewhere in the western Mediterranean. It is occasionally found on wasteland, having perhaps escaped from cultivation in ancient times when it was grown, as mentioned, for medicinal purposes. The plant has densely hairy stems, compound basal leaves with triangular leaflets, their margins irregularly toothed, which are prickly and white-veined. The cauline leaves become gradually smaller and lanceolate, while the upper ones are very closely packed, almost covering the flower head. The latter, solitary, is formed of yellow, violet-streaked flowers, and has a receptacle with spiny bracts and long hairs covering it. The fruit is an achene of ½ in (1 cm), ridged and furnished with a pappus. It is easily grown in loose, fertile soil, seeds being sown outside in spring, the rows 20 in (50 cm) apart. The leaves are harvested when flowering starts. Zones of cultivation are central Europe, Russia, and the Balkan peninsula.

Bitter principles extracted from the plant are used for the preparation of herbal liquors and aperitifs. St Mary's thistle (*Silybum marianum* Gaertn.) has big leaves, but smooth and white-streaked, with yellowish thorns along the margins. The flower heads are formed of tubular red flowers, covered by spiny bracts. The plant has tonic, aperient properties.

---

42 COCHLEARIA OFFICINALIS L.

Cruciferae

Scurvy-grass, (G) Löffelkraut, (F) cranson, (I) coclearia

This species, originally from northwestern Europe, is widely naturalized in wet and brackish areas of the continent, thanks to its diffusion as a medicinal plant. The typical form of the rounded, long-stalked basal leaves resembles a spoon, and this explains the generic name; the cauline leaves are oval, their base clasping the stem (amplexicaul). It is a herbaceous plant with a smooth stem that divides into compound racemes. The flowers are small, about ¼ in (6 mm) in diameter, with white corollas; they produce oval, delicately marked silicula. Seeds are sown in spring in virtually any type of soil. It is a hardy plant, resisting cold, the green parts even surviving under the snow. The cultivated form, therefore, is a biennial, and has long been prized in northern Europe.

The complete herb is harvested, crushed or chopped, and gives out an aroma, like many other crucifers, of mustard oil, but milder. It has a high content of vitamin C and was once used against scurvy (hence the common name). It also has tonic, diuretic and digestive properties.

The leaves of other crucifers are eaten in the same way, as for example those of large bitter-cress (*Cardamine amara* L.), which grows on river banks; the leaves are pinnate-lyrate and the small flowers white with violet stamens. Another is lady's smock (*C. pratensis* L.), which has violet flowers with yellow stamens, and grows in wet places. Both can be used for seasoning mixed salads.

43 COFFEA ARABICA L.

Rubiaceae

Coffee, Arabian coffee, (G) Bergkaffee, (F) café, (I) caffè

The coffee plant comes originally from Abyssinia and was brought to Arabia in the thirteenth century, from where it spread rapidly thanks to pilgrims returning from Mecca to their homelands. Coffee has been enormously popular, initially in the world of Islam, where it proved pleasant to drink and was reputed to stimulate the physical and intellectual faculties (bearing in mind that the Koran forbids alcoholic beverages). The Turks were the first to use coffee on a wide scale, and in the sixteenth century it found general acceptance throughout Europe. The coffee then drunk was bitter and fairly light, and it was first sweetened in Austria. In the eighteenth century coffee houses were opened all over Europe and soon became centers of cultural life and social activity (one of the most famous, then and now, is Florian's, in Venice). But the raw material was very expensive and this was a check to its diffusion; its consumption was at first limited to the wealthy but later became genuinely popular. At the same time the medicinal properties of coffee as a stimulant were revealed.

The coffee plant is a small evergreen tree that does not grow taller than 16 ft (5 m), with divided branches and opposite leaves, leathery, oval, and dark green. In spring the plants are covered with showy tubular, white, scented flowers, which open in five long perpendicular lobes. The fruits, formed from the inferior ovary, are spherical drupes, red when ripe, containing two pale green horny seeds that are covered by a soft involucre and that lie with their flat faces together, with a central groove. In addition to *Coffea arabica*, which is the most highly valued, there are other species, with very large seeds such as *C. robusta* (= *C. canephora*), cheaper and with more caffeine, *C. liberica*, less fragrant and not in such demand, and *C. stenophylla*, the celebrated highland coffee; as a rule all are mixed with Arabian coffee.

Coffea arabica is the species most widely cultivated, growing in fertile soil above a height of 3,000 ft (900 m), between the two tropics, at an optimum temperature of 60°–70°F (15°–20°C) and with alternating periods of rain and drought. Coffee plantations go into production after their third year and productivity increases up to the tenth or fifteenth year, after which it falls off. The principal producers of *arabica* and *robusta* in 1981, in order, were Brazil, Colombia, Mexico, Ethiopia, Uganda, and India.

Hybrids (arabusta) are considered important because of their resistance to fungal diseases such as rust. On the market the gap in price between *arabica* and *robusta* has gradually narrowed, although the former is still more expensive because of the superior quality. The fruit consists of a leathery pericarp, a fleshy pulp (mesocarp) and a papery endocarp that encloses the seeds. These have a soft tegument and are constituted mainly of the endosperm, containing principally starch and the alkaloid caffeine. The ripe fruits, which are harvested, require careful handling; they are laid out in thin layers in the sun where they dry for two to three weeks. In rainy zones, where this procedure is difficult, the pulp is crushed and then, in a short fermentation, the seeds are liberated, to be dried in a current of hot air. The seeds, separated according to quality, are sold and roasted only where they are to be consumed; when roasted, the grains take on a brown color and characteristic aroma, and can then be ground.

44 COLA ACUMINATA Schott. et Endl.

Sterculiaceae
Cola, (G) Kolabaum, (F) colatier, (I) cola

The plant comes originally from West Africa, where it is locally known as *cola*. It is an evergreen tree growing to about 65 ft (20 m), with stalked leaves of 8–10 in (20–25 cm), whole, sparse, elliptical with a pointed tip. The dense clusters of stellate flowers are whitish; the fruits are made up of a mass of follicles, each 4–5 in (10–12 cm) long, enveloping ten fairly large, oval seeds, white or reddish, each weighing up to ½ oz (25 g). The seeds, about 1¼ in (3 cm) long, are called cola nuts. There are other cola species: *C. nitida* Schott. & Endl., with yellow-red flowers and somewhat smaller leaves, which produces nuts that are highly valued, and *C. verticillata* Stapf ex A. Cheval. The plants are cultivated in countries round the Gulf of Guinea and in the tropics.

The seeds, which contain principally caffeine, are fairly bitter because of the presence of tannin; caffeine, associated with the polyphenols, has marked stimulant and tonic effects, while negative secondary actions are curbed. The fizzy non-alcoholic drinks commonly called cola retain a name associated with the former procedure of extracting the seeds, tonic in effect, the use of which has now been largely replaced by other aromatic principles. The seeds were once chewed by natives to assuage hunger and weariness; the sharp taste is gradually annulled by the enzymic separation of the sugars in the starches and the action of ptyalin.

---

45 COMMIPHORA MIRRHA Holmes

Commiphora molmol Engl.
Burseraceae
Myrrh, (G) Myrrhe, (F) myrrhe, (I) mirra

The name of the genus comes from the Greek *kómmi*, gum, in the sense of a sticky material, and from *phóros*, a carrier.

This is a thorny tree with light bark which grows in East Africa from Sudan to Somalia, and in southern Arabia, together with the species *C. abyssinica* and *C. schimperi*, very similar, which produce leaves only in the rainy season, remaining bare for the rest of the year.

The resin, contained in lysigenic ducts in the trunk, is obtained by making cuts in the trunk, usually near the ground, and collecting the yellowish fluid, which hardens into tears when exposed to air. The myrrh gives out a penetrating aromatic and balsamic scent. The resin can be treated with benzol to obtain the resinoid, which serves as a fixative; direct extraction with alcohol produces the very dense absolute, which remains liquid only by addition of appropriate solvents. The essence is obtained by distillation in a current of steam. This forms an ingredient in strong, floral, exotic perfumes. The slightly pungent taste of the myrrh is suitable for use in toothpastes and mouthwashes, as well as scented ointments. The gum resin and fluid extract have marked antiseptic and aromatic qualities, and as such are utilized for perfumes and liquors.

A similar resin, Mecca balsam or balm of Gilead, is obtained from a shrub growing in Arabia, *C. opobalsamum* (L.) Engl., and is used for medicinal purposes or as incense.

46 CONVALLARIA MAJALIS L.

Liliaceae
Lily of the valley, (G) Malglöckchen, (F) muguet, (I) mughetto

The specific name refers to the plant's flowering period, May, or perhaps to Maia, Roman goddess of fertility. It grows throughout the northern hemisphere in cool deciduous woods of hill and valley, as the name of the genus indicates. The lily of the valley is noted for its fragrant bell-like flowers. It is a perennial rhizomatous plant, with floral scapes 8–12 in (20–30 cm) tall, from the base of which a pair of elliptical leaves with parallel veining tightly clasp the stem. The flowers, with tepals joined in a campanulate perigonium and six outward-jutting lobes, are borne on a one-sided raceme; they are delicate and strongly scented, with a short bract beneath the peduncle. The fruit is a round, bright red berry.

Cultivation, particularly as an ornamental garden plant, is easily achieved by dividing the rhizomes. The plant, nevertheless, is poisonous, with a cardiac action; so great care must be taken not to taste the berries and to mistake it for any of the other edible lilies, as for example ramsons. The leaves of the wild plant can be picked for medicinal purposes; they have spasmolytic, cardiotonic, diuretic, emetic and purgative properties. The flowers, with their unmistakable fragrance, serve as raw materials for absolute and concrete extracts, used in perfumery to produce scents for nuances of rose, orange or lemon, though not precisely of lily of the valley. Such perfume, in fact, is mainly obtained by chemical synthesis.

---

47 COPAIFERA spp.

Leguminosae
Copaiba, (G) Kopaiva, (F) copayer, (I) copaive

The plants that furnish copaiba belong to various species of the genus *Copaifera* which grow wild in the forests of Brazil and other countries of South America. The resin-bearing ducts, 0.2 mm (c. ⅟₈₀ in) in diameter and up to ¾ in (20 mm) long, secrete a balsamic resin that hardens to produce copaiba after evaporation of the essential oils.

Among the principal species are *C. reticulata* Ducke from Brazil, *C. guyanensis* Benth. from South America, *C. officinalis* L. from Venezuela and the West Indies, and *C. multijuga* Hayne from the basin of the Amazon River.

The finest product, Parà or Manàos, comes from the lower Amazon and is exported from Belem-Parà.

Each tree may furnish more than 17–18 kg of copaiba in a year. The exit hole of the resin can be sealed and reused; in *C. multijuga*, the trunk is pierced at the height of about 3 ft (1 m), yielding 20–30 liters of liquid which is directly usable as diesel fuel, without any treatment. The balsam, yellow-brown, has components that are soluble in alcohol and other insolubles, an aromatic odor, and a bitter, burning taste. Essence is extracted from the balsam.

Both the oleoresin and the essence were once used for preparing ointments; today they are utilized only in perfumery as a fixative, for scenting soaps and in pine, violet, wood, and spicy perfumes. Copaiba is used, furthermore, in making lacquers, varnishes and carbon paper.

48 CORIANDRUM SATIVUM L.

Umbelliferae
Coriander, (G) Koriander, (F) coriandre, (I) coriandolo

The name comes from the Greek word for this umbellifer, a species originally from North Africa, nowadays cultivated in most temperate regions, notably Russia, Bulgaria, Morocco, and from the United States to South America. There are numerous cultivars obtained by genetic improvement.

This is an annual or biennial herbaceous plant, with tap-roots, which has flower stems up to 20 in (70 cm) in length. The basal leaves are pinnatisect, the upper ones reduced to linear laciniae. The inflorescences, in umbels, bear small flowers with five bilobed petals that bloom in June–July. The fruits have ten ridges, and the two parts of the schizocarp are not separated, producing a single spherical fruit. There are two varieties of coriander; one with a small fruit (microcarp), growing in temperate zones, and one with a large fruit (macrocarp), cultivated in warm countries.

The fruits, when being harvested, give out a disagreeable odor that subsequently disappears. The essence, obtained by steam distillation, is colorless and highly scented. The essential oil is used in the pharmaceutical, cosmetics, and food industries. Its commercial value is due to the high linalol content (60–70%). The fruits are used for flavoring vegetables and pickles and as ingredients for curry and seasonings.

---

49 CRITHMUM MARITIMUM L.

Umbelliferae
Samphire, rock samphire, (G) Meerfenchel, (F) criste marine, (I) finocchio di mare

The generic name is the one used by the Greeks to describe this plant. The species, originating in the Mediterranean area, grows on rocks exposed to the sea, on cliffs and on jetties washed by sea spray. The plant is perennial, woody at the base, forming a small hemispherical shrub, the upper part with herbaceous stems. The fleshy, glaucous leaves are all pinnatisect, the basal ones with lanceolate or linear leaflets, the cauline ones becoming gradually smaller. The smaller greenish yellow flowers are inconspicuous, arranged in umbels made up of numerous rays. The fruit is a cremocarp and the single element, long and oval, is slightly grooved. Cultivation is difficult because of the rocky environment needed. It may be propagated by division of clumps or by seeds. The plant is useful as an ornamental shrub, for adorning a sunny wall or a corner of the rock garden; but it is averse to standing water. Centuries ago it was grown in the stony kitchen gardens of southern France and used as a vegetable.

The young fleshy leaves have a pleasant salty aroma, rather like celery, and can be used as a salad ingredient or pickled. The essential oil can be extracted from all parts of the plant. Like many other umbellifers, it can be used medicinally for its choleretic, vermifugal, antiscorbutic and remineralizing properties.

50 CROCUS SATIVUS L.
Iridaceae
Saffron, (G) Safran, (F) safran, (I) zafferano

Saffron is from the Arab word *assfar*, yellow, while the generic name is derived from the Latin and Greek names for the plant. Known since antiquity, this is a crocus of oriental origin, cultivated widely in the West above all for the valuable dye contained in the flower stigmas. This is a particularly deep and luminous shade of yellow, traditionally used for the clothing of the privileged classes and therefore acquiring ritual or caste significance. The saffron crocus has long been associated, especially in the East, with fertility and harvest rites, with physical strength, sexual, and psychic powers, and with royalty. It is a perennial plant, with a rounded bulb and leaves longer than the ciliate flowers. The flower, which opens in autumn, is formed of six lilac-colored tepals and with orange-red clavate stigmas, longer than the stamens, protruding from the lobes of the perigonium; it gives out a marked perfume and has a bitter taste. Cultivated in Italy, Spain, and the Balkans, it rarely grows wild. The bulbs are planted in rows some 6 in (15 cm) apart, at a depth of 4 in (10 cm), in June.

The stigmas constitute the commercial product, which contains a bitter principle (picrocrocin), a glycoside from which is liberated safranal (which gives the aroma) and the carotenoid crocin, which is the dye. It is used both as a dye and flavoring agent in the food, drinks, and cosmetics industries, and in the kitchen with meats, fish, and rice dishes. It is good for the digestion and has eupeptic, carminative and emmenagogic properties.

51 CUMINUM CYMINUM L.
Umbelliferae
Cumin, (G) Kreutz-, Mutter-, Römischer Kümmel, (F) cumin, (I) comino, comino romano

A species originally from the Mediterranean region, where it has been cultivated since ancient times, this plant now grows mainly in Morocco, Egypt, Syria, India, North America, and Chile.

Both the generic and specific names derive from the original Greek *kyminon*, referring to an umbellifer similar to caraway. It is an annual, fairly small, up to 20 in (50 cm) high, with laciniate leaves; the inflorescence, a loose umbel, bears only a few flowers with white or pink petals; it produces mericarps $^3/_{16}$ in (5 mm) long, furrowed like those of caraway, which have a strong, warm aroma and a slightly bitter flavor. The seeds should be sown under glass and the seedlings transplanted out early, preferably in sandy-calcareous soil. Fruits appear after two months.

The inflorescences are removed when the plants begin to wither and are dried before they are fully ripe. They are used, like caraway, for flavoring vegetables, sauerkraut, meats and sausages, bread and biscuits, cheese and curries. Cumin is also used for flavoring various drinks. In Arab countries, particularly Morocco and the Middle East, it is employed for seasoning kid, chicken, and sweetbread, and in India for preparing digestive infusions, with mint, camomile, lemon, salt, sugar, and tamarind water. Cumin essence is obtained by distilling the chopped fruits; the oil is used for spices and scents.

52 CURCUMA LONGA L.

Zingiberaceae
Turmeric, curcuma, (G) Gelbwurz, (F) curcuma, (I) curcuma

The name of the genus comes, through Spanish, from the Arabic *kurkum*, meaning saffron, a yellow dye. The plant grows widely in India, China, Taiwan, Indonesia, Vietnam, and the Philippines. India produces 12,000 tons of the spice annually, of which 10,000 tons are exported. The plant is a monocotyledon, similar to ginger, which produces shiny lanceolate leaves with innate veining, in tufts that stem from the tuberous rhizome. These are the parts of the plant that are used, boiled, skinned, dried, and ground, to give the spice which, in powder form, has a characteristic yellow color, due to curcumin, a carotenoid produced during cooking of the tubers. As a pigment, turmeric is used for edible purposes and also for dyeing materials and leather. The dark yellow powder, tasting similar to ginger, slightly bitter and pungent, gives a pleasant flavoring and a golden yellow color to food. Whereas the color is long-lasting, the flavor is fleeting; the spice is therefore consumed in small quantities, prepared as required.

Turmeric is one of nine standard ingredients (the others being ginger, cardamom, coriander, cumin, nutmeg, cloves, pepper, and cinnamon) of Indian curry. It is also an essential ingredient of Worcestershire sauce. The related species *C. zedoaria* Rosc. is cultivated in Sri Lanka, the leaves being edible; an aromatic oil, bitter and camphorated, is extracted from the rhizome and used in pharmacy for flavoring.

53 CUSPARIA TRIFOLIATA Engl.

Galipea officinalis Hancock
Rutaceae
Angostura, (G) Angostura, (F) angostura, (I) angostura

This tree grows wild in the tropical regions of Central and South America (Colombia, Venezuela, West Indies). It bears trifoliate leaves (hence the name) with a long stalk, and panicles of flowers with a pink-white corolla, producing capsule-like fruits containing two spherical black seeds. The innermost section of the bark, known as angostura bark, ⅛ in (2–3 mm) thick, contains alkaloids (cusparine), essential oils and a bitter principle. Commercially it is cut into oblique strips; the outer part is gray and spongy, the inner part brown, due to the presence of small crystals of calcium oxalate. The essential oil is obtained by steam distillation of the bark; as a rule, for use in liquors, the bark is directly treated with alcohol. The tincture is used for giving a bitter flavor to aperitifs and cocktails, giving them a characteristic taste. Whereas the color is long-lasting, the aromatic odor is fleeting and is therefore not used in perfumery. It has febrifugal, carminative and aperient properties.

Another member of the Rutaceae, which grows in woods of pubescent oak, dry zones and among limestone rocks, is the fraxinella, dittany or burning bush (*Dictamnus albus* L.). The leaves, when rubbed, give off a scent of lemon but cannot be used for edible purposes because they contain a poisonous alkaloid, dittamine. The flowers and roots, however, secrete an essence used in perfumery.

54 CYMBOPOGON FLEXUOSUS (DC.) Stapf.

Andropogon nardus var. *flexuosus* Hack.

Graminaceae

Lemongrass, (G) Lemongrass, (F) lemongrass, (I) lemongrass

This grass, smelling strongly of lemon, grows wild in the subtropical zones of Asia, Africa, and America. It is specially cultivated, with several harvests a year, for the extraction of its active principles. The essential oils are found in parenchymatous cells or in the interstices of the cells themselves.

There are diverse forms of lemongrass, including the Indian (*C. flexuosus*), with citral and camphene; the oil is extracted by distillation, lasting about three hours. The quantity of citral diminishes the longer it is kept, and has to be stored in the dark. The oil has antiseptic properties (against gram-negative bacteria). *C. citratus* (DC.) Stapf., cultivated in Tanzania, contains 75–80 percent citral, from which a violet scent (ionone) is extracted, used both in the cosmetics and liquor industries. Pamarosa or geranium oil is obtained from gingergrass, (*C. martinii* [Roxb.] W. Wats.); it has a high content of geraniol, sometimes called East Indian geranium oil, which is used to make inexpensive perfumes and in the food industry. Ceylon citronella oil is obtained from *C. nardus* (L.) Rendle, in Sri Lanka, India, and Taiwan, and is the source of geraniol for perfumery. Java citronella oil is derived from *C. winterianus* Jowitt, cultivated everywhere in the tropics; this is the principal source of citronellal, used in perfumery.

---

55 DAUCUS CAROTA L.

Umbelliferae

Carrot, (G) Möhre, Karotte, (F) carotte, (I) carota

The Greek word *dáukos* was used to describe various wild umbelifers, related to parsnip, as did *karotón*. The wild carrot is a polymorphous plant, found everywhere in dry areas, on loose and often arable soil. It is a biennial plant, almost 3 ft (1 m) high, with an erect, hairy, branching stem that bears bi- or tripinnatisect leaves, with lanceolate-linear leaflets; the white flowers form dense, compact umbels with a crown of characteristic laciniate, divided bracts at the base. The fruits are bristly mericarps with uncinate wings; after ripening the umbel folds back on itself like a small basket. In the wild species the root is thin, whitish, and woody.

The cultivated carrot (*D. carota* ssp. *sativus* ([Hoffm.] Arcang.), on the other hand, has a fleshy tap-root, full of carotenes and thus orange in color, probably originating in the Near East following successive crosses with *D. maximus* Rouy & Camus. It is sown outside in rows, in a well-exposed spot and well-worked soil, and the seedlings should be thinned out. The roots are harvested in the first year because by the second year they are exhausted after producing the inflorescence. There are numerous varieties, differing in the form of the tap-root and the quantity of woody heart in relation to the outer pulp.

The plant contains sugars, pectin, vitamins, particularly vitamin A, mineral salts and, like all umbelifers, an essential oil. Apart from its culinary use as a vegetable, it is used for coloring various foods and drinks and in the manufacture of fine perfumes.

56 ELETTARIA CARDAMOMUM (L.) Maton
Zingiberaceae
Cardamom, (G) Cardamon, (F) cardamome, (I) cardamomo

Along the Malabar coasts this plant is known as *elettari*, and the specific name may be connected with the Greek *kárdamon*, cardamine, a crucifer with a sharp taste.

The species was known in Mediterranean Europe at the time of the Greeks and Romans. The most valuable cardamom comes from the rainforests of Malabar, obtained from a rush-like shrub growing to a height of 6½ ft (2 m), furnished with sturdy rhizomes and stems covered in lanceolate leaves. The inflorescences, shorter than the sterile stems, are racemes with a dozen or so yellow-tipped, blue-streaked flowers. The fruits are trilocular, nut-sized capsules with 4–8 seeds. The species grows wild in the tropical mountain forests of southern India and is nowadays cultivated in India, Thailand, and Central America; India and Sri Lanka produce more than 1,000 tons of the spice. The small dark greenish brown seeds, covered by an aril, are dried in the incompletely ripe capsules and kept in them, away from the light, until ready to be used. They have an aromatic odor and a sweetish, warm, pungent taste.

Cardamom is used in the kitchen, for sausages, pastries, and in curry. The Arabs use it in coffee, as a symbol of hospitality, for it is one of the most costly of spices, after saffron and vanilla. The seeds may be chewed to sweeten the breath and for digestion. The agreeably scented oil is used in perfumery.

---

57 ERUCA SATIVA Miller
Eruca vesicaria L.
Cruciferae
Garden rocket, (G) Raukenkohl, (F) rouquelle, (I) rucola

The scientific name was used by the Romans to indicate the sharp, burning taste (from *urere*, to burn); in addition to growing wild, it was cultivated in ancient times around the Mediterranean. It is an annual or biennial branching plant, distinguished from similar crucifers by its white, violet-streaked flowers, in bloom from late winter to early summer. The leaves are dentate and more or less deeply divided; the fruits are straight siliquae with a short beak. The plant is adapted to all types of climate and soil and reproduces by seed, simply requiring light weeding. The leaves may be harvested all through the growing season and are used raw for seasoning salads, their pungent and stimulating flavor are due to mustard oils. The seeds, too, contain a certain amount of oil which can be extracted.

Many other crucifers are used in the same way as garden rocket. They include wild rocket (*Diplotaxis muralis* DC.), the basal leaves of which, usually in a rosette, are harvested in spring; and shepherd's purse (*Capsella bursa-pastoris* Med.), with a less sharp flavor and an aroma rather like that of cabbage. Whereas the roots of these plants are of little interest, the swollen turnip-shaped roots of the radish (*Raphanus sativus* L.) are edible and known everywhere for the bright red skin which contrasts vividly with the white flesh.

58 ERYNGIUM MARITIMUM L.

Umbelliferae

Sea holly, (G) Strandmannstreu, (F) panicaut, (I) eringio marino

The scientific name comes from the Greek word *eryngion* for thistle, underlining the similarity of the two thorny plants. As the specific name suggests, it grows on sea coasts, in brackish areas and on dunes along the shore, virtually all over Europe. It is perennial in the form of a globose bush, light blue-green, up to 3 ft (1 m) tall. Strongly ramified, it has flexible, grooved branches that bear stalked basal leaves, leathery and kidney-shaped, with a wavy border and large teeth terminating in stiff, sharp spines; the cauline leaves are similar but smaller. The hemispherical flower heads at the tips of the branches are surrounded by large thorny bracts; the single flowers are blue-green and produce fruits in the form of mericarps.

The swollen tap-roots of the wild plants are harvested in autumn; as with other umbellifers, they contain essential oils with a penetrating aroma, saponin, and mineral salts. Although rather fibrous, they have a pleasant taste and are used for flavoring cooked vegetables. The young shoots, in moderation, can be used in salads, but are often bitter and best boiled in plenty of water; and the leaves just in bud can be pickled.

The crystallized roots are also a herbal product, used against chills and as a diuretic.

---

59 EUCALYPTUS GLOBULUS Labill.

Myrtaceae

Eucalyptus, Blue Gum, (G) Eucalyptus, (F) eucalyptus, (I) eucalipto

The Greek name refers to the particular form of the flowers, consisting of a receptacle enclosed by a lid, which is discarded when the stamens appear, hence literally "well hidden." The genus comprises hundreds of species, all originally from Australia, where they represent the principal element of the forest cover. Eucalyptus also grow in California, southern Europe, and much of North and tropical Africa, demonstrating their adaptability to arid or semi-arid conditions.

They are evergreen trees of considerable dimensions. The leaves of the young branches are thick and rolled at the base, those of the adult branches are curved and full of glands, which are also numerous on the inflorescences and the bark of the trunk. This bark comes off in light brown strips. The flowers, in terminal corymbs, have a broad cup-like receptacle, without a perianth. Eucalyptus has a variety of uses, as a source of timber for building, fencing, etc., wood pulp, and fuel. The essence of *E. globulus* Labill. is produced mainly in Spain, India, Brazil, and Argentina; the oil extracted from the leaves, used in perfumery, contains geraniol, citral, and limonene.

All the other varieties are suited to industrial purposes, for they principally contain cineol and are used for the production of disinfectants, deodorants, and oils for mineral flotation. The essence, with a balsamic, expectorant and bacteriostatic action, is utilized as an antiseptic of the urinary tract and in soothing ointments.

60 EUGENIA CARYOPHYLLATA Thunb.
Syzigium aromaticum (L.) Merr. & L. M. Perry
Myrtaceae
Cloves, (G) Gewürznelkenbaum, (F) clous di girofe, (I) chiodi di garofano

The generic name *Eugenia* commemorates Prince Eugene of Savoy (1663–1736) who, apart from being a statesman and field-marshal of the Austrian empire, was also a patron of the arts and sciences. The synonym of the genus, *Syzigium*, is associated with the Greek for "closed together," alluding to the fact that the petals close in a tuft over the flower. Cultivated widely in Indonesia, Sri Lanka, Madagascar, Tanzania (Zanzibar), and Brazil, the species came originally from the Moluccas in the Indian Ocean.

This spice was familiar in ancient times to the Chinese and the Romans, who prized it very highly. But only in 1500, with the increase in trade resulting from European sea voyages to the Indies, did cloves become better known and more widely used. The tree normally grows to over 50 ft (15 m), although in Zanzibar the cultivated form is restricted to about 25 ft (8 m), and is evergreen with opposite, lanceolate, leathery, and glossy leaves. The flowers, with an inferior ovary, have a purple calyx and numerous white stamens that emerge in a dense pompon after the corolla cap formed by the linked petals drops off. The fruits are dark red berries with one or two black seeds.

Trees are cultivated from one-year old seedlings and harvested for the first time after five years. Each plant produces some 7 lb (3 kg) of the essence/spice midway through the year. The cloves are the flower buds (about ⅝ in [15 mm] long) which contain the largest quantity of active principle. After harvesting, they are immersed in boiling water for a few seconds and then, with the stalk removed, dried in the sun or near a source of heat. Beneath the epidermis of the buds are glandular cavities which contain up to 20 percent of ethereal oils, especially eugenol (70–90 percent). The cloves are used as they are or in the form of powder. The odor is aromatic, the taste pungent and burning because of the eugenol. They are used for flavoring desserts, fruit salads, mulled wine, and liquors. Sometimes they are stuck in oranges hung in cupboards as a freshener. Whole or in powdered form they also help to relieve toothache.

The essential oil is obtained by steam distillation, mainly of the discarded parts, young shoots, and leaves. More than 22 lb (10 kg) of essence can be obtained each year from a single plant; this is the basis for the synthesis of vanilla. The liquid is pale yellow and tends to become darker with time. It has antiseptic, stimulant, stomachic and digestive properties. As an anti-infectant, cloves are effective against coli bacilli, streptococci, staphylococci, pneumococci and as an antimycotic. The oil, too, is used in dentistry for its antiseptic and analgesic properties, and, like the whole cloves and powdered cloves, for local pain-relieving purposes.

61 FERULA ASSA-FOETIDA L.

Umbelliferae
Asafoetida, (G) Asant, (F) asafetide, (I) assafetida

The numerous species of the genus *Ferula* are very similar, as is typical of many umbellifers. A gum resin is obtained from their roots. They include *F. gummosa*, *F. narthaex* and *F. scorodosoma*; but the most important of them is *F. assa-foetida*. The generic name is Latin for umbellifers of this type, and the specific name means "stinking mastic," from the Persian root *aze*. The plant grows in western Asia from Iran to Kashmir. It is a herbaceous perennial, up to 6½ ft (2 m) tall when in flower; the leaves are tripinnatisect, and finely laciniate, and the tap-root is thick and fleshy. The inflorescences, produced in summer, are yellowish.

At the beginning of summer the stems and roots are cut, producing a dense, odorous sap that congeals when exposed to air. This material is either sold as it is or after being ground to powder. The spice is used in fairly small quantities and is, among other things, an ingredient for Worcestershire sauce. It has calmative, carminative, diuretic, digestive, and anthelminthic properties. From it can also be obtained a resinoid, a tincture using alcoholic extraction. Steam distillation eliminates the garlic-like smell of the spice and furnishes a product for use in perfumery, with good fixative capacity.

The green parts of asafoetida, including the inflorescences in bud, can be used as a vegetable.

---

62 FILIPENDULA ULMARIA (L.) Maxim.

Spiraea ulmaria Maxim.
Rosaceae
Meadowsweet, (G) Mädesüss, (F) reine des près, (I) filipendula

The name of the genus refers to the characteristics of the root of *Filipendula vulgaris* Moench, which has tuber-like swellings interconnected by thin strands; in *F. ulmaria* the leaves resemble those of the elm. It is a rhizomatous plant, growing in ditches and wet, shady places throughout the northern hemisphere. The leaves are compound, with unequal sections, and oval serrated leaflets, pale and downy underneath. The reddish flower stem is more than 3 ft (1 m) tall and bears compound panicles of numerous small white flowers that give out a strong scent of honey and almonds. The plant can be propagated by division of the sturdy rhizome. Leaves and flowers, especially when fresh, are highly aromatic, with a smell that is somewhat like that of wintergreen. The leaves, which contain cumarin, emit a pleasant, lasting odor as they dry, and these, absorbed by appropriate fixatives, are used for scenting hydromel or mead (made by alcoholic fermentation of honey and water) or for making aromatic beers. Harvesting is done when the flowers start to appear and the entire plant is dried. Meadowsweet has astringent, antirheumatic, febrifugous, diuretic, and diaphoretic properties; the flowers contain salicylates. In northern Europe it was once used for perfuming homes and the flowers were used as a dye, forming a greenish yellow tincture in the presence of alum, while the root dyes wool black.

63 FOENICULUM VULGARE Mill. ssp. **vulgare**

Umbelliferae

Fennel, (G) Fenchel, (F) fenouil, (I) finocchio

The Latin name of the plant comes from *foenum*, hay, because of the appearance of the finely divided leaves. The species is originally from the Mediterranean area but has spread throughout the rest of Europe. It is found growing wild on wasteland, by roadsides, and in dry places close to kitchen gardens. Fennel has been cultivated since antiquity as a herb, both for its green parts and its seeds.

A perennial umbellifer, growing up to 4 ft (1.5 m) or even more, it has an erect bright green stem, thickened by rings at the nodes, bearing leaves with swollen sheaths, pale-edged and three or four times pinnatisect, in the form of very fine, thread-like segments. The general appearance of the leaves is of delicate lace. The inconspicuous yellow flowers are borne in dense, compact umbels. The fruits are oval, ridged mericarps, almost ½ in (1 cm) long and slightly curved, like caraway. The fruits of var. *dulce* contain ethereal oils, among them anethole and, in smaller quantities, fenchone. The latter principle is more abundant in var. *vulgare* (bitter fennel), giving it a distinctive taste. Fennel has many properties, calmative, bechic, carminative, digestive, vasomotorial, cardiac, galactagogue and diuretic. Balsamic time coincides with the start of maturation.

Fennel is used for edible purposes in the preparation of pickles, in pastries and as a flavoring; bread is sometimes baked with fennel seeds. Anethole is employed in the liquor industry to produce aperitifs and drinks similar to anise. Essential oil is extracted from the turnip-like root. The variety *dulce* (Mill.) Batt. & Trab. (Florence fennel, sweet fennel or finocchio) is cultivated for herbal purposes whereas var. *vulgare* is used medicinally.

The seeds are sown in spring in rows 20 in (50 cm) apart. Water is needed to encourage germination. Thinning and hoeing operations are also necessary to keep down weeds. Var. *dulce* is cultivated annually, while in the case of biennial varieties the mericarps should be collected at intervals in late summer, when the leaves start to fade; in order not to lose the seeds, umbels with fruit should be cut as soon as they begin to ripen, and then the fruits must be carefully destalked and thoroughly dried so that nothing goes wrong with the fermentation processes. For herbal use the leaves may be removed several times before flowers appear, while the roots, harvested in autumn, require washing and subsequent drying. Fennel is most frequently cultivated for eventual extraction of the essence known as fennel oil.

Florence fennel is grown as a vegetable; the base of the foliar sheaths are enlarged and swollen and attached to a short shoot situated on the turnip-like root; this constitutes a sort of bulb which has an anise-like flavor and a fleshy consistency, both cooked and raw. It is often used in salads. The foliage can also be chopped and used to flavor salads. It is becoming more well known in the United States and Great Britain.

64 GALIUM ODORATUM (L.) Scop.

Asperula odorata L.
Rubiaceae
Sweet woodruff, (G) Waldmeister, (F) aspérule odorante, (I) stellina odorosa

The root of the name *Galium* is *gála*, milk, because of the curdling properties contained by plants of this genus. All the *Galium* species are much alike: herbaceous plants with whorled leaves and small flowers with four lobes, often delightfully scented. The sweet woodruff, a perennial species of beech and mixed conifer woodlands in central and northern Europe, is a herb up to 18 in (45 cm) tall, with a thin rhizome bearing several roots; the glossy quadrangular stem produces inflorescences of white flowers (much larger than those of other *Galium* species) with a funnel-shaped corolla. The fruit is a pair of hairy mericarps. The plant is cultivated in the U.S. by sowing the mericarps in cool, sandy soil or by dividing the rhizome, in a shaded spot. No particular care is necessary. It is harvested in the second year, when flowering starts, dried in the shade and kept well away from light. It contains glycosides, which in the course of drying release cumarinic compounds that possess a scent similar to vanilla; it also contains bitter principles, tannins, and vitamin C. In Germany it was formerly used for scenting wines, by simple maceration. In the liquor industry it can be used as a corrective or, by reason of its tonic-digestive properties, even to flavor drinks. *G. verum* L., with panicles of yellow flowers, contains cumarinic principles and gives out a sweet perfume; this was once used primarily to curdle milk and to color cheeses yellow.

65 GAULTHERIA PROCUMBENS L.

Ericaceae
Wintergreen, (G) Waldmeister, (F) aspérule odorante, (I) stellina odorosa

This prostrate evergreen perennial species, 4–8 in (10–20 cm) in height, is found only in its wild form. It is common in North America, growing in woods along the U.S.–Canadian border, in markedly acidic soil; it is harvested principally in eastern Pennsylvania. The leaves are dentate-serrate, the white flowers urceolate, similar to those of the myrtle, appearing in summer; the fruits are red berries that ripen in autumn. The leathery leaves are heavily scented, with astringent and stimulant properties, containing mineral salts and pain-killing principles.

The leaves are harvested during the summer, from June to September; distillation of the fresh or fermented product yields wintergreen essence, the principal constituent of which is methyl salicylate. In pharmaceuticals this is used as a corrective, or as a flavoring agent for confectionery and crystallized fruit. Infusions can be obtained from the leaves and drunk like tea. Wintergreen essence and methyl salicylate are used in the manufacture of perfumes and to flavor toothpastes. There are other species, *G. punctata* Blume., *G. fragrantissima* Wall. and *G. fragrans* D. Don, from India, Java, and Sumatra, from which Indian wintergreen is distilled. Nowadays methyl salicylate is produced by synthesis, replacing wintergreen extract. Various species of *Gaultheria* are also grown as ornamental subjects.

66 GENTIANA LUTEA L.

Gentianaceae

Yellow gentian, Bitterwort, (G) gelber Entian, (F) gentiane jaune, (I) genziana maggiore

According to Pliny and Dioscorides, the name is derived from the last king of an Illyrian people, Gentius, who was the first to reveal its medicinal properties. It is a mountain plant from southern Europe, an area thus extending over the northern Mediterranean. It grows wild in pastures, on calcareous soil, above a height of 3,300 ft (1,000 m). Excessive harvesting of the roots has jeopardized the survival of the species. In the same habitat grows the false helleborine (*Veratrum album* L.), a member of the lily family which is difficult for non-specialists to distinguish in the absence of flowers. The yellow gentian is a large herbaceous perennial, more than 3 ft (1 m) in height, glabrous, pale green, produced by a hypogean system comprising a large rhizomatous root. The stem bears opposite leaves, the lower ones with a small stalk and the others sessile, elliptical-oval, with parallel main veins. The flowers consist of deeply lobed yellow corollas, and are arranged in axillary and terminal tufts, protected by large leaf bracts, forming a spike. The fruit is a capsule that contains many small seeds.

The rhizome and roots are harvested in autumn and spring; they are fleshy, give out a penetrating odor of damp earth and have a very bitter taste. With stomachic and digestive properties, these parts have numerous uses, in caramels and digestive pastilles and in tonic preparations. Fermentation and subsequent distillation of the root produces "gentian grappa." It is used in the liquor industry to prepare aperitifs, syrups, and sparkling drinks, and is an ingredient of vermouth and angostura. Aperitifs can also be prepared quite easily by infusing the root in white wine. In folk medicine it is exploited because it stimulates the appetite and is good for the digestion as well as for dispelling fever. The bitter principles are glycosides.

Because the seeds do not easily germinate, the plant is difficult to cultivate. The seeds require a period of vernalization at a low temperature or treatments to stimulate germination. In spring, after some two months of germinating in a substratum of sand and peat, the seedlings may be transplanted, ten to the square yard, taking care to water and weed, given the gentian's inability to compete during the early years. Efforts have been made to propagate by division of rhizomes but the technique has not been as successful as was hoped, due to the insufficient strength of the secondary roots. Harvesting is carried out in the fifth or sixth year, in late summer, or before the renewal of plant growth. The entire hypogean apparatus is removed and after cursory cleaning this is dried; for herbal use swift action is necessary, in an oven at about 120°F (50°C); in the liquor industry the plants have to be slightly fermented before drying.

Infusions with gentian roots can be attempted with other species of the genus, e.g. the following: *G. punctata* L., similar to the yellow form, but with larger and black-flecked campanulate flowers; *G. purpurea* L., which is similar but with purple corollas, common in the western Alps; *G. asclepiadea* L., found in woodland, with opposite leaves and campanulate blue corollas; *G. kochiana* Perr. & Song., a stemless gentian, growing in fields and meadows, the large single campanulate blue flowers having five pointed lobes and green spots in the throat; and *Gentianella amarella* (L.) Borner, a herb with a branched stem, violet flowers and hairs in the throat.

67 GERANIUM MACRORRHIZUM L.

Geraniaceae

Geranium, cranesbill, (G) Felsenstorchschnabel, (F) géranium, (I) geranio

The plant derives its name from *géranos*, which is the Greek word for a crane, because of the similarity of the beaked fruit to this wading bird and some species of *Geranium* are called cranesbill. This showy and decorative geranium grows in arid surroundings of rocks and calcareous gravel, in hill and mountain zones. Originally from the mountains of southern Europe, it is not a very common species but, when present, grows densely. A herbaceous perennial, it is 20–28 in (50–70 cm) in height, with erect, massed stems and a sturdy creeping rhizome; the leaves are large, the basal ones palmate and divided, the cauline ones long-stalked, gradually becoming smaller and sessile. The fairly big flowers have reddish peduncles and are formed of deep red sepals, purple-red petals and violet stamens. The fruit is composed of five mericarps that separate by breaking off at the base when ripe. The plant may be multiplied by seed or by division of rhizomes, on fertile but moist soil.

This is the only wild geranium with a strong scent. It also has astringent and vulnerary properties.

The dried leaves are put in sachets to repel household insect pests. The essence is extracted by distilling various parts of the plant in steam, especially in Bulgaria, where it is cultivated. The essential oils of the geranium are of considerable commercial importance, containing, among others, geraniol, citronellol, and linalol. Like the extracts from the various species of *Pelargonium*, they are used in the production of cosmetics, perfumes, and soaps.

---

68 GEUM URBANUM L.

Rosaceae

Wood avens, herb bennet, (G) Nelkenwurz, (F) benoîte, (I) cariofillata

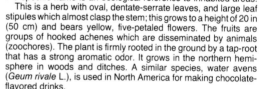

The significance of the Latin name *Geum* for this plant is not clear; the specific name is an ecological reference to inhabited areas.

This is a herb with oval, dentate-serrate leaves, and large leaf stipules which almost clasp the stem; this grows to a height of 20 in (50 cm) and bears yellow, five-petaled flowers. The fruits are groups of hooked achenes which are disseminated by animals (zoochores). The plant is firmly rooted in the ground by a tap-root that has a strong aromatic odor. It grows in the northern hemisphere in woods and ditches. A similar species, water avens (*Geum rivale* L.), is used in North America for making chocolate-flavored drinks.

The root of *G. urbanum* smells of cloves (for which it can be a substitute) and its taste is slightly astringent. These roots contain eugenol, tannins, and bitter substances and have tonic, stomachic, astringent, and febrifugous properties, most evident in decoctions. Once dried they should be stored, to be chopped or ground only when ready for use. Wine, tasting somewhat like vermouth, may be prepared from the infusions, with the addition of orange peel. Apart from the roots, used for flavoring, the leaves can also be eaten in salad.

69 GLYCYRRHIZA GLABRA L.

Leguminosae
Licorice, (G) Süssholz, (F) réglisse, (I) liquerizia

The "sweet root," which is the translation of the generic name, grows widely from the Mediterranean eastward to China and is cultivated in Italy, especially the central and southern regions, Spain, Turkey, and Russia, both for medicinal and culinary purposes. Licorice has the habit of a weed, rapidly infesting cultivated land. It is a herbaceous perennial with pinnatisect leaves and racemes of violet butterfly-like flowers. The small lomentaceous pods contain 3–5 seeds. The plant has strong roots from which woody rhizomes, colored yellow inside, develop horizontally.

Licorice is harvested either wild or in cultivated form. In the past for every 220 lb (100 kg) of roots that were harvested and treated about 44–55 lb (20–25 kg) of juice were extracted. The extension of citrus plantations, however, led to the progressive elimination of licorice, regarded as a weed. It has been growing in Britain since the sixteenth century, Pontefract at one time being an important center, remembered now in the licorice-flavored Pontefract cakes.

As it cools, the blackish brown mass solidifies. The sweet taste is determined by the glycoside glycyrrhizin, which has a sweetening property fifty times greater than that of saccharose; the flavor is extremely characteristic, so licorice cannot be used as a substitute for ordinary sugar. From the roots and the rhizomes, harvested in autumn, the essence is extracted by boiling and subsequent filtration. The bundles of roots, used industrially, are made up from the straightest pieces of root and sold as such; the remaining roots and other parts for extraction. The solidified product is prepared in the form of sticks. The decorticated roots, cut into pieces, are used medicinally. Licorice is utilized in the confectionery and pharmaceutical trades, in the latter case primarily to make cough-relieving products. In the liquor industry it is an ingredient for bitters and herbal liquors, and is also used to flavor certain beers and pipe tobaccos. The medicinal properties of licorice, notably emollient, diuretic, and expectorant, have been known since antiquity.

A wild "sweet root" of the temperate zones of Europe is the polypody or mountain licorice (*Polypodium vulgare* L.). This is a vascular fern with a sturdy, gnarled horizontal rhizome covered with brown scales and whitish inside, from which stems an almost pinnatisect frond with finger-like lobes. The rhizome, when chewed, tastes sweet and fresh, rather like licorice; it has cholagogic, purgative, vermifugal action.

An exotic legume, used as a herb, is the tamarind (*Tamarindus indica* L.); this is a tall tree originally from tropical Africa, which produces berries with a fleshy pericarp and a bitter-sweet, refreshing taste. The extract from the pulp is used to flavor drinks, thirst-quenching syrups, caramels, and sauces (Worcestershire sauce); it also has laxative properties. The tamarind is grown for its fruit in India and elsewhere as an ornamental shade plant.

70 HAMAMELIS VIRGINIANA L.

Hamamelidaceae
Witch hazel, (G) Zaubernuss, (F) hamamélis, (I) amamelide

This plant is very common on the Atlantic coast of North America (in the state of Virginia, as the specific name suggests), and can be cultivated as an ornamental in temperate climes. It is an undemanding species, only needing acidic soil. It takes the form of a small tree or a shrub up to 13 ft (4 m) tall, with scattered branches and leaves resembling those of the hazel, hence the English common name. It is deciduous and in winter looks something like the strawberry shrub. The flowers, with four narrow yellow petals, spiral in shape and ¾ in (1.5 cm) long, are sessile, similar to those of the strawberry shrub, in loose axillary inflorescences; they bloom in autumn, after leaf drop. The fruit is a capsule ½ in (1 cm) long that bursts open to eject two oval, glossy black seeds.

The Indians of North America were familiar with the properties of the plant; the bark and leaves possess valuable haemostatic and astringent qualities. The bark is sold in 4-in (10-cm) strips. Distillation of the leaves and the young shoots produces a distilled water that contains very little essence, but by decanting and subsequent separation it is possible to obtain small quantities of a fatty green substance with a strong smell. As a rule the distilled water, colorless and with an agreeable odor, is used in the manufacture of scented soaps, creams, astringent lotions, and eye washes.

---

71 HELICHRYSUM ITALICUM Don.

Compositae
Helichrysum, everlasting flower, (G) Helichrysum, (F) hélichrysum, (I) elicriso

The generic name describes the bright yellow flower heads, from the Greek, literally "golden sun." This Mediterranean plant grows in open, dry, sunny areas. It is a shrub, at most 20 in (50 cm) tall, with numerous erect and branched stems; the straight leaves are gray and hairy. The flower stems are simple, divided only at the top to produce corymbs of some 30 small, conical, flower heads covered by dry, bright yellow scales that may be dried and used in winter flower arrangements. The flowers, with a tubular corolla, are also yellow; the fruit, an achene, has a whitish pappus. The plant is propagated by division of clumps or by cuttings. Like many other composites, it contains principles which repel insects and thus has no problems with parasites; the Romans used the plant for keeping moths out of their homes.

The flower heads and young shoots of the plant, which have a strong, slightly disagreeable smell and a bitter taste, are harvested. Soon after collection, these parts are distilled to produce a yellow essential oil with the scent of roses.

Helichrysum is used in cosmetics in compositions with iris and orange-flower oil. In the kitchen it can be used to flavor jellies and drinks. In the pharmaceutical industry its properties are recognized as being effective against respiratory problems and allergies.

72 HERACLEUM SPHONDYLIUM L.

Umbelliferae

Hogweed, cow parsnip, (G) Wiesen-Bärenklau, (F) berce, (I) panace

According to legend, Heracles, mythical hero of ancient Greece, discovered the healing qualities of this plant, hence the generic name. The specific name is Greek for vertebra, after the jointed, angular appearance of the stem. Originally from temperate zones of the ancient world, the plant grows widely in grassland, woods, and in any ground with plenty of nitrogen substances.

It is a hairy perennial herb which may grow to a height of 6½ ft (2 m), with a thick reddish rhizome that gives out an aromatic odor. The erect, grooved, stiff and hollow stem, with swollen nodes, bears compound leaves, divided and pinnatisect, with large lobate, tooth-edged leaflets. The white or pink flowers are arranged in large, sturdy umbels. The fruits are flat mericarps, with a papery wing; like those of other umbellifers, they have a marked aromatic, bitter taste and can therefore be used, in small amounts, for seasoning. The roots, scented and pungent in flavor, are sometimes used, again in moderation, for the same purpose. The young stems and shoots (turions), after being scraped, can be served as a vegetable and have a slightly mandarin-like smell.

In eastern Europe (Poland, Russia) leaves and young stems are fermented in a little water to produce the soup known as "borshch," which keeps for a long time because of its lactic acid content. It is also used in sauerkraut, which has a very distinctive aroma due to the plant's essential oils.

---

73 HIBISCUS SABDARIFFA L. var. **sabdariffa**

Malvaceae

Roselle, (G) Karkade, (F) karkadeh, (I) carcadè

Hibiscus is from the Greek *ibiskos*, a form of mallow, but the origin of the specific name is uncertain. It is an annual species, originally from Africa, about 6½ ft (2 m) high, with a reddish green stem and sparse, long-stalked, palmate-lobate leaves, with a dentate margin. The calyx of the single, axillary flowers is strengthened by an outer calyx with five yellow, red-flecked petals; the stamens are joined in a tube around the style. The fruit is a round, pointed capsule, covered by a broad, fleshy calyx. This plant grows in many of the world's tropical regions and is cultivated in Asia, India, the Philippines, Malaysia, Senegal, and Ethiopia.

The fleshy calyces which enfold the ripe fruit are harvested at intervals and dried in the open air; they contain citric acid, tartaric acid, vitamins, and mineral salts. They are mainly used in a deep red, aromatic infusion that can be drunk hot or cold as a tonic, stimulating the intestinal and kidney functions. The calyces are also used in jellies and ice creams, and to color foods and cosmetic products. The best varieties are the African, which contain a higher proportion of citric acid to tartaric acid.

The musk mallow or abelmusk (*H. abelmoschus* L.) is cultivated in tropical zones for its seeds, from which an essence smelling of musk is extracted and used as an ingredient of perfumes and liquors.

74 HUMULUS LUPULUS L.

Cannabaceae

Hop, (G) Hopfen, (F) houblon grimpant, (I) luppolo

The name of the genus is from the Latin, while the specific, (meaning "small wolf") refers to the aggressive habit of the plant, which tends to smother those around it. The hop is quite common, growing in hedgerows and thickets and by roadsides. The stems twine in a clockwise direction; when young they are fleshy and herbaceous but later they look like ropes. The leaves are palmate-lobate, rough to the touch, usually with three lobes arranged opposite on the stem. The plants are of separate sexes: the males bear loose panicles of fairly small greenish flowers; the females' modest inflorescences, situated at the leaf axils, are in the form of drooping spikes. The female flowers, reduced to a single pistil, are covered, in groups of four, by two oval-lanceolate scales. Pollination is effected by the wind. The female fruits are eventually formed by overlapping papery bracts, at the base of which is an achene. The perennial root annually produces new shoots that may grow to a length of more than 33 ft (10 m). The hop is cultivated in many countries for flavoring beer, the major producers today being Germany (especially Bavaria), U.S., USSR, Czechoslovakia and Yugoslavia.

Only female specimens are planted, these being taken from the mother plant with 4–5 shoots, and flowering only in the third year. Supporting stakes and wires, up to 25 ft (8 m), have to be provided; and in autumn the plant is cut at the base. The bracts of the female inflorescences have tannic properties and are comprised of small yellow glands that contain the aromatic principles. Among the many compounds contained in the hop essence are, above all, hydrocarbons and 10–20 percent resins which give strength to the aroma, rich and somewhat spicy, with calmative and antibiotic properties.

Harvesting is done in September–October; the plants are cut a meter from ground level, all shoots are removed and the inflorescences (cones) are separated for drying and eventually for production of beer; thus prepared, they are cooked in the sugary liquid obtained from the malt and flavored during fermentation. In central Europe hops were used as early as 1200 for making beer, while in England, up to 1600, bogbean, *Menyanthes trifoliata* L. (a water-plant related to the gentian family) and the legume *Cytisus scoparius* (L.) Link (broom) served the same purpose. In former times the application of various principles to stabilize and flavor the beer led to the use of many other plants, including dropwort, licorice, sweet clover, mace, ginger, mugwort, and wormwood. The hop also serves to acidify bread. The infusion obtained from the cones is a calmative and a tonic and can be mixed with sweet liquors to produce aperitifs. The essential oil, moreover, is used to flavor sauces and tobaccos.

The hop is also an ancient textile plant, long utilized for making ropes and sacks. Nor should its edible properties be overlooked as a wild vegetable. In spring the young leaves, still closed, can be picked like wild asparagus and boiled; and the tips of the shoots are good for giving flavor to risottos, soups, and omelets.

75 HYSSOPUS OFFICINALIS L.
Labiatae
Hyssop, (G) Ysop, (F) hysope, (I) issopo

The Greek word for the genus means a sacred plant. Originally from Asia Minor and the Mediterranean, the hyssop is found on dry, stony ground. It is a small perennial shrub with woody stems, at most 3 ft (1 m) tall; the sessile or decussate leaves are lanceolate-linear with a slightly revolute margin, covered with hairs and oil-bearing glands. At the stem tips and leaf axils are spike-like inflorescences of bilabiate violet-blue flowers. Because of the long flowering period bees can gather plenty of nectar. In cultivation it is an undemanding species, requiring well drained, calcareous soil. Propagation is by cuttings or seed. Harvesting of the leaves and terminal shoots is carried out just before or at the time of flowering; they should then be dried in the shade. The aromatic, bitter, penetrating flavor of the leaves is similar to that of thyme and they should therefore be used in moderation.

A very ancient medicinal plant, hyssop has stomachic and digestive properties. The leaves can be eaten fresh with meat and fish or in sauces, ground up as an ingredient for spicing sausages, and used fresh or dried for preparing an infusion with a digestive action. The oil, obtained by distilling the leaves and the flower tips, contains pinene and has bechic, expectorant, and balsamic properties; it is one of the ingredients of eau de Cologne and oriental-type perfumes, and is used for flavoring Chartreuse-type liqueurs.

76 ILEX PARAGUARIENSIS St. Hil.
Aquifoliaceae
Maté, (G) Matebaum, (F) arbre à maté, (I) matè

In South America the Incas gave the name *matè* to the hollow gourds or calabashes used (to this day) as receptacles for drinking this tea, sucked through a special tube. In Latin *ilex* is the holm oak, whose young leaves are prickly like those of holly. This species is originally from Brazil and Paraguay, growing in the forests as far as Argentina. An evergreen shrub or small tree, it has sparse, short-stalked leaves with serrate-crenate margins. The flowers have four white petals and the fruits are red berries which turn black when ripe. Once used in its wild form, the plant is nowadays cultivated, mainly in southern Brazil.

The leaves are picked from the third year and subjected to heat treatment in order to preserve the green color and enable them to acquire their characteristic aroma. They are subsequently used to produce a stimulating drink similar to tea, either prepared by pouring hot water over powdered leaves or by cold maceration, using a filtering cane; the drink, pleasant and thirst-quenching, contains caffeine, vitamins, and green pigment. It has stimulant, diuretic, digestive, and diaphoretic properties. An extract from the leaves is also used in the manufacture of floral perfumes. Despite the popularity of the beverage in South America, *matè* is virtually unknown in the rest of the world.

77 ILLICIUM VERUM Hook. f.
Illicium anisatum L.
Illiciaceae
Star anise, (G) Sternanis, (F) anis étoilé, (I) anice stellato

The generic name comes from the Latin *illicere*, to attract, due to the pleasant scent of the capsule. This is an extremely ancient species, known in China as far back as 100 B.C. The principal producing regions are Kwangsi and North Vietnam. It is a tree of some 33 ft (10 m), evergreen, with white bark, similar to that of the birch, with glossy lanceolate leaves, growing through southeast Asia (from China to India). It produces rayed flowers with numerous yellow or reddish petals, from which come compound fruits of 6–8 follicles, shaped like a star, hence the common name. The plant is productive only after 15 years, yielding three annual harvests. The fruits, rough and brown outside, are smooth and shiny inside, each follicle normally containing one seed, and they are picked just before they ripen, to be dried in the sun. The pericarp contains the active principles, notably anethole and anisole, which are long-lasting provided they are kept in sealed containers. The odor is strongly aromatic, the taste similar to that of aniseed but somewhat more bitter. The drug can be used as it is or ground in the kitchen. It is used in the liquor industry as a tincture or distillate. The properties are carminative, stomachic, and sedative. The smaller fruits produced by *I. anisatum* L. (= *I. religiosum* Sieb. & Zucc.) are poisonous, smelling not of aniseed but cardamom. In Japan the bark of star anise is burned to release perfumed smoke.

---

78 INULA HELENIUM L.
Compositae
Elecampane, (G) Alant, (F) aunée, (I) inula campana

Originally from Eurasia, the plant is now found in temperate zones everywhere, growing wild in ditches, wet fields and waste places. At the base of the stems are rosettes with lanceolate leaves up to 20 in (50 cm) long; the leaves clasping the stem are oval, downy underneath. Flower heads 2 in (5 cm) in diameter, with radial, ligulate yellow flowers, appear in the summer; the latter drop when ripe, leaving only the tubulous central flowers. The roots and rhizomes are fleshy and aromatic.

Elecampane can be cultivated (especially in the Balkan peninsula) on cool, light, clay soil rich in organic substances, being propagated by seed or clump division in autumn. The ground needs hoeing and the flower stems have to be removed in order to stimulate root development. The roots, harvested at the end of the second year, have a strong, warm, bitter taste, and are washed, scraped, and dried in the sun or other suitable surroundings. At one time the leaves were eaten in salads or to produce a tea with the effect of stimulating the appetite; the roots, boiled in plenty of water, were sliced for seasoning salads.

The roots contain a fair quantity of inulin and the essence extracted from them takes the form of crystals with a little dark oil; this in turn contains azulene, alantolactone and other principles, which are used for scenting perfumes and liquors. A similar species is *I. conyza*, with aromatic leaves and roots.

79 IRIS GERMANICA L. var. florentina Dykes

Iridaceae

Iris, (G) Schwertlilie, (F) iris, (I) giaggolo

Irises, with their gaudy, spectacular colors are linked etymologically to the Greek word *ireos*, a rainbow. The genus comprises numerous species, including some that grow wild, found all over the northern hemisphere. Genetic improvement has produced dozens of varieties that are cultivated as ornamental garden plants. The essence, extracted by distillation, is obtained from irises raised in central and southern Europe, such as *I. germanica* L. var. *florentina* Dykes, to var. *germanica*, cultivated mainly in France, Morocco, and Italy; *I. pallida* Lam., however, comes originally from the Balkans.

Irises are perennial rhizomatous plants which in flower can reach a height of 32 in (80 cm). The superficial rhizomes are tuberous, with numerous adventitious roots; they bear the traces of the fallen leaves and branch sideways, terminating in a shoot. The leaves, stemming directly from the rhizomes, are sword-shaped, with parallel veining and smooth margins, their base sheathing the shoot. The flower stems are cylindrical, slightly angular, divided above into three or six branches, each of which carries a large, showy flower, in the axil of two scarious bracts; the buds are typically fusiform. The six tepals are arranged in two series, the three outer ones (falls) folded down and the three inner ones (standards) turned upward, around the petaloid stigma. The color in var. *florentina* is white, in other varieties various shades of violet-blue. The ovary is inferior and produces a loculicidal capsule with numerous large, rough seeds. Rhizome development is dichotomous, with one terminal flower shoot and two lateral vegetative shoots. Cultivation proceeds by planting pieces of rhizome furnished with shoots, taken from adult plants after flowering stops, in marly, sandy, and chalky soil. Hoeing is necessary at first to contain weeds and limited amounts of organic fertilizer should be given. Harvesting is done by pulling up the entire plants after 2–3 years, during the summer, and separating the rhizomes from the vegetative parts. The rhizomes are washed and then scraped. These operations are time-consuming and require a large work force, which explains why large-scale cultivation is nowadays on the decline. The cleaned rhizomes are dried in the sun for some 10 days and a long maturation period is then necessary in storage (4–6 months) for the orris root to develop and give the characteristic sweet violet fragrance to the flower.

The yellowish white essence, through steam distillation of the rhizomes, produces the substance, known as iris butter, which contains myristic acid (85 percent), irones (alpha and beta), furfurol and other principles, starch, fatty oil, resins, and mucilages.

The rhizome, in powder form, is used for scenting talcum and face powders; the essence has marked fixative properties and serves as the basis for manufacture of violet perfumes together with other essences such as lily of the valley, sandalwood, and geranium; it is found in toothpastes and toilet waters. Dried rhizomes can be put inside cupboards for giving a scent to the contents. Both the rhizome, in conjunction with other herbs, and the liquid essence are used for making certain liquors. In some cases the roasted seeds are used as coffee substitutes.

The fresh rhizome has emetic properties and can be chewed by children while teething. The drug has an aromatic, diuretic, and laxative action.

80 JASMINUM GRANDIFLORUM L.

Oleaceae

Spanish jasmine, (G) Jasmin, (F) jasmin, (I) gelsomino

The genus *Jasminum* contains more than 300 species of shrubs and climbers, deciduous or evergreen. They bear rotate flowers, with a long tube that opens in 5–6 lobes arranged perpendicularly above it. The leaves are opposite and usually pinnate.

Jasminum grandiflorum L., the Spanish jasmine, is a very ancient perfume plant, originally from India, a climber with imparipinnate leaves of 7 leaflets, the flowers initially pink and then white. Other species include *J. officinale* L., the white jasmine, growing from Iran to China, also a climber, deciduous, with imparipinnate leaves of 5–9 leaflets; the flowers, in axillary corymbs, are white. Common in temperate zones, and cultivated only for ornament, *J. nudiflorum* L., the winter jasmine, is a shrub with trifoliolate leaves and a 6-lobed yellow corolla which flowers from winter to spring. All these species can be propagated by layering or by cuttings and are normally grown only as ornamental plants. They need a mild climate. Flowering is between June and October; in Egypt the flowers are picked in the morning before the sun rises for extraction by the enfleurage method, which does not remove the more volatile components. The concrete has a waxy consistency and is reddish brown; the absolute is yellow, with the characteristic scent. The essential oil is obtained from the absolute by distillation.

Jasmine is one of the basic ingredients of many floral perfumes and in the manufacture of scented soaps.

81 JUGLANS REGIA L.

Juglandaceae

English walnut, Persian walnut, (G) Walnussbaum, (F) noyer royal, (I) noce

The generic name is from the Latin, meaning "Jove's acorn," indicating the quality of the seed, reiterated in the specific name, royal.

This is a tree with a rounded shape, with gray bark and slightly curving branches; the leaves are imparipinnate, with 5–7 leaflets, the apical one often larger than the rest. The leaves have a characteristic pleasant odor due to the presence of numerous glands secreting aromatic oils, the scent being similar to the laudanum or the rockrose (*Cistus ladanifer* L.) which has a balsamic odor like that of ambergris. The inflorescences are of separate sexes; the males are drooping catkins, with inconspicuous green flowers, the females, borne at the base of the branches at the leaf axils, are one or two flowers reduced to pistils with a large bifid stigma. Flowering is in May when the leaves appear. The fruits are drupes, with an outer green part that covers the woody endocarp, enclosing the seed. In the course of harvesting, in autumn, the fleshy part (hull) is removed and the seeds enclosed in the endocarp (kernel) kept.

Apart from being highly prized for its seeds, which yield a valuable edible oil, the tree produces excellent timber. The leaves and hull produce the fluid extract that possesses tonic, bitter properties, and an ethereal fluid extract used as a sun-tan oil. The green (but dry) hulls are used as flavoring in the preparation of walnut liquor.

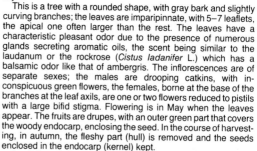

82 JUNIPERUS COMMUNIS L.

Cupressaceae

Juniper, (G) Wacholder, (F) genévrier, (I) ginepro

The generic name juniper was used by the Romans. A long-lived woody plant, it usually assumes a shrubby habit but sometimes grows into a columnar tree over 30 ft (10 m) tall, though usually with a divided trunk. The bark is gray-brown and the leaves are pointed and needle-like, about 1 in (1.5 cm) long, blue-green, arranged in groups of three. It is a dioecious species, the males bearing inconspicuous inflorescences at the tips of the branches, the females rounded cones formed of three fertile scales which, after being fertilized, produce a fleshy bluish berry with three triangular seeds. The pulp contains ethereal oils, particularly pinene, camphene, and other terpenes. The plant reaches maturity after two or three years, depending on climatic conditions.

The berries are harvested by hand in late summer; the sugars they contain bring about a fermentation process and subsequent distillation produces juniper-based liquors (Steinhäger). The essential oil is separated during distillation and is used industrially for the manufacture of gin and other liquors.

Juniper may be cultivated, though with difficulty, growing very slowly but adapting to any type of soil. The eastern red cedar or pencil cedar (*J. virginiana* L.) produces cedar oil, used in perfumery and pharmacy. And from the green parts of the Italian *Cupressus sempervirens* L. an essence is obtained which is used in perfumery for its scent of laudanum and ambergris.

---

83 LAURUS NOBILIS L.

Lauraceae

Bay laurel, sweet bay, (G) Lorbeerbaum, (F) laurier commun, (I) alloro, lauro

The origin of the name is uncertain but may be derived from the Celtic *laur*, green, or from the Latin *laudo*, honor or praise. The species comes from the Mediterranean where it grows widely in mild climates, tolerating relatively low winter temperatures. The laurel is a tree with an erect trunk that may grow to a height of 15–25 ft (5–8 m); it is often found in the form of a shrub, especially as an ornamental or in areas not enjoying a warm climate. The persistent leaves are leathery and dark green, shiny above, opaque below; the blade is entire, lanceolate, with a short curving stalk attached to the stem; the margin is wavy, slightly rough and streaked with a paler line; and the base is cuneate with a pointed tip. The small male and female flowers are separate, with yellow petals, and arranged in short umbels which open in March–April. The fruit is an oval black berry, about ½ in (1 cm) long.

The leaves, both fresh and dried, are strongly fragrant, containing 1–3 percent ethereal oils with pinene, cineol, lauric acid, and tannins. They are dried and lightly pressed in the dark. The fruits also contain fatty oils that are extracted to produce the ointment laurin. The leaves are used either fresh or dried in the kitchen for seasoning, and often cooked with meat to make it more easily digestible by stimulating the gastric and liver functions. They also have carminative, sudorific, antiseptic, sedative, and stimulant properties. The distilled oil is utilized in the perfume and liquor industries.

84   LAVANDULA ANGUSTIFOLIA Mill.

Lavandula officinalis Chaix

Lavender, (G) Lavendel, (F) lavende, (I) lavanda

Lavender is a species that grows wild on grassy slopes, dry fallow ground, and scrubland, and is cultivated in France, Dalmatia, Algeria, and Italy. It derives its name from the fact that the Romans added the flowers to bath water. It has a bushy habit and in its rounded form may reach a height of 4 ft (1.5 m). A perennial woody plant, it is covered with gray down and emits a pleasant scent when touched. The stems bear opposite, straight leaves with a slightly curved margin. The spikes of bilabiate violet flowers, on long stalks with a few leaves, stem from the leaf axils.

Lavender has been cultivated since ancient times for its aromatic properties and has reverted to the wild well beyond its original range. Among the wild species are *L. latifolia* Med. (synonym *L. spica* DC.) from western regions of the Mediterranean, similar to *L. angustifolia* but with broad leaves and branched, drooping inflorescences; *L. stoechas* L. (French lavender), which grows on scrubland, especially along the Mediterranean coasts, and possesses spikes with a corolla of very showy, sterile violet bracts; *L. multifida* L. (Egyptian lavender), from the western Mediterranean coasts, in Italy only in Calabria and Sicily, with pinnatisect leaves; and *L. dentata* L., originally from the Balearics and Spain, with straight, finely dentate-crenate leaves. A natural sterile hybrid formed from *L. officinalis* and *L. latifolia* is the lavendin (*L. hybrida*). It is cultivated in Mediterranean mountain zones, on dry calcareous soil. It may be propagated from seed, but preferably from woody or herbaceous cuttings. In spring or autumn twigs are taken from second-year individuals and set to root in light soil, to be transplanted the following year in rows 4 ft (1.5 m) apart. There are many cultivars of the hybrid lavender that require closer attention, especially with regard to feeding. One planting lasts 5–10 years, according to species. Harvesting is done when three-quarters of the flowers have already bloomed. Care is taken to cut off the whole inflorescences with a small part of the branch. The yield of the lavendin is almost double that of lavender (12–15 t/ha as against 5–7 t/ha).

The parts, gathered in sacks, are distilled by steam to produce lavender oil, widely used in perfumery. The percentage of essential oil and its composition varies according to species; the essence contains linalol, linalyl acetate, cineol, camphor, and other principles. The essences from warm countries are richer in esters (linalyl acetate, smelling of bergamot), while those from temperate zones contain more cineol, with a stronger odor of camphor.

Because of its fragrance, lavender is used in the cosmetics industry for the production of creams, soaps, lotions, and a vast range of scents and toilet preparations, including lavender water and colognes. In pharmacy it is utilized as an odor corrective and as a scent for creams. Finally it has varied culinary uses, as a flavoring agent and to enrich the taste of meats, jams, tea, etc.

Lavender has antispasmodic, stimulant, sedative, carminative, and antiseptic properties. Bunches of lavender and lavender bags are kept in drawers and wardrobes; besides giving out a delicate perfume they help to repel insects. Flowering lavender attracts hordes of bees that produce a sweet-smelling, clear white honey.

85 LEPIDUM SATIVUM L.

Cruciferae
Garden cress, (G) Gartenkresse, (F) cresson alénois,
(I) crescione dei giardini

The name of the genus probably refers to the one used by the
Romans, perhaps associated with the scaly form of the pods, and
derived from the Greek *lepidon*. The specific name indicates that
the plant sows itself and therefore grows wild. The wild forms
originate in the Middle East, where it has been cultivated since
antiquity; seeds have been found in remains from ancient Egypt.
Cress is cultivated nowadays in temperate regions all over the
world. It is an annual plant with a tap-root and an erect stem, up to
20 in (50 cm) in height, glabrous, divided above by long flower
branches. The basal leaves are oval, the cauline leaves pinnatisect; the inflorescences of compound racemes bear small
pinkish white flowers from May to September, producing barely
winged siliculae. The cultivated varieties differ principally in the
shape of the leaves. The species is adaptable to all soils, provided
they are moist, and may be sown from spring to autumn. Use is
made prevalently of germinated seedlings, easily distinguished
from the others by their trilobate leaves. After a few weeks the
leaves, about 4 in (10 cm) tall, can already be harvested.
   The leaves, with a pungent taste, possess a high vitamin
content (carotene, group B vitamins, vitamin C) and are used for
salads, with vegetables, stewed meats, and as garnishing.
   A similar species is winter cress (*Barbarea vulgaris* R. Br.),
likewise grown in moist, sandy soil but also found wild along
seashores.

---

86 LEVISTICUM OFFICINALE Koch

Umbelliferae
Lovage, (G) Liebstöckel, Maggikraut, (F) livèche, (I) levistico,
maggi

In the ancient world many aromatic umbellifers were called
ligusticum, with which the common names in various languages
are associated. The herb probably originated in western Asia and
spread to Europe during the Middle Ages, where it was cultivated
as a medicinal plant, known for its diuretic, emmenagogic, digestive, and carminative properties. It is found almost exclusively in
herb gardens, seldom in the wild. A perennial plant, with a
rhizomatous root, its large, glossy blue-green leaves, bi- or tripinnatisect, with reddish stalks, measure over 20 in (50 cm); the tips
of the leaflets are deeply dentate. The inflorescences are borne on
tall, glabrous, grooved, reddish stems, 3–6½ ft (1–2 m) in height;
the yellow flowers are arranged in double umbels and the fruit, a
mericarp, is oval and slightly ridged. The whole plant gives out an
aromatic odor which is like that of celery. For cultivation it needs
deep, rich soil and cool surroundings. It can be sown directly
outside or under glass with later transplanting. Given the considerable size of the plant, it is best to keep plenty of space
between the rows. The leaves are harvested when ready for use,
taking care of the central shoot. Roots can be lifted in the second
or third year, in autumn, then washed, sliced, and dried. Stems
and leaves are used for seasoning, in cubes or concentrates for
soup, and in the liquor industry for digestive infusions. In the
kitchen the leaves and shoots give flavor to salads, soups,
sauces, cheese, fish, and meat. The essence is used in exotic
perfumes.

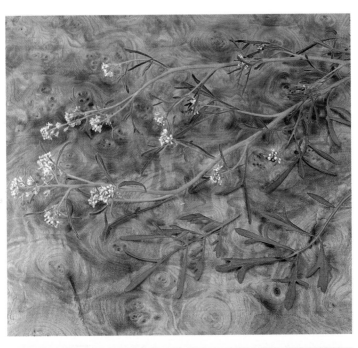

87 LIPPIA CITRIODORA Kunth
Aloysia triphylla Britt.
Verbenaceae
Lemon verbena, (G) Zitronenstrauch, (F) verveine odorante, lippia, (I) cedronella, erba cedrina, erba Luigia, verbena odorosa

The name of the genus commemorates A. Lippi (1678–1704), the French botanist and physician, while the specific name alludes to the aromatic character of the plant; the synonym *Aloysia* is after Maria Luisa, wife of Charles IV of Spain (1788–1808). The plant comes from Central and South America where it grows in the form of a tree or shrub. In temperate climes it grows to about 6½ ft (2 m) but cannot withstand frost. Introduced to Europe at the end of the eighteenth century to be utilized in perfumery, it is today replaced industrially by essence of lemongrass (*Cymbopogon*); but it is still cultivated in France (Grasse), Algeria and China. The leaves are opposite, lanceolate, gray-green above, downy and abundantly furnished with glands; the violet and purple labiate flowers are arranged in terminal spikes. Verbena requires a sunny spot and average, well-drained soil; it is propagated in summer from cuttings, and in winter it is advisable to give it shelter. The leaves smell of lemon and are harvested throughout the growing period; they are dried in the shade and stored in sealed containers. They are used for infusions and for flavoring food because of their stomachic properties, or for home-made liquors. The scent is strong and penetrating, useful for perfuming drawers and cupboards. The fresh twigs, gathered just before flowering, are used for distillation, and from it Spanish verbena is obtained. The essential oil is an ingredient of colognes and can be mixed with lemon, orange, and geranium essences.

88 MALVA SYLVESTRIS L.
Malvaceae
Mallow, (G) Algiermalve, (F) mauve, (I) malva

The Latin name of the plant indicates that it belongs to the mallow family. It originated in the Euro-Siberian regions and has become common everywhere, in built-up areas, by roadsides, in fields and on wasteland.

A herbaceous perennial, up to 3 ft (1 m) tall, it has long-stalked palminerved leaves, slightly hairy with five round lobes and a crenate margin. The large flowers, with the calyx strengthened by an epicalyx, are in axillary clusters, the petals are pink and the stamens tube-like. The fruit is a schizocarp derived from the carpels of the ovary, arranged in a circle, which break up when ripe and separate into numerous mericarps. The mallow is cultivated mainly for its flowers, but leaves can also be collected from wild plants. It is quite undemanding with respect to soil and is sown in April–May with 24 in (60 cm) left between the rows. Some hoeing is required to keep down the weeds; and to prevent leaf rust it is best to use treated seeds.

The flowers are harvested in stages, and for the leaves the entire plant should be lifted and the stems removed. The flowers are used for tisanes and infusions, especially against chills. All parts of the mallow contain mucilage and the leaves, in particular, are used externally for soothing inflammations of the mouth and skin. The inflorescences and young leaves give a distinctive flavor to soups and salads.

89 MATRICARIA CHAMOMILLA L.

Chamomilla recutita (L.) Rauschert
Compositae
Camomile, (G) echte Kamille, (F) camomille, (I) camomilla

Camomile (chamomile) is a species that has been widely cultivated in the herb garden since ancient times, being used medicinally against a range of illnesses, including menstrual
disorders, as suggested by the generic name *matrix* signifying
uterus; the specific name is derived from *khamaimelon*, small
apple tree, because the flowers give off a scent similar to that of
ripe apples. The common camomile is a medium-sized herbaceous plant that grows in fields, as a weed among cereal crops,
along roads and on wasteland. The stem is erect and branched,
with tripinnatisect leaves and filiform, finely laciniate leaflets. The
heads of very small flowers are convex and hollow inside (this
characteristic distinguishes them from those of the perennial or
English camomile ([*Anthemis nobilis*]). The yellow disk florets are
tubular about 1/16 in (2 mm) long, the ray florets white, 3/16 in (5 mm)
in length. When fully out, the ligulate flowers tend to curve
downward. The involucre is made up of green bracts with a
scarious margin. The fruits are small brown achenes. The fresh
plant gives out a pleasant odor that becomes heavy after drying.

Camomile grows wild through the Mediterranean zone and can
be harvested; in the herb garden, in cultivated form, it tends to
spread like a weed. It is not particularly demanding about climate
but prefers calcareous soil, even when hard and dry. It reproduces
by seed and, if need be, can be transplanted; hoeing is necessary
if the ground is too rich. When harvested wild, care should be
taken to check on local and/or national regulations.

The drug is found in the flower heads as they open, so harvesting is in May–June; the best method is to remove the heads from
the stalk snipping them so that only about 1/2 in (1 cm) of the
peduncle remains; the heads are then dried in the shade, laid out
in thin layers and turned so that they do not become gray or brown,
bearing in mind that too much handling may detach florets and
devalue the product. In fact, flowers that do fall off can be
powdered. The dried flowers should be stored in well sealed glass
containers, away from direct light.

Camomile contains many active principles, including essential
oils, principally derived from azulene which gives the essence its
blue color. It has a bitter taste and is good for the digestion; and it
also has sedative and antispastic actions, mild though effective,
and febrifugal and sudorific properties. In perfumery it is used for
soaps and bath salts but especially for shampoo preparations for
general care and lightening of the hair. Camomile has limited use
in the liquor industry, but is employed in pharmacy because of its
azulene content, for skin liniments and mild mouth disinfectants.

There are various wild species that look much like the common
camomile but which do not possess the latter's properties. They
include: the so-called false camomile (*M. discoidea* DC. = *M.
suaveolens* = *Chamomilla sauveolens*), with no ligulate florets
and yellowish hemispherical heads, and some medicinal use as
an anthelminthic and antispastic; the odorless camomile (*M.
inodora* L. = *Tripleurospermum inodorum*), similar in appearance
but with larger heads, a full receptacle and hence no aroma; and
the bastard camomile (*Anthemis arvensis* L.), again resembling
the common camomile but without scent and with small pointed
scales on the conical receptacle, among the tubular flowers.

90 MELILOTUS OFFICINALIS (L.) Pall.

Leguminosae
Yellow sweet clover, melilot, (G) gelber Steinklee, (F) mélilot, (I) meliloto

This wild herb, common in Europe, was introduced in ancient times from Asia. Today the species is found everywhere. The name indicates the honey-producing properties of the plant, which grows by roadsides, in fields, and on poor, stony ground. It is a herbaceous annual or biennial, with trifoliolate leaves, similar to those of the medicinal herb, with attractive erect spikes of golden-yellow flowers; the fruits are small pods. The several flower stems grow to about 3 ft (1 m). The flower heads are harvested and dried, during which process they take on the typically pleasant smell of hay, due to the formation of coumarin, with the sweet taste of almonds, similar to that of sweet woodruff (*Galium odoratum*). The leaves contain 2 percent melilotin and a coumarinic glycoside, which in large amounts can be poisonous; for this reason the species cannot be used as fodder but only as a soil improver.

In minimal quantities the essence can be used in sweets, compotes, and salads, and for seasoning sauces; also for flavoring sausages, marinating meat, and for flavoring beer. In Switzerland it is added to "Green Cheese" and Gruyère. The infusion prepared with the dried parts has digestive and carminative properties. The dried leaves have a scar-forming action and also repel moths.

The similar species, white sweet clover (*M. alba* Medik.), with white spikes, also contains coumarinic principles but varieties have been selected that are free of these substances and can therefore serve as fodder.

91 MELISSA OFFICINALIS L.

Labiatae
Lemon balm, sweet balm, melissa, (G) Zitronenmelisse, (F) citronelle, (I) melissa

The name of the genus is an abbreviation of the Latin *melissophyllum*, meaning bee plant or leaf. It may have been harvested in the belief that the branches, rubbed over new hives, would attract swarms of bees. The plant, originally from southern Europe, has characteristic opposite heart-shaped leaves, with a dentate-crenate margin, full of oil-bearing glands. The inconspicuous creamy white flowers are arranged in a terminal spike. The herb is in the form of a perennial rounded shrub. It is easily cultivated, with seedlings transplanted into open ground, in sunny surroundings. It can also be multiplied by clump division, in autumn or spring; the plants should be replaced every five years.

The leaves are harvested just before or at the time flowers appear; they are then dried in the shade, quickly, to keep them from turning dark. They give out a characteristic scent of lemon, slightly bitter and aromatic, due to the presence of ethereal oils, notably citral and citronellal; they can be used fresh to flavor salads, soups, meats, sauces, custards, and puddings, and also in the preparation of aromatic vinegars, refreshing drinks, and Chartreuse-type liqueurs. The distillate is used commercially in conjunction with other oils such as lemon, citronella, and lemongrass.

Lemon balm has antipyretic, refreshing, cholagogic and stimulant properties; and melissa water is a well known calmative.

92 MENTHA x PIPERITA L.

Labiatae

Peppermint, (G) Pfefferminze, (F) menthe poivrée, (I) menta piperita

Plants of the genus *Mentha* have been known and appreciated since antiquity, so much so that the Romans introduced them from the south, where they originated, to other parts of Europe. In the Middle Ages they were cultivated in monastery gardens and much used locally. Minthe was the name of a nymph who was seduced by Pluto, and whom the jealous Persephone turned into a seedling. The natural hybrid *Mentha* x *piperita* is derived from the crossing of *M. aquatica* L., *M. spicata* L. and *M. longifolia* (L.) Huds., the most common of the European wild species, and was discovered for the first time in England in the seventeenth century by the naturalist John Ray; today it is cultivated all over the world.

This perennial herb, about 20 in (50 cm) high, has a branching rhizome that produces long stolons. The erect quadrangular stem is branched above; the long-stalked leaves are opposite, lanceolate-elliptical, with a dentate margin. The flowers, with an almost regular pink corolla, are in dense terminal spikes; they appear around July, but are sterile. For this reason plants are propagated by vegetative means, rooted stolons with shoots being lifted in autumn or spring. The ground must be fertile, cool, and light, and it should be noted that the plant needs plenty of potassium; given its tendency to spread, only light hoeing is needed at the start. Peppermint is cultivated as an annual, even though the plant is long-lived, for if it is left in the ground it is likely to take over the whole garden in irregular fashion, hindering cultivation of other species. The entire vegetative part is removed prior to flowering if intended for herbal use, but in full flower if required for distillation.

Special glands in the leaves secrete an essential oil that consists mainly of menthol (50–80 percent), menthone, menthofurane, and limonene, flavonoids, carotenoids, and tannins. The essential oil is obtained by steam distillation, producing the so-called crude essence which, before being used commercially, must be further decanted and filtered. The dry leaves are used to prepare a highly aromatic and stimulating infusion (peppermint tea).

In the pharmaceutical industry the oil is used for flavoring syrups, pastilles and ointments. In cosmetics it serves as an ingredient for toothpastes and mouth washes because of its refreshing taste, and for soaps, shampoos, and scents. It is very widely used, of course, for the preparation of foodstuffs, to flavor confectionery (sweets, chocolates, and chewing gum) and preserved foods, and in the manufacture of syrups and liqueurs. Menthol is often used to flavor tobaccos. In the kitchen it may be used, sparingly, in various ways. Peppermint has stomachic, carminative, stimulant, antiseptic, and anaesthetic properties.

The perennial mint known as pennyroyal does not belong to the genus *Mentha*; its scientific name is, in fact, *Calamintha officinalis* Moench (= *Satureja calamintha*). This plant grows wild on uncultivated ground in Mediterranean regions, although often found nowadays on arable land and in the herb garden. It has terminal spikes of violet-pink tubular bilabiate flowers and small round to oval leaves, slightly dentate and downy. It contains pulegone, mentone, and pinene, and is used on a modest scale for preparing stimulating infusions.

93 MYRISTICA FRAGRANS Hout.

Myristicaceae

Nutmeg, mace, (G) Muskatnuss, (F) noix muscade, (I) noce moscata, macis

The name is derived from the Greek *myristicós*, fragrant; in fact, the scent of nutmeg has been compared with that of myrrh. The common name, in various languages, is explained by the fact that only the inner part, similar in size to a nut and smelling of musk, is actually used. This species furnishes the seeds, which constitute a highly prized essence, brought in ancient times by the Arabs to the Mediterranean region. The Portuguese, having circum-navigated Africa, had a trade monopoly in the spice, later taken over by the Dutch, who limited cultivation of the tree to the Moluccas. Today this area has expanded to include Indonesia, Sri Lanka, India, the West Indies, and Brazil. Indonesia, the world's leading producer, sells 5,000 tons of nutmeg annually, followed by Grenada (West Indies) with 2,700 tons a year.

An evergreen tree of 20–35 ft (6–10 m) in height, *Myristica fragrans* is dioecious, with single individuals, being either male flowers or female flowers only. The oval leaves, dark green above, light green below, are scented. The flowers, which appear in June, are not conspicuous. The male flowers, in clusters, display numerous stamens fused into a column; the female flowers, furnished with a single carpel, are solitary or grouped. The fruit is a spherical dehiscent berry.

Cultivation of this species is extremely difficult and is possible only in warm, humid climates, with temperatures of not less than 55°F (13°C), or in a hothouse. It can be propagated from cuttings or from seed. However, this is not always successful as the seedlings tend to be delicate and difficult to handle.

When the fruits are harvested, the fleshy part is removed, thus freeing the seed, covered by a fleshy pink involucre (aril) which, when dried, is sold as mace and used for seasoning food, in perfumery, and for liquors, notably beer. The inner part, after being dried, breaks up to liberate the seed proper, oval and pink, 1–1½ in (2–3 cm), wrinkled on the surface; this is the actual nutmeg, which is treated with slaked lime and marketed.

The aroma is very strong and penetrating, so nutmeg has to be used sparingly, all the more because large amounts may prove hallucinogenic and ultimately toxic. The drug contains 30 percent fatty oils, 30 percent starch, 7–16 percent ethereal oils, composed of pinene, camphene, terpene, and borneol, and 8 percent myristicin and other phenols.

Small seeds or any that are damaged while being harvested can be used for the extraction of an oil used for cosmetic creams.

Finally, an oil utilized in the liquor and perfumery trades is obtained by distillation.

94 MYRRHIS ODORATA (L.) Scop.
Umbelliferae
Sweet cicely, (G) Süssdolde, (F) cerfeuil musqué, (I) finocchio dei boschi

A plant of large dimensions, sweet cicely commonly grows in woodland clearings and mountain meadows of southern Europe and is widespread in northern England and southern Scotland; it has a strong, pleasant aroma that resembles that of other officinal umbellifers such as aniseed, and this explains the generic name that refers to myrrh, in the sense of a perfumed product. A herbaceous perennial, more than 3 ft (1 m) high, its stem is erect, grooved, and densely pubescent, with basal leaves more than 20 in (50 cm) long, pinnatisect, the lobes with dentate margins. The umbels of white flowers produce mericarps 1 in (2 cm) or more long, with distinct ridges, which turn brown as they ripen. The plant only grows wild but can be cultivated solely for ornamental purposes in shady corners of the garden; multiplication is by seed or clump division.

All the parts contain anethole. The leaves, fruits, and roots can all be used, the last as a vegetable. The leaves, with their odor of aniseed, can be served fresh (if dried they lose much of their aroma) for flavoring soups, omelets, drinks, and liquors; the fruits, collected while unripe and then dried, can garnish meat, giving it a sweet spicy taste like licorice. The entire plant is used to prepare infusions from which are obtained herbal liquors. The plant, especially the fruits, has tonic, carminative, aperitive, antiseptic, and freshening properties.

95 MYRTUS COMMUNIS L.
Myrtaceae
Myrtle, (G) Brautmyrte, (F) myrte, (I) mirto

This plant, sacred to Venus, was used for garlands and coronets in wedding cremonies as a symbol of love; its delicate perfume is derived from the Greek *myrtos*, having a common root with myrrh. It is a typical species of the Mediterranean flora, common along the seashore, in hedgerows and in scrubland. It revels in warmth and light, growing freely in acid and subacid soils. It is frequently cultivated in many varieties, differing in the size of their leaves, sometimes for ornamental purposes. The myrtle is an evergreen plant in the form of a shrub or small tree, with light reddish brown bark that flakes off in fibers. The oval, pointed, coriaceous leaves are simple, 1½ in (3 cm) long, with entire margins, set opposite or in whorls. The white pedunculate flowers stem from the leaf axils, solitary or in pairs. The calyx is persistent and numerous stamens with long filaments and yellow anthers stem from the rayed corolla, 1½ in (3 cm) in diameter. The fruits are round blue-black berries of ½ in (1 cm), with the remains of the calyx at the tip. The plant is propagated either from seed, in the greenhouse and then transplanted, or from cuttings. In cold climates plants should be protected in winter.

The leaves and flower heads are used for the extraction of "angel water," used in the cosmetics trade for soaps and scents. The leaves are used for flavoring meat, sausages, game, wines and liquors. The essential oil obtained from the leaves and fruits contains myrtol and various principles.

96 NASTURTIUM OFFICINALE R. Br.

Rorippa nasturtium-aquaticum Hayek
Cruciferae
Watercress, (G) Brunnekresse, (F) cresson de fontaine, (I) crescione

The highly individual odor of the nasturtium accounts for the generic name from the Latin *nasum torquere* ("to twist the nose"); the plant was already known to the Romans for its medicinal and aromatic properties. This is a wild species growing in streams or in ditches with clean water, cultivated for centuries in France and northern Europe, especially Holland; and where thermal water is available, production and harvesting can continue all year long. The plant is aquatic with a submerged stem and pinnatisect leaves that appear at the surface; the stems have adventitious roots at the nodes; an erect raceme of white flowers is produced from May to July.

The winter shoots, cut some 4 in (10 cm) from the tip, possess a sharp, bitter taste; they contain mustard glycosides and various vitamins. When cultivated, the plant is multiplied by dividing the clumps and burying them in the direction of the current. It is also possible to obtain seedlings by sowing seed directly under glass. Care must be exercised when harvesting the wild plants, for cysts of *Fasciola hepatica*, a flat parasite of mammals, usually sheep, which can be passed on to humans, sometimes appear on the surface.

Watercress can be eaten in salads together with other vegetables or cooked as an accompaniment to fish.

---

97 NICOTIANA TABACUM L.

Solanaceae
Tobacco, (G) Taback, (F) nicotiane, (I) tabacco

This plant, of North American origin, is widely cultivated throughout the world for the tobacco industry and also for its medicinal properties and ornamental qualities. It was brought to Europe in the mid-sixteenth century by a French diplomat, J. Nicot, hence the generic name. Tobacco comes from the Indian name for the plant; some authors maintain, however, that it existed before the discovery of America and may refer to other aromatic plants used for smoking.

It is an annual herbaceous plant, up to 6½ ft (2 m) high, hairy and sticky, with an erect stem, branched only to produce the inflorescences, with pointed oval leaves up to 20 in (50 cm) long. The flowers have a tubular calyx, like the corolla, which is colored red, pink or yellow, up to 2 in (5 cm) in length. The fruits are capsules with small seeds.

Venice was the first power to impose a monopoly on its cultivation, followed by the Papal States. Today it is grown in many temperate countries. The leaves contain up to 4.8 percent nicotine, a stimulant of the nervous system and a toxic alkaloid. Because of this nicotine was extracted for use as an insecticide, although today it is produced by synthesis. Part of the leaves, particularly of Virginia tobacco, is used in perfumery, notably masculine, oriental-type scents with nuances of tobacco. In addition to furnishing material for smoking, tobacco is widely chewed but the practice of sniffing tobacco has practically disappeared. However, snuff is still made; users generally tuck it between the lips and gums.

98 NIGELLA DAMASCENA L.

Ranunculaceae

Nigella, black cumin, love-in-a-mist, (G) Schwarzkümmel, (F) nigelle, (I) nigella

The seeds account for the generic name, from Latin, *niger*, black, and the specific name alludes to Damascus, the region where the plant originated. It grows in fields and on uncultivated ground in the Mediterranean area. Nigella is an annual herbaceous plant, up to 20 in (50 cm) high, with a delicate erect stem with pinnatisect leaves and laciniate leaflets. The solitary flowers, with five black-spotted blue petals, are unmistakable because they are surrounded by an involucre with deeply laciniate, lacy bracts. The fruit is formed of five swollen follicles that contain four tetrahedral black seeds that constitute the spice. This is used for flavoring confectionery and liquors because of its sharp, pungent taste and because it gives out the faint scent of strawberries.

The related fennel-flower (*N. sativa* L.), which is cultivated from North Africa to India, has seeds containing the bitter principle nigellin and ethereal oils, used for flavoring bakery products. Similar to *N. damascena*, it has creamy blue-flushed petals and finely grooved follicles. It is also cultivated in temperate zones as an annual ornamental plant and is seldom found growing wild. It adapts well to poor soils and can be sown in open ground, merely requiring some weed control. The seeds of both plants should be used sparingly because of their irritant effects; they have hypertensive, carminative, anthelminthic and emmenagogic properties.

99 OCIMUM BASILICUM L.

Labiatae

Basil, sweet basil, (G) Basilienkraut, (F) basilic, (I) basilico

The specific and common names are derived from the Greek *basiléus*, king, and the herb, by reason of its special properties was given regal status; the generic name may also come from the Greek *ókimon*, fragrant-lipped. It is a labiate herb, much branched, with oval, dentate, bright green leaves and terminal spikes of white flowers. The oval nutlets contain mucilage and swell up in water. Basil is grown in the garden or in pots; it requires rich, loose soil and can be sown in April–May directly outside or under glass, as early as March, with subsequent transplanting of seedlings. Growth may be encouraged by trimming the plants. They need a fair amount of water and early treatment against various cryptogamic diseases, to which they are prone.

The green parts of sweet basil are cultivated for use, either fresh or dried, as a seasoning, or for extraction of essence. Harvesting is in summer when the inflorescences appear. These are dried in airy, shaded surroundings. The leaves are used in the kitchen for flavoring soups, omelets, sauces and vinegar.

The essence, golden-yellow and with a delicate aroma, is extracted by steam distillation. The essential oil is used in soaps, toothpastes, mouthwashes, and perfumes. It is also a basic ingredient for the manufacture of Chartreuse-type liqueurs.

100 OENOTHERA BIENNIS L.

Onagraceae

Evening primrose, (G) Nachtkerze, (F) onagre, (I) enotera

Although the scientific name is derived from Greek, it would not seem to have historic or cultural associations as the plant came from the New World in the eighteenth century. The genus is also known because the botanist De Vries studied it in relation to mutations (O. erythrosepala, 1901).

The species grows widely on sandy, gravelly soil, by roadsides, on banks, and on wasteland. It is a tall biennial plant, up to 5 ft (1.5 m) high, with a swollen root and an erect stem. The basal leaves are in rosettes, the stem leaves sparser, bright green with reddish veining. The flowers, in terminal racemes, are large, the calyx with drooping sepals, the corolla formed of four free sulfur-yellow petals; they have a pleasantly sweetish smell and bloom throughout the summer. The inferior ovary produces a long capsule attached to the cauline axis. Seeds are sown in light, permeable soil and the roots are harvested in spring of the second year.

The scraped yellow root is edible in small quantities, either raw or cooked, with an agreeable taste like that of a parsnip, and can be used for seasoning various dishes. It has to be harvested at the end of the first year, with the basal leaf rosette only, because in the second year the flowers use up the accumulated reserves. The leaves and the stem have astringent properties and, thanks to the presence of mucilage, are effective against coughs.

101 ORIGANUM MAJORANA L.

Majorana hortensis Moench

Labiatae

Marjoram, sweet marjoram, (G) Majoran, (F) marjolaine, (I) maggiorana

This species, originally from Africa, is much cultivated and grows wild in grassy areas; in olden times it was believed, because of its aroma, to guard against all types of illness and misfortune. The generic name, from the Greek, refers to a wild labiate; the specific name is from Latin *major*, greater, and in later Latin, *mezurana*. Marjoram is a perennial, but cultivated as an annual, with a downy stem and oval or lanceolate, opposite gray leaves. The flower stems, reddish near the top, terminate in graceful spikes of flowers with an almost regular white or pink corolla, producing 4 nutlets. Marjoram is sown in spring in a sunny position, in loose, humus-rich soil; hoeing is necessary and, in the event of drought, continual watering. The plant is cut off at the base, before flowering; because the plant will regrow a second harvesting can be made in the autumn, after which the plant should be dug up. After harvesting, it is dried in the shade or kept fresh for immediate use in the kitchen. Marjoram contains an essential oil rich in terpenes and tannins which is used to season sauces, vinegars, salads and cooked dishes. In perfumery it is employed for scenting soaps, lotions and creams, and in the drinks industry as an ingredient for herbal liquors. It has digestive, antispasmodic, carminative, diaphoretic and diuretic properties. The essence is used in limited doses because it is a narcotic and may have adverse effects in larger quantities.

102 ORIGANUM VULGARE L.

Labiatae

Oregano, origanum, wild marjoram, (G) Dost, (F) origan, (I) origano

Although the generic name is somewhat fancifully said to be derived from the Greek *óros* and *gános*, meaning "shining mountain" or "mountain splendor," it is more likely to have come from the ancient name for a wild labiate. This species grows in sunny, rocky places, on arid slopes and in dry, sparse woodland from the plains to the mountains. Widely found in eastern North America, Europe, and Asia, it is a perennial herb, up to 20 in (50 cm) in height, with a strong scent. The stems are hairy, densely branched and orange-red above. The short-stalked, opposite leaves are elliptical-lanceolate with dentate margins; the pink flowers, with a 2-lipped corolla, are arranged in pedunculate clusters at the terminal leaf axils and are covered by violet-red bracts. The plant is much frequented by bees for its nectar.

The plants are harvested in the wild or are cultivated, like sweet marjoram, from seed or division of clumps. Sowing, however, is done earlier, directly outside or in rows, since the seedlings are more resistant to cold; the soil should be light and well-drained, in a sunny spot. The plants can be left in for several years, especially in more temperate areas. The young shoots are collected when ready for use or the entire clumps cut off for drying in the shade.

The species usually cultivated is the pot marjoram (*O. onites* L.), a plant originally from the eastern Mediterranean region. The white flowers are in compact spikes lengthened by hairy bracts at the margins. The winter marjoram (*O. heracleoticum* L.) grows wild and is cultivated in the southern Mediterranean; it is similar to origanum but the bracts of the inflorescences are green, not reddish, shiny, and full of glands. Kept in dried bunches, it is used for its aroma, more powerful than that of other species.

The flowering herb of origanum is rich in essential oil which includes thymol, borneol, pinene, tannins and bitter principles, used for flavoring bread, pizzas, dressings, sauces, oils, and vinegars; in perfumery it is used in fresh-scented soaps. *O. onites* is also used as an ingredient for liquors. The essence serves as a disinfectant for skin and mouth infections and also has carminative, digestive, tonic, sudorific, and expectorant properties.

A common labiate found in dry zones, growing in hedges and by roadsides, is catmint (*Nepeta cataria* L.), originally from the eastern Mediterranean and now widely cultivated. The specific name comes from the late Latin *cathus*, because the scent is a feline aphrodisiac, while the generic name refers to an ancient Etruscan city. The plant has an erect, divided, hairy stem with opposite stalked leaves, whitish below, oval in shape with a dentate margin. With its aromatic scent and taste of mint, it is used in the kitchen for seasoning salads, soups, omelets, sauces and various main dishes, and as an officinal plant with sedative, spasmolytic, and emmenagogic properties; the dried leaves can be prepared as medicinal cigarets. All these plants, moreover, are used for infusions and aromatic tisanes, with an expectorant and diaphoretic action. Their essential oil is used in perfumery.

103 OXALIS ACETOSELLA L.

Oxalidaceae
Wood sorrel, (G) Sauerklee, (F) alléluja, (I) acetosella

This plant grows in damp woodlands, from plains to mountains, throughout the northern hemisphere. The name of the genus comes from the Greek óxos, vinegar, due to the characteristic flavor of the leaves, and the term is reinforced by the specific name. It is a perennial with a long, slender creeping rhizome which has fleshy swellings. The characteristic trifoliolate leaves have a reddish petiole and heart-shaped leaflets with an emarginate tip. Like all species of the genus, it is notable for its nastic movement which enables the leaflets to fold up so as to adhere to the stalk at night or in bad weather. The flowers, on a short peduncle, are solitary with five white or pinkish petals and violet veining. The fruit is an oval capsule. The leaves contain oxalates that give them their typically acidic, astringent taste. A handful of freshly ground leaves, added to salad, give it a stimulating flavor, and they can also be used for flavoring vegetable soups and sauces. The plant, noted for its stimulant properties since antiquity, must be used in moderation since an excess of oxalates may prove harmful.

The leaves of sorrel (*Rumex acetosa* L.) and sour dock (*R. acetosella*), two common field plants with a strong tap-root, can be used in a similar way. The former is cultivated in the var. *hortensis* Dierb. and contains fewer oxalates than spinach or beetroot. The flower shoots of both species can also be served in salads or, candied, as a substitute for rhubarb.

---

104 PANAX PSEUDOGINSENG Wall.

Panax ginseng L.
Araliaceae
Chinese ginseng, (G) Ginseng, (F) ginseng, (I) ginseng

The generic name, from the Greek *panakés*, means panacea, a cure for all ills; the Chinese specific name is *jen-shen* (plant-man), because the root looks like a human figure. Chinese ginseng grows in wet woodland mountain zones of eastern Asia, where it is used as a medicinal plant. American ginseng (*P. quinquefolius* L.) is found in the forests of northeastern America. The leaves are palmatosect, divided into five oval, pedunculate leaflets. The inflorescences are like those of ivy, in the form of spherical umbels, the flowers greenish and the berries red. From the late nineteenth century the plant has been cultivated and sold abroad (in China and Europe).

The roots, more than 20 in (50 cm) long, are harvested six years after seeds have been sown. Among the active principles contained in them are saponin, bitters, a few ethereal oils, phosphates, and tannins. Ginseng is reputed to have the effect of prolonging life and it certainly activates the neurophysical functions because of the presence of a glycoside (ginsenin) and group B vitamins; it also undoubtedly has tonic, sedative, stimulant, digestive, and aromatizing actions. It is used in powder form or as an infusion; it is used in elixirs, or tonic and bitter cordials.

Ginseng is especially highly prized in Asia and many people go in search of it rather like truffle hunting in Europe.

105 PAPAVER SOMNIFERUM L.

Papaveraceae
Opium poppy, (G) Mohn, (F) pavot somnifère, (I) papavero

The opium poppy is widely distributed and is cultivated to produce aromatic seeds and for ornament (ssp. *hortense* Huss.). The generic name is from the Celtic word *pap*, pulp or mash; in fact, the fruits can be ground into a pulp and mixed with baby food as a mild sleep-inducer.

An annual plant, more than 3 ft (1 m) tall, it is glaucous and waxy, with large, lobed and dentate, curly, amplexicaul leaves. The long-stalked, solitary terminal flowers are reclinate before opening; they have two deciduous sepals and four violet-white petals with a black spot on the claw, and the margins are entire or wrinkled, according to variety. The dark flower stamens are visited by bees for collection of pollen. The fruit is a round capsule of about 2–3 fused carpels which open by means of pores (the capsule is thus described as poricidal). Cultivated varieties produce capsules that do not open and that can be picked when ripe. It is grown in alpine areas of Europe, in Slav- and German-speaking countries, for its seeds, which are used as fillings for cakes and as garnishing for bread and rolls. The oil contained in the seeds is made up of glycerides of linolenic acid and is used for edible purposes but also in the manufacture of expensive oil paints. The seeds contain no alkaloids.

An ancient medicinal plant, the opium poppy is noted for its calming, soothing and sleep-inducing properties. It cannot be grown legally in the United States.

---

106 PASTINACA SATIVA L.

Umbelliferae
Parsnip, (G) Pastinak, (F) panais, (I) pastinaca

Linnaeus gave this umbellifer the name used by the Romans, emphasizing, in the specific name, the fact that it was once widely cultivated. It is found almost everywhere, on cultivated and waste land, in fields and woods, and by roadsides, and has also been grown since the Middle Ages in improved varieties (ssp. *sativa*). It is a biennial herb, up to 3 ft (1 m) tall, with a tap-root which is woody in wild forms. The stem bears leaves with a single row of leaflets, oval with a dentate margin; the cauline leaves are fewer and smaller towards the top. The yellow flowers are in fairly small, compound umbels. The fruits are flattened paired mericarps with a thin wing. The tap-root is used in the same way as that of the carrot; growing to a length of 16 in (40 cm) and weighing more than 3 lb (1.5 kg), it is whitish yellow and has a pleasantly sweet, aromatic flavor. Seeds are sown in deep, heavy, well-manured soil. The roots are harvested in autumn of the first year because the plants are worn out in the second year by the production of flowers. However, the flavor and texture of the roots are improved if the roots are not harvested until after the ground has frozen; in fact, the best parsnips are those that are left in the ground until spring of the second year.

The parsnip contains sugars, starches, vitamins, and essential oils; the agreeable smell is more noticeable after keeping for several weeks. The essence extracted from the fruits contains coumarinic derivatives and esters of organic acids, while those extracted from the flowers and roots respectively bear a resemblance to sweet sultan and vetiver.

107 PELARGONIUM SUAVEOLENS L'Hérit.
Geraniaceae
Geranium, (G) Geranie, (F) géranium, (I) geranio

As in the case of the genus *Geranium*, the etymology of *Pelargonium* refers to the shape of the fruit, similar to a swan's beak, *pelargós* in Greek; *suaveolens*, sweet-smelling, alludes to the aroma of the green parts. The essence-producing geraniums, which include the garden geranium cultivated as an ornamental plant, come from southern Africa, growing in rocky areas; they were introduced to England in 1710 and from there to the rest of Europe. All plants of the genus *Pelargonium* have a shrub-like habit, with opposite, palmate-lobate leaves, full of glands; the inflorescences are umbels, the flower calyx having a nectar-producing spur and the corolla petals of varying size, red, white, pink or streaked. The fruit is a schizocarp of five achenes linked by a long beak-shaped appendage.

Oil is extracted from the species *P. graveolens*, *P. odoratissimum*, *P. fragrans*, *P. capitatum*, *P. roseum*, and *P. radens*. In warm climates they are all perennials, elsewhere they need shelter. Propagation is from seed or cuttings, the latter technique being more common in temperate zones. In spring the green parts are harvested, before flowering, and then, during dry, warm weather in summer and autumn, steam distillation produces a delicately scented essential oil comprising geraniol and citronellol, as well as menthol, linalol, and other components. It is used in the cosmetics industry in place of rose essence

---

108 PETROSELINUM CRISPUM (Mill.) A. W. Hill
Petroselinum hortense auct.
Umbelliferae
Parsley, (G) Blattpetersilie, (F) persil, (I) prezzemolo

This plant probably originated in the eastern Mediterranean region and later spread virtually everywhere in its cultivated form. One of the commonest herbs, it is sometimes found growing wild on waste ground. The name of the genus comes from the Greek *petrosélinon*, but it is not certain which, of so many, was the actual umbellifer concerned. It is a biennial herb, up to 28 in (70 cm) tall, with a tap-root. The glossy, striate, erect stem bears compound leaves, usually with three rows of leaflets. The bright yellow, pentamerous flowers are in small umbels; the mericarps are oval and slightly ridged. The curly-leaved variety (var. *crispum*) is the one most commonly cultivated; there is also the turnip-rooted parsley (var. *radicosum*), used like celery. Plants are sown outside in well-manured soil; to hasten germination, which takes four weeks, the seeds can be soaked for 24 hours before use. The leaves can be served fresh or as a seasoning for meats, preserves, sauces, and dressings; they should be added after cooking so that the aroma is not lost; this property disappears when the parsley is dried.

The green parts contain an ethereal oil, composed of apiol, pinene, and myristicin. Since apiol is toxic, it is safe to eat only small quantities of parsley as a vegetable; because of this it was regarded with suspicion in antiquity and believed to possess magical properties. The essence from the seeds is used in the manufacture of certain strong, masculine scents.

109 PIMENTA DIOICA (L.) Merr.
Pimenta officinalis Lindl.
Myrtaceae
Allspice, pimento, (G) Nelkenpfeffer, (F) toutépice, (I) pepe di Giamaica, pimento

The name comes from the Spanish, meaning pepper. This is a small evergreen tree, growing to a height of about 30 ft (9 m), with opposite, oval, leathery leaves, found wild and cultivated in Central America, particularly Mexico and the West Indies. The principal producers are Jamaica, Mexico, India, and Réunion. The tree bears corymbs of white flowers; the inferior ovary produces a dark reddish brown berry. It is very easy to grow and only requires regular weeding; multiplication is by seed. Every plant remains productive for some 100 years.

The berries are picked and dried before they are fully ripe so that the pulp becomes as soft as membrane; in this form they resemble grains of pepper. In the pulp, but even more in the seeds, there are active principles constituted of ethereal oils, mainly eugenol. The scent is similar to that of nutmeg, cloves, and cinnamon, and the taste is pungent, like pepper.

It is possible to extract an oil with digestive and slightly narcotic properties. The leaves, dried or fresh, are used for preparing aromatic infusions; the spice is used in sausages and fish preserves, and also as an ingredient for curry. The Aztecs used to flavor chocolate with pimento seeds.

---

110 PIMPINELLA ANISUM L.
Anisum vulgare Gaertn.
Umbelliferae
Anise, (G) Anis, (F) anis, (I) anice

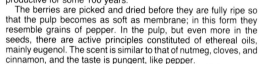

This plant, originally from the eastern Mediterranean, has been cultivated since antiquity for its aromatic qualities. It grows on fallow ground and near kitchen gardens. Mentioned by Pliny and Theophrastus as *ánison*, hence the specific name; the name of the genus comes from the transformation, as time passed, from *piperina* (grass) to *piperinella* and *pipinella*. An annual, with a hairy, striate stem, up to 20 in (50 cm) tall, it has divided basal leaves, with oval, toothed leaflets, while the stem leaves have lanceolate leaflets. The white pentamerous flowers are arranged in small compound umbels; the fruits are hairy, oval, pear-shaped mericarps and are strongly scented. Anise can be sown in open ground in rows 20 in (50 cm) apart. The fruits or seeds (aniseed) are harvested just before they are quite ripe, from late July to August; they contain an essential oil, composed mainly of anethole, isoanethole, and anisic aldehyde, and the aroma appears only after seasoning. Aniseed is used for flavoring bread, cakes, fruit salads, sauces, and for marinating meat and fish. It is also used as the basis for liqueurs such as Anise and Pernod.

Among wild umbellifers, masterwort (*Peucedanum ostruthium* (L.) Koch) is a tall herb, found in mountainous grassy zones, with aromatic rhizomes: these are harvested in autumn or spring to be used in herbal liquors, with digestive properties.

111 PINUS MUGO Turra

Pinus montana Mill.
Pinaceae
Mugo pine, (G) Latsche, (F) pin mugo, (I) mugo

The mugo pine has a very distinctive appearance, with branches up to 16 ft (5 m) in length, at first growing prostrate on the ground, then erect, with gray-black bark. The stiff and pointed needle-like leaves, in pairs, are dark green, about 2½ in (4–5 cm) long. Like all pines, the tree bears separate inflorescences; the male flowers are yellow, in terminal catkins, the female flowers are reddish violet, in axillary pairs. The cones are round, about 1½ in (3 cm) across, and the blackish, short-winged seeds take several years to ripen. The *Pinus mugo* group also includes the mountain pine (*P. uncinata* Mill.) which grows to a height of up to 65 ft (20 m) and is found on calcareous-dolomitic terrain from the Pyrenees to the central Alps; and *P. mugo* ssp. *pumilio* Franco grows in the marginal zones. These trees, apart from their habit, differ in the form of their cones and particularly the pattern of the scales.

The mugo pine is found in mountain zones throughout Europe from 2,250 ft (700 m), rarely less, to 9,000 ft (2,700 m), forming alpine woods and thickets. The species is well able to withstand heavy snowfalls because of its flexible branches. Of the various pines, it is most commonly used for extraction of pine oil. The young branches, lopped during the summer in high mountain zones, are brought to collection centers where distillation by steam produces this essential oil, which has medicinal properties. It has a balsamic action, containing pinene, limonene, fellandrene, and other principles, and is used for respiratory disorders and as an antiseptic for skin complaints. It is utilized in the perfumery trade, too, for toilet waters, deodorants, and bath foams and salts.

Similar extracts are obtained from the Scots pine (*P. sylvestris* L.), a tree that grows naturally from the Alps across northern regions of Eurasia. The freshly cut branches are taken to the distillery when woodland is thinned out. In both cases, however, production is on the decline as balsamic products are now obtained from other essences.

Certain pines produce edible seeds with an aromatic flavor, much used in the kitchen and in baking; they include the stone pine (*P. pinea* L.) and the arolla pine (*P. cembra* L.). The former is commonly found on sandy Mediterranean shores, and cultivated as an ornamental subject in parks and gardens; it produces a large, glossy, oval cone 6 in (15 cm) in length, with pairs of seeds, covered by a woody tegument, between the scales. The arolla pine is found in the central and western Alps and is able to withstand much harsher climatic conditions; unlike other European pines, its needle-like leaves are borne in bundles of five, and the violet cone is not completely woody, while the tiny seeds are particularly aromatic, with a balsamic, resinous taste.

Resin is in fact an important product of many pines, collected from cuts made in the trunks. Conifer resin, also known as turpentine, serves as a natural defense for the tree against traumas and parasites. It consists of more or less fluid materials, insoluble in water but soluble in alcohol; the components are terpenic derivatives, tannins, sterols, and aromatic acids. Turpentine has antiseptic, balsamic and revulsive properties; it is obtained by steam distillation and the residue is known as colophony or rosin, a light resin used for the production of varnishes and glues. The principal sources of turpentine in the United States are the longleaf pine (*P. palustris* Mill.) and slash pine (*P. Caribaea* Morelet), both of which grow along the Gulf Coast northwest to South Carolina.

112 PIPER NIGRUM L.

Piperaceae

Black pepper, (G) Pfeffer, (F) poivre, (I) pepe

Pepper originated in the Indian equatorial and tropical forest regions, especially along the Malabar Coast. Today it is cultivated in India, Indonesia, Malaysia, and Brazil. The genus *Piper* comprises a very large number of species, of which only *P. nigrum* has any importance as a spice, and has become enormously popular in Europe. The plant is a climber, with stems bearing green oval to heart-shaped leaves, 3–7 in (8–18 cm) long, and adventitious roots anchoring it to the ground. The inconspicuous flowers, with no perianth and formed of two stamens and a pistil, are arranged in drooping spikes. The fruit, or peppercorn, is a berry-like drupe about 3/16 in (1/2 cm) in diameter, green when unripe, then red. The seed consists of a small embryo enclosed in a horny perisperm, which contains 5–9 percent piperine.

Cultivated plants are propagated from seed or cuttings; the developing seedlings need to be staked and are kept low so that growth is horizontal; in the wild the plant will grow to some 20 ft (6 m). Production commences five years after planting and the spikes are harvested before they mature so as not to lose the fruits.

The spice that is obtained from the fruits is made up of black, white, and green pepper. Black pepper comes from whole fruits picked just before they are completely ripe, white pepper from ripe fruits with the endocarp of the pulp separated for fermentation, and green pepper by pickling the unripe fruits, to keep them from turning dark. The fruits contain the pungent alkaloid piperine, oils, and resins. White pepper contains a higher percentage of piperine but fewer aromatic principles, particularly important in black pepper.

Ground pepper quickly loses its aroma, so that it has to be stored whole; its taste is unique and unmistakable. The spice also has stimulant, digestive, and eupeptic properties.

Cultivated and used only in their various countries of origin are *P. longum* L. (India), *P. retroflexum* Vahl (Indonesia) and *P. cubeba* L.f. (Malaysia), with a burning, bitter taste. *P. betle* L. (Indonesia, Malacca, Iran, and Arabia) is a stimulant and the fresh leaves are chewed together with the seeds of the betel palm (*Areca catechu* L.) and the juice of the gambier (*Uncaria gambir* (Hunter) Roxb.).

Red pepper is obtained from *Schinus molle* L., family Anacardiaceae, and is also known as false pepper and Peruvian pepper. Growing widely from Central America to Brazil, it is an evergreen tree with imparipinnate leaves, also cultivated as an ornamental in the temperate dry lands of the Mediterranean. It produces red drupes that contain a seed with pungent principles. In Peru they are used, after fermentation, for making vinegar and alcoholic drinks.

Japanese pepper or anise pepper (*Xanthoxylum piperitum* DC.) belongs to the Rutaceae. It is a dioecious shrub from northern China, Korea, and Japan, with pinnatisect leaves, stipular thorns, and red fruits with a shiny black seed. The seed is used as a spice in Chinese and Japanese cuisine.

113 PISTACIA VERA L.

Anacardiaceae
Pistachio, (G) echte Pistazie, (F) pistache, (I) pistacchio

The name is derived from the Persian *pistah*, then the Greek *pistáke* and the Latin *pistacia*. The plant originated in the Middle East and is today cultivated in various parts of the Mediterranean region and in the southern United States. It is a hardy species that can withstand drought and cold winters but not spring frosts.

Apart from the pistachio, other species of the genus *Pistacia* are *P. terebinthus* L. and *P. lentiscus* L., the latter is an evergreen that is used as stock for grafting. The pistachio is a tree which in natural conditions may grow to some 33 ft (10 m). The leaves are pinnate and deciduous, leathery, with pointed leaflets. The plants are dioecious, so that when cultivated it is necessary to keep one male plant to every 5–6 female plants so as to fertilize them by wind pollination and to form fruits. The inflorescences are inconspicuous flowers that lack petals; the fruit is an oval drupe with a thin mesocarp.

The fruits are harvested when fully ripe, many of them having opened to reveal the nut inside. After being picked, the fleshy part of the drupe is separated and placed in receptacles with moving water in order to detach the mesocarp. The nuts are dried with their shell and the kernels then removed. The seed has cotyledonal leaves with chlorophyll, which gives the green color to the products used for confectionery, and also a characteristic flavor like that of the almond.

---

114 POGOSTEMON CABLIN (Blanco) Benth.

Pogostemon patchouli Pellet
Labiatae
Patchouli, (G) Patchouly, (F) patchouli, (I) patchouli

The name of the genus alludes to the characteristic anatomy of the stamens which possess hairy filaments (from the Greek *pógon*, beard, and *stémon*, thread); the common name comes from Tamil *patch*, green, and *ilai*, leaf. Cultivated mainly in Indonesia and Malaysia, the major producer today is Sumatra (90 percent); others used to be Malacca and Singapore.

This herbaceous plant has elliptical leaves with a dentate margin and a very hairy lower surface. The inflorescences are verticels of flowers in terminal or axillary spikes. After harvesting, the leaves are dried, baled, and the essences distilled by steam. Patchouli essence is constituted of benzoic aldehyde, eugenol, cinnamic aldehyde, and so-called patchouli alcohol. It is used for producing oriental-type perfumes and combines well with other essences. It is also used in soap manufacture.

Among other aromatic species of Labiatae is Oswego tea or bee balm (*Monarda didyma* L.), a perennial originally from North America, now cultivated more or less everywhere. It is a herb with oval leaves and terminal capitula of 2-lipped scarlet flowers. Both the leaves and flowers are used, the fresh leaves for seasoning salads and the dried leaves for preparing an infusion similar to tea, with a typically refreshing taste. Also from North America is the mint anise or anise hyssop (*Agastache anethiodora* (Nutt.) Britton), with terminal spikes of blue flowers, used like the preceding species, and also for flavoring cordials.

115 POLYANTHES TUBEROSA L.

Amaryllidaceae
Tuberose, (G) Tuberose, (F) tubéreuse, (I) tuberosa

The tuberose comes originally from Mexico, where it grows wild. The plant is cultivated in France (Grasse) and the Mediterranean basin, in Morocco and also in Taiwan, Sri Lanka, and Java. In the French Maritime Alps (Cannes, Pégomas) double-flowered species for ornament and single-flowered species for essence are both grown. In southern Italy, where temperatures are mild until December, it is raised for its bulbs.

The tunicate, fleshy, conical, elongated bulbs are attached to a short rhizome. The central bulb is bigger than the others, which closely encircle it. The sessile leaves are linear, light green, and glabrous; the simple flower stem, 2–5½ ft (60–170 cm) high, has an apical spike of white flowers, flushed pink outside; the plant flowers from August to December. The large bulbs are cultivated for display and flower only once; essence is extracted from the earlier flowering single varieties. The plants need plenty of feeding and extract as much as possible from the soil; harvesting is carried out during flowering, in the latter half of August, and the buds are removed from the main stem early in the morning.

The crop is treated in France by enfleurage but otherwise with volatile solvents. The scent of tuberose essence is sweet but so powerful that it can become cloying. It is used for preparing delicate but penetrating perfumes of the oriental type.

---

116 PORTULACA OLERACEA L.

Portulacaceae
Purslane, (G) Portulak, (F) purslane, (I) porcellana

Purslane is a weed found on arable land, especially wet and heavy ground, on roadsides and embankments, under walls, and on wasteland. The generic name comes from the Latin *portula*, little door, referring to the manner in which the capsule opens; the specific name alludes to its use as a kitchen vegetable.

It is a prostrate annual plant with succulent reddish stems and opposite, spathulate, fleshy leaves 1 in (2 cm) in length. The flowers are arranged in pairs or in axillary fascicles; they are inconspicuous with two sepals and small yellow petals. The fruit is a round capsule ¼ in (6 mm) in diameter, with a lid that opens when ripe to reveal small black seeds. The subspecies *sativa* can be cultivated as an aromatic vegetable, sowing the seeds (in May) on loose, sandy soil. It looks slightly different from the wild subspecies *oleracea*, in that the stems are climbing and erect. They contain mucilage, vitamins, and organic compounds. The young leaves can be pickled or eaten in mixed salads; their taste is refreshingly salty.

The ice plant (*Mesembryanthemum crystallinum* L.), belonging to the Aizoaceae and originally from South Africa, grows in southern California and along the Mediterranean coasts, on rocks and walls, and is similarly used as a kitchen herb. It is a succulent creeping annual with fleshy oval-lanceolate leaves, covered with small crystalline papillae.

117 PRUNUS DULCIS D. A. Webb
Amygdalus communis L.
Rosaceae
Almond, (G) Mandelbaum, (F) amandier, (I) mandorlo

The almond originated in the Near East and then spread through the entire Mediterranean region, being cultivated together with the olive. It is now grown on a large scale by Californian farmers. It is an undemanding species, adapting to poor ground but not able to withstand frost and strong winds. The tree has dark gray bark and sometimes a few spines in the wild. The short-stalked deciduous leaves are lanceolate with a toothed margin; the fairly small flowers are in pairs, almost sessile, with five pink petals, and they appear early before the leaves. The fruits are green drupes of 2 in (5 cm), with a velvety hull. The useful part is the seed, enclosed in the woody endocarp; during harvesting the outer parts are discarded, leaving only the nuts. The kernel is rich in fats (over 50 percent), proteins, carbohydrates, vitamins, and salts. Sweet almonds are used for making almond paste for confectionery; and the milk of almonds (the syrup of crushed almonds, with water and sugar) is a thirst-quenching drink; it is used, too, for other aromatic liquors. The fatty oil extracted from almonds is used for expensive soaps. Bitter almonds contain the glucoside amygdalin which, through the action of the enzyme emulsin, splits into glucose, benzoic aldehyde and hydrocyanic acid, making them poisonous. They are used, like sweet almonds, for the extraction of oil for cosmetic purposes, as well as in the confectionery trade to flavor syrups and pastries. Almost all seeds of the genus *Prunus* contain amygdalin and must therefore be eaten with caution.

118 RHEUM spp.
Polygonaceae
Rhubarb, (G) Rhabarber, (F) rhubarbe, (I) rabarbaro

The genus takes its name from the Greek word *rhéon* or *rha*, meaning a root, this being repeated in the specific name, which indicates it as being a "foreign root." The genus comprises several species which have been cultivated in China since ancient times particularly for the laxative properties of the root (in particular that of *R. palmatum* L.). In Britain and the U.S. the leafstalks are used as stewed fruits. The plant *R. rhabarbarum* L. is originally from Siberia and possesses a main root that forms lateral rhizomatous rootlets that bury the shoot further in the ground as they contract. The yellowish rhizome has a penetrating smell, but less strong than Chinese rhubarb (*R. officinale* L.). The very big, long-stalked, heart-shaped leaves develop in spring and contain a large quantity of oxalic acid. In early June a large inflorescence appears – in *R. officinale* it is up to 6½ ft (2 m) and in *R. rhabarbarum* and *R. rhaponticum* 3 ft (1 m) – in the form of a compact panicle, with numerous creamy flowers. It is easily cultivated in mid-mountain areas; the inflorescence is discarded so as not to wear out the root. The rhizome is decorticated and cut into pieces; it is orange, with a pleasant odor and a bitter, astringent taste. The properties depend on the concentration of the drug; if small, it is tonic, if high, purgative. Tinctures from it are used in the drinks industry. Chinese rhubarb is originally from Tibet and is cultivated only in China, where it is highly esteemed. The rhizome has a rough surface, covered with yellow dust; its odor is strong and astringent.

119 ROSA x DAMASCENA Mill.
Rosaceae
Rose, (G) Rose, (F) rose, (I) rosa da essenza

From time immemorial rose essence has been used in the preparation of cosmetic products; although imported in ancient times into Europe from eastern Asia, it was only after the Crusades that the rose began to be cultivated for this purpose. Nowadays it is grown in Asia Minor, Morocco, and Bulgaria, where the low cost of labor keeps production expenses down. The morphology of the plant is similar to that of other species belonging to this vast genus, which contains innumerable hybrids. A woody shrub, its shoots bear thorny, alternate, unpaired pinnatisect leaves, and flowers in terminal corymbs with a swollen receptacle that produces the fleshy false fruit or hip, which contains the true fruits or achenes.

Cultivated roses for extraction of essence are the hybrids *R. damascena* (damask rose), *R. centifolia* (cabbage rose), and *R. gallica* (Provence rose). They are all propagated from cuttings, by layering, grafting, and clump division. No particular attention is needed apart from spraying against diseases.

The essential oil is extracted from the flowers by distillation with water or in steam, or by the enfleurage method. The yield is around 1/30 oz (1 g) of pure oil from 2 lb (1 kg) of petals. It is used, in addition to perfumery, in the food (marzipan) and drinks industries. The petals can be utilized for making pancakes and jams, the hips likewise for jams, aperitifs, and cordials, and the essence, after being dried, for pleasantly astringent infusions.

120 ROSMARINUS OFFICINALIS L.
Labiatae
Rosemary, (G) Rosmarin, (F) romarin, (I) rosmarino

Rosemary is a plant from the Mediterranean region, part of the characteristic scrubland; its generic name derives from the Latin *ros marinus*, meaning sea dew, referring to its natural habitat. It is a woody evergreen shrub of ascending prostrate habit, rather untidy, with cracked gray bark. The persistent, straight, leathery leaves are green above and white below, opposite or in fascicles. The blue 2-lipped flowers are borne in spikes at the leaf axils.

Commonly cultivated since antiquity for its medicinal and aromatic properties, the plant needs an open, sunny position. It has therefore spread well outside its original range as it multiplies easily from cuttings and by layering during the summer. It requires well-manured clay or sandy soil. It can also be raised easily on a terrace or balcony. Among the active principles are eucalyptol, pinene, borneol, camphor, and cineol; the taste is rather pronounced, so it should be used only in small quantities.

Among kitchen herbs, this is the most frequently used for roasts and fat meats, for producing salt, aromatized oil and vinegar, and for flavoring bread, buns, and cakes. It is employed with other spices for seasoning canned foods and sausages. In perfumery the distillate is used in the manufacture of soaps, scents, eau de Cologne, and deodorant sprays. Dry twigs serve to repel insects and are useful in cupboards. It has digestive, stimulant, choleraic, and carminative properties.

121 RUBUS IDAEUS L.
Rosaceae
Raspberry, (G) Himbeere, (F) framboisier, (I) lampone

The raspberry is a species of the northern hemisphere, growing in hills and mountains, woods, scrub, and heathland. In temperate regions hybrids and varieties are cultivated for fruit. The specific name refers to Mount Ida, on the island of Crete. A perennial plant, it produces glaucous-green herbaceous shoots up to a height of 6½ ft (2 m) in the first year, which become woody and turn brown, fruiting in the second year. The stems, initially upright, bend under the weight of fruit, and bear soft reddish prickles. The leaves are compound, tri- or pentapinnate, with oval leaflets that are whitish underneath, with a dentate or lobate margin, a petiole and slender stipules. The white flowers, in terminal clusters, have five petals and a calyx with widespread lobes. They produce compound hairy red fruits that separate from the receptacle when ripe.

Raspberries are cultivated mainly for the fruits, which are eaten fresh and often used for making jams, jellies, and syrups. An extract, with the characteristic raspberry scent, can be produced to give an aroma used as a flavor corrective in the food and pharmaceutical industries. The essential oil contains principally aldehydes, ketones, and alcohols, all of which go to make up the so-called fruity aromas.

The blackberry (*R. fruticosus* L.) produces black fruits, which in addition to being eaten raw and in jams, are used for coloring food; so too is the blackcurrant (*Ribes nigrum* L.).

122 RUTA GRAVEOLENS L.
Rutaceae
Rue, (G) Raute, (F) rue, (I) ruta

This herb from the Mediterranean area grows in fields, on calcareous rocks, and on old walls. The name of the plant comes from the Latin and also alludes to the heavy odor it emits. The species takes the form of a small shrub, woody at the base, standing up to 3 ft (1 m) tall, with erect, glaucous branches and a penetrating, somewhat sickly smell. The pinnatisect leaves have spatulate leaflets with shiny glands; the flowers have yellow concave petals, curly at the edge, in groups of four in the loose terminal racemes, in fives lower down. The fruit is a rough, angular capsule.

Rue is an ancient medicinal plant that can be cultivated without difficulty in seed beds, in loose soil, and later transplanted into pots or outdoors; it can also be multiplied by clump division. The whole plant is used when it comes into flower. Rue contains essential oils, resins, tannins, and the glycoside rutin. It is employed in minimal doses in the liquor industry for its bitter taste; in the kitchen, in moderate quantities, for flavoring bread, meat, eggs, and sauces. In Italy grappa alla ruta is produced by inserting the whole plant in the bottle and allowing it to infuse the liquor, the essence is used in vermouth and bitters.

Rue has emmenagogic, carminative, digestive, and anthelminthic properties; it is dangerous to use it during pregnancy and it is toxic in large quantities. The essential oil is utilized in the cosmetics trade for soaps, creams, and scents.

123 SALVIA OFFICINALIS L.

Labiatae
Sage, (D) Salbel, (F) sauge, (I) salvia

Known since antiquity, sage is renowned for its medicinal properties, hence the generic name, from the Latin *salvus* meaning healthy. The plant grows wild in the Mediterranean region, especially in coastal scrubland, together with cistus, rosemary, and asphodel. It is commonly cultivated in herb gardens throughout the Old and New Worlds, and is indeed the most frequently grown medicinal plant. Sage is a perennial shruub, hemispherical in shape, with woody branches divided from the base and herbaceous shoots of the year which are quadrangular in cross-section. The pedunculate leaves are oval-lanceolate, rough in texture and light grayish green, with a dense covering of down that makes them look silvery. The flowers, in whorls on terminal spikes, have a bell-shaped violet-brown calyx and 2-lipped violet-pink corollas. The fruits are composed of 4 single-seeded nutlets. The leaves, long utilized for infusions and for flavoring, contain an ethereal oil, the principal component of which is thujone (30–50 percent), with pinene, borneol, camphor, and cineol.

Although the species comes originally from the Mediterranean area, it does well in cold regions as long as there are not too many successive frosty days; and as a general rule it needs to be sheltered from the wind. It is easily cultivated in well-drained soil. The plants can be propagated from cuttings, rooted in sandy ground, fertilized and transplanted in the autumn; where conditions are favorable, clump division and direct sowing are also commonly practiced. Harvesting can commence the third year after planting, mechanically over large areas. The tops are cut 4 in (10 cm) from the ground, either just before flowering for herbal use or while in flower for extraction of the essence. The properties of sage are antiseptic, tonic, digestive, and stimulant.

Sage has varied uses as an accompaniment to food; in the kitchen as a spice and seasoning, in moderate amounts, for cooked dishes, condiments and sauces, in drinks (aperitifs and bitters), and especially in the form of oil. It is employed in cosmetics for toiletry products and together with other essences (rose, rosemary) for scenting lotions. In addition to *S. officinalis*, similar use is made of *S. triloba* L., which grows in Greece and Turkey, and *S. lavandulaefolia* Vahl, from Spain.

Clary (*S. sclarea* L.) differs from common sage both in appearance and use. The specific name may be a deformation of the late Latin *ascia reja*, from the Latin *hastula regia*, referring to the inflorescences used to adorn the images of the divinity; or it may be associated with clearing the vision. It has an aroma similar to the muscat grape. This too is a shrub of spreading habit. The quadrangular stems bear very big leaves, about 8 in (20 cm) long, with a cordate base; their surface is rough, with sparse down but not silvery. The spikes are formed of whorls of flowers with lilac-pink corollas and characteristic oval bracts, hairy at the base. Originally from the Mediterranean, it is now widely cultivated; the flower tops emit a scent quite different from that of sage, for the essential oil contains acetate of linalyl. It is used mainly for scenting vermouth and for cosmetics and perfumes along with lavender and bergamot.

124 SAMBUCUS NIGRA L.

Caprifoliaceae

Elder, (G) Schwarzer holunder, (F) sureau noir, (I) sambuco

The origin of the generic name is not clear; it may either have Aegean or Etruscan roots or it may refer to an ancient wind instrument, the sambuca. It is a small hemispherical tree, found in built-up areas and on wet, fertile ground. The leaves are opposite, imparipinnatisect; bearing 4–7 leaflets with a toothed margin. The inflorescences are umbel-like corymbs about 8 in (20 cm) across, and when in bloom the tree is covered with small creamy white flowers, the five-lobed flat corolla being easily detached; depending on altitude, these appear from May to July. The wine-red fruiting branches bear round black berries, over ³⁄₁₆ in (5 mm) in diameter. As the flowers appear, the leaves, which repel many harmful insects, can be harvested and used either fresh or dried. The flowers have a pleasant scent and go well with fruit salads, jellies, and aromatized vinegars; they also possess a large amount of strongly scented nectar that can be used for making refreshing drinks. Bark, leaves, and fresh fruit are strongly laxative and should not be taken internally but the stewed fruit is popular, especially in northern England. The sap of the leaves, cooked for a quarter of an hour in a little water, has a soothing effect on skin complaints, burns, and sprains. The tea made from the flowers has a calming effect and relieves headaches.

125 SANGUISORBA MINOR Scop.

Poterium sanguisorba P.

Rosaceae

Salad burnet, (G) Bibernelle, (F) sanguisorbe, (I) pimpinella

The bright red inflorescences of the salad burnet were, according to the medieval Swiss physician Paracelsus, reputed to staunch bleeding, and this supposed haemostatic property is reflected in the generic name. The species grows in temperate zones of the Old World, on wasteland, embankments, dry fields, and loose soil at most altitudes. It is a perennial herb with a strong tap-root and pinnatisect leaves in basal rosettes, with elliptical, dentate leaflets; the stem leaves are similar but progressively smaller. The flowers, without a corolla and with a four-sepal calyx, display showy, feathery red-violet stigmas; they are arranged in rounded terminal capitula. The plant commonly grows wild but can be cultivated as a herb, sown in rows outside and if necessary thinned out; later the plants multiply autonomously from seed. The basal rosettes are harvested when they are young and tender, to be eaten in mixed salads, giving them a characteristically fresh, bitter flavor. The chopped leaves are used for seasoning cheeses, soups, and sauces. It has astringent, carminative, and scar-forming properties. At one time the root was used as a tanning agent and black dye.

The great burnet (*Sanguisorba officinalis* L.) has a long, cylindrical, purple inflorescence; it grows in wet places.

126 SANTALUM ALBUM L.

Santalaceae
Sandalwood, (G) Sandelholz, (F) bois de santal, (I) sandalo

The sandalwood is a large tree that grows in India and Malaysia. Like many other species of the family Santalaceae, it lives in conditions of hemiparasitism; in fact, even though it is photosynthetic, it relies on other plants, via sucker roots, for its food requirements. For this reason it can be cultivated only in a semi-wild state, so that the tree can develop alongside its natural host. It has evergreen, opposite, lanceolate leaves, and panicles of reddish yellow flowers. After some 50 years the trees are felled for their heartwood and roots. These parts are then cut up and consigned for distillation; all the other parts are discarded. Every 220 lb (100 kg) of this material yields about 12 lb (5.5 kg) of essence, consisting mainly of santalol and santalene. The predominant product is Indian oil, which is used in religious ceremonies as a body unguent. In some cases the wood is exported for distilling in Europe.

Extracts similar to sandalwood oil are obtained from an African plant of the same family, *Osyris tenuifolia* L.; in Australia *Santalum spicatum* is used, and in the West Indies a species of the Rutaceae, *Amyris balsamifera* L. Sandalwood, once employed in pharmacy, is much used in the perfumery trade for making soaps and flowery compositions because of its fixative power and lasting fragrance. The wood is carved into boxes and small items of furniture which retain the pleasant sandalwood scent for a long time.

---

127 SASSAFRAS ALBIDUM (Nutt.) Nees

Sassafras officinale Nees
Lauraceae
Sassafras, (G) Fleberbaum, Sassafras, (F) laurier sassafras, (I) sassafrasso

The generic name is probably derived, via the Spanish, from the original South American name. It is a hardy deciduous species, up to 65 ft (20 m) tall, with a straight trunk, rough bark, and a conical crown. The leaves differ in shape and size, either entire, ovate or bilobate, or trilobate, darker on the upper side. The species is dioecious, and from April to June bears inconspicuous flowers with a yellowish calyx and no corolla; the male flowers display nine stamens. The fruits, derived from the female flowers, are bluish drupes with a red peduncle, covered by a persistent calyx. The leaves (when rubbed), branches, and bark give out a spicy, fragrant odor of orange and vanilla.

The sassafras is native to the eastern United States and is used for producing an essential oil extracted from the roots, harvested in summer and autumn; the active principles are found chiefly in the bark of the roots, less in the wood. Synthetic essence of sassafras is obtained from brown oil of camphor.

The chemical industry makes use of sassafras oil, which contains safrol, iso-safrol, and heliotropin; it is utilized too in the cosmetics trade for scenting soaps and deodorants. In America sassafras also serves to flavor confectionery and soft drinks. The bark extract contains an orange dye for wool.

128 SATUREJA HORTENSIS L.
Labiatae
Savory, (G) Bohnenkraut, (F) sariette, (I) santoreggia, erba cerea

A herb of Asiatic origin, it grows in the Mediterranean area, on dry and stony ground, old walls, and uncultivated land. The etymology of the name is uncertain but is probably that used by the Romans to describe labiates.

The plant is an annual that has a violet or gray-green overall appearance and is strongly scented. It has an erect, branched stem up to 16 in (40 cm) high, with opposite, narrowly lanceolate, entire leaves. The flowers, in loose spikes, are lilac, with a calyx and campanulate 2-lipped corolla. The fruit is composed of 4 nutlets. Savory is commonly grown from seed in herb gardens on light, well-drained soil. Feeding should be kept to the minimum, since too much results in the loss of aroma. Rooted plants will seed themselves spontaneously in autumn and can, in due course, be cultivated, to be harvested when flowers appear.

Savory contains an essential oil with carvacrol, pinene, and tannins. The herb is widely used in the kitchen for its slightly sharp, stimulating taste, but always in limited amounts, for otherwise it drowns all the other flavors; it is used in omelets, cooked vegetables and soups, and to season meat and fish. It is also included in the preparation of herbal liquors and vermouth. Savory has carminative, digestive, astringent, antiseptic, and vermifugal properties.

---

129 SATUREJA MONTANA L.
Labiatae
Winter savory, (G) Winterbohnenkraut, (F) sarriette des montagnes, (I) santoreggia d'inverno

Unlike the preceding species, this is a perennial, in the form of a small, slightly downy shrub. It grows on calcareous soil, and on stony, rocky ground in the western Mediterranean regions. The leaves are lanceolate, opposite, and glabrous, though with a ciliate margin. The pinkish white flowers, with a 2-lipped corolla, are in terminal spikes, dense at the tips of the branches. Winter savory can be sown in a seed bed and transplanted to a sunny corner; and propagation can also be by division of the plants when not in flower. The seedlings must be thinned out to eliminate weeds. It can stand up quite well to winter frosts provided they are not too prolonged. Some feeding is advisable after the main cutting back. The young shoots with leaves and the flower tops are harvested; this can be done in the second year on two or three occasions, the last in late summer so that there is time for the plant to recover before winter. Uses are similar to those for common savory, to flavor meat, fish, risottos, soups, omelets, and sauces. The essence, mixed with others, is used for herbal and digestive liquors. It has spasmolytic, aperient, and eupeptic properties.

White horehound (*Marrubium vulgare* L.) is another perennial labiate, highly aromatic, with stems that bear dense axillary fascicles of white flowers; its bitter and stimulating taste dictates its use in the kitchen.

130 SEDUM REFLEXUM L.

Crassulaceae

Rock stonecrop, yellow stonecrop, (G) Tripmadam, (F) orpin, (I) erba pignola

The numerous wild species of *Sedum* that form part of the European flora are all succulents, usually with cylindrical leaves, sausage-shaped or spatulate. They grow on poor soil, old walls, shingle, and dry, rocky ground. The etymology of the name is uncertain; it may come from the Latin *sedere*, because of the plants' ground-hugging habit, or from *sedare*, in the sense of calming or soothing. Rock stonecrop is cultivated mainly in Holland, to be eaten in salads and soups. A perennial plant, woody at the base, it needs only a very small area in which to grow; the stems and leaves are succulent, the stellate yellow flowers form a corymb, the fruits are dry and dehiscent. The green parts contain mucilage, organic acids, and tannins, giving them a bitter taste and astringent action, which are diminished slightly with cooking; the juicy green parts can be chopped or crushed, for seasoning. The herb is cultivated in warm sandy soil; it is multiplied from seed or by division.

Wall-pepper (*Sedum acre* L.) has slender stems which break off at the top after flowering; the fleshy leaves are spiraled, with a peppery taste, due to the presence of alkaloids, tannins, and glucosides; it is used sparingly for seasoning and flavoring, since in large doses it is emetic. Orpine (*S. telephium* L.) has spatulate oval leaves about 1½ in (3–4 cm) long, slightly toothed, and corymbs of purplish flowers, up to 12 in (30 cm) tall; the plant has similar uses.

131 SESAMUM INDICUM L.

Pedaliaceae

Sesame, (G) Sesam, (F) sésame, (I) sesamo

Sesame, which has been cultivated from ancient times, comes originally from lands on either side of the Indian Ocean, Africa, and India; the phrase from *The Thousand and One Nights* – "Open Sesame" – is associated with the rich seed content of the plant capsule. It is an annual species with a stem up to 6½ ft (2 m) tall, and opposite, oval leaves. At the leaf axils are one or three campanulate flowers with a white or pink corolla and five lobes at the claw. The superior ovary produces a quadrilocular capsule ½–1 in (1–3 cm) long, which opens at the apex. The seeds are small, oval, and flattened.

The cultivated plant is found in warm, dry regions. It is grown in India, China, Sudan, and Mexico; in Egypt sesame is regarded as a cereal rather than an oil-bearing species. Its seeds, which are also called benne seeds, are used for bread and pastries, as a spice, and as a medicinal substance. They contain fatty oils (50 percent), proteins (30 percent) and starch. The seeds are exported to the West where large quantities are utilized in the manufacture of margarine.

The presence of various principles (sesamin and sesamol) gives the oil, rich in unsaturated oils, an anti-oxidant property. The oilcakes that are the residue of the pressing are also particularly rich in protein and used as cattle feed.

132 SMYRNIUM OLUSATRUM L.

Umbelliferae

Alexanders, (G) Pferdeeppich, (F) ombrelle jaune, (I) macerone, smirnio

According to Pliny, the name *smyrnion* indicates a plant that smells of myrrh (Greek *smyrna*); *olusatrum* means black (*ater*) cabbage (*holus*). Originally from the Mediterranean area, the plant is cultivated in temperate countries as an aromatic herb and vegetable, particularly in northern Europe. It has become naturalized over much of Britain and grows in shady places and makes a good pot plant. The medieval name was *Petroselinum alexandrinum*, hence the English name. A biennial or perennial umbellifer, it bears a slight resemblance to angelica or lovage, with large, thick ternate leaves, glossy and aromatic, and oval, tooth-edged leaflets covered by large sheaths. The umbels of yellow flowers, often so full of nectar that they glisten, appear in spring; the mericarps are dark and grooved. They are sown in a seed bed and the seedlings transplanted outside in the summer, their scented leaves ready for use the following year. All parts of the plant are utilized for their aromatic content and are an especially good accompaniment to fish dishes and soups. The leaves are also used, after being blanched, like asparagus; the inflorescences, when in bud, can be served in salads or, when in flower, breaded and fried. The seeds can be used for seasoning. Because of its aromatic qualities it can serve as a substitute for celery. The roots, too, can be eaten, like those of other umbellifers.

133 STYRAX OFFICINALIS L.

Styracaceae

Storax, (G) Storax, (F) styrax, (I) storace

The plant gets its name from the agreeably perfumed gum resin storax, which seeps from cuts made in the bark. The tree, found in eastern Mediterranean regions, is small and highly valued for ornamental purposes, with a spherical crown, alternate short-stalked leaves, ovate and downy underneath. The few flowers (3–6) are in racemes, with a white sympetalous corolla, divided into numerous laciniae. The fruits are aromatic drupes. The resinous, sweet-smelling balsam smells somewhat like vanilla, and this furnishes the solid storax. The resin benzoin is obtained from the bark of various trees in southern Asia, notably the Thai benzoin (*S. tonkinensis*), in the form of yellow-brown tears or gray-brown amygdaloids, and the Sumatra benzoin (*S. benzoin* Dryand.), which produces gray-brown almonds. Benzoin is used in cosmetics for manufacturing soaps and as a fixative in perfumes. It is also used in confectionery.

Liquid storax is produced from the sweet gum (*Liquidambar styraciflua* L.), of the family Hamamelidaceae, and has similar uses to solid storax. This big, beautiful tree grows from New England south to Central America (in Guatemala it forms whole forests). It possesses pockets of oleoresin which is collected by making incisions in the bark. The species *L. orientalis* Mill. grows wild in Asia Minor, and the balsam that seeps from cuts in the bark is gathered in special containers.

134 TANACETUM PARTHENIUM (L.) C. H. Schultz
Chrysanthemum parthenium (L.) Bernh.
Compositae
Feverfew, (G) Mutterkraut, (F) grande camomille, (I) erba madre, camomilla grande

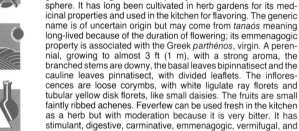

Originally from the Balkan peninsula and western Asia, the herb grows wild, though not too frequently, all over the northern hemisphere. It has long been cultivated in herb gardens for its medicinal properties and used in the kitchen for flavoring. The generic name is of uncertain origin but may come from *tanaós* meaning long-lived because of the duration of flowering; its emmenagogic property is associated with the Greek *parthénos*, virgin. A perennial, growing to almost 3 ft (1 m), with a strong aroma, the branched stems are downy, the basal leaves bipinnatisect and the cauline leaves pinnatisect, with divided leaflets. The inflorescences are loose corymbs, with white ligulate ray florets and tubular yellow disk florets, like small daisies. The fruits are small faintly ribbed achenes. Feverfew can be used fresh in the kitchen as a herb but with moderation because it is very bitter. It has stimulant, digestive, carminative, emmenagogic, vermifugal, and insectifugal properties.

Costmary or alecost (*Tanacetum balsamita* L.) has entire leaves, finely toothed and of leathery texture, the basal leaves petiolate, the smaller cauline leaves sessile. The corymbs bear small yellowish flower heads, all tubular. It is a bitter herb, with a pleasant, penetrating odor, long cultivated for medicinal and kitchen use. The specific name refers to its balsamic, preservative, and antiseptic properties.

---

135 TANACETUM VULGARE L.
Chrysanthemum vulgare (L.) Bernh.
Compositae
Tansy, (G) Rainfarn, (F) tanaisie, (I) tanaceto

At one time the genus *Tanacetum* was included in *Chrysanthemum*, because of the golden color of the flowers. Tansy, like costmary, has tubular yellow flowers but without ligulate florets, so that the heads look like golden buttons. Probably of Asiatic origin, the species was introduced to Europe and cultivated for its medicinal properties, growing wild on river banks, in hedgerows, and on waste ground. A perennial herb, over 3 ft (1 m) tall, the stem is erect and ridged, the leaves characteristically pinnate, petiolate, with lanceolate segments, uniformly toothed. The flower heads ½ in (1 cm) across, the centers indented, arranged in broad corymbs that are cut when flowering commences and can be kept dried; in fact the old name of the plant, *athanasia*, means immortal. The fruits are short, ridged achenes. Tansy is propagated by clump division and also from seed in a seed bed, with subsequent transplanting.

The flowering herb contains an essential oil with thujone, tannins, bitter substances, and resins. Because of the high content of thujone, tansy can be used only in moderate quantities, if at all, for seasoning. The flower extract serves as a flavor corrective in the liquor industry; and in perfumery, although rarely, it may be an ingredient for highly-prized scents. It is very effective against insects in the home and was once used as an insecticide; when grown in orchards it wards off aphids and other parasites.

136 **TARAXACUM OFFICINALE** Weber

Compositae
Dandelion, (G) Löwenzahn, (F) pissenlit, (I) tarassaco, sof-
fione

The dandelion is found more or less everywhere and is a very
common composite of fields, meadows, lawns, paths, and wasteland. The generic name probably derives from the Persian word
tharakhachakon, bitter herb; the genus contains a large number of
species that look very much alike and are thus hard to identify. A
perennial, without visible stem, it has a strong, fleshy, whitish tap-
root surrounded by a rosette of leaves which vary in form, usually
runcinate or dentate, with a conspicuous central vein, sometimes
reddish. The large solitary flower heads are on a hollow scape, and
all the florets are ligulate and bright yellow. The tapering
brown achenes bear a white umbel-like pappus.

The root contains inulin and the whole plant exudes a white
latex with bitter principles; the green leaves are rich in vitamin A
and mineral salts.

The dandelion is generally picked wild but in some cases it is
cultivated, mainly for its roots. These are harvested in autumn
before the vegetative rest period, and used, roasted, and ground,
as a coffee substitute, like chicory. The young leaves, gathered in
spring, make an excellent salad, either cooked or raw, with a
pleasantly bitter taste. The flower buds can be pickled like capers
and used for seasoning other foods. The dandelion has bitter,
cholagogic, digestive, depurative, and diuretic properties. Roots
and leaves constitute a brown dye.

---

137 **THEOBROMA CACAO** L.

Sterculiaceae
Cocoa, cacao, chocolate, (G) Kakaobaum, (F) cacaotier,
(I) cacao

Cocoa came originally from Central and South America and was
cultivated by the Mayas. In pre-Columbian civilizations it was a
very important food and drink, given its high energy content. The
regard in which it was held is reflected in the generic name which
means "food of the gods," while the specific name is derived from
the Aztec word *kakawa*. Nowadays it is cultivated in equatorial
lands, the major producers being the Ivory Coast, Brazil, Ghana,
and Malaysia.

This small evergreen tree of the rainforest grows to a height of
16–20 ft (5–6 m), bearing oval petiolate leaves. The small,
pentamerous whitish flowers are borne in clusters directly on the
trunk or branches. The fruit, green, red or yellow, is a berry of 8 in
(20 cm), longitudinally ridged, of a fibrous texture outside, fleshy
inside, with many large lenticular seeds.

The seeds are extracted from the fruits after the rind and pulp
are removed for fermentation; this process gives them a richer
aroma and also releases alcoholic substances from the pulp. The
seeds, heat-dried and ground, yield the basic paste, extremely
rich in fats, which are partly separated by pressing (cocoa butter),
making it more suitable for grinding (cocoa powder); the cocoa
butter, with milk and sugar, gives white chocolate. Cocoa contains
theobromine, caffeine, proteins, sugars, and fats. It is used as an
energy food, as a hot drink, and in candies, cakes, cookies,
liquors, etc.

138 THYMUS VULGARIS L.

Labiatae
Thyme, (G) Thymian, (F) thym, (I) timo

Thyme is a prostrate shrub of modest size, growing wild in dry areas, notably the scrub of the western Mediterranean. The genus contains species that are difficult to identify because they all look very similar. It has woody main stems, more or less creeping, with terminal spikes of leafy branches. The ½-in (1-cm) leaves are gray underneath and lanceolate; the flowers, with a pale pink 2-lipped corolla, produce a fruit of 4 nutlets. The plant is commonly grown in herb gardens, sown in seed beds, on sandy soil, and then transplanted. In addition to its use as a herb, thyme makes an attractive border for the rockery. The whole plant contains aromatic substances, an essential oil composed of thymol, cymol, carvacrol, and others. Thymol has a marked antiseptic action. The fresh or dried leaves, whole or chopped, are used in the kitchen with meat, fish, sauces, and mushrooms. The fresh parts also serve to flavor salads, cheeses, and aromatized salt; and the herb has many other uses in the food, liquor, cosmetic, and pharmaceutical industries. In perfumery, especially, it is an ingredient for soaps, bath salts and foams, and toothpastes. In addition to being antiseptic, it has tonic, digestive, and carminative properties.

Related species have similar uses: wild thyme (*T. serpyllum* L.) is one of the commonest wild herbs found in dry areas, lemon thyme (*T. x citriodorus* Schreb.) is a hybrid with a strong lemony scent; and caraway thyme (*T. herba-barona*), originally from Corsica and Sardinia, smells of caraway.

---

139 TILIA CORDATA Mill.

Tiliaceae
Small-leaved linden or lime, (G) Winterlinde, (F) tilleul, (I) tiglio

The linden or common lime is a tree that grows from Europe to the Caucasus. It bears the old name used by the Romans which may be derived from the Greek *ptilon*, wing, because of the characteristic winged bract which supports the inflorescence. It has an oval crown, with a dark gray trunk, cordate leaves with an asymmetric base, finely toothed and sharply pointed. The flowers, formed of five ivory white petals and numerous stamens, are in drooping fascicles, on a long peduncle joined to a membranous bract, free at the tip. The fruits are pointed nuts. In May–June the scented flowers appear, visited by swarms of insects intent on sipping their nectar. Bees, in fact, produce a delicately aromatic honey from this tree.

The flowers, harvested with the bracts and dried in the shade in small quantities to prevent fermenting and turning dark, are the parts commonly used. An infusion can be made from them, an excellent aromatic tea, pleasant-tasting and thirst-quenching; it also has sedative, anti-spasmodic, hypotensive, and sudoriferous properties. The flowers, rich in mucilage and tannins, are utilized in cosmetics for decongestive and anti-wrinkle poultices. Wild species include the large-leaved linden or lime (*T. platyphyllos* Scop.); and among the cultivated species, used as ornamental subjects for parks and roads in town and countryside, are the silver linden (*T. tomentosa* Moench.), with thickly pubescent gray leaves, and the American linden (*T. americana* L.) with large leaves, up to 8 in (20 cm) wide.

140 TRIGONELLA FOENUM-GRAECUM L.

Leguminosae
Fenugreek, (G) Bockschornklee, (F) fénugrek, (I) trigonella

The trifoliolate leaves, the leaflets of which are three-cornered, probably explain the name of the genus, while the specific name, meaning "Greek hay," may be derived from the fact that in ancient times the Greeks used the plant as fodder. The species is found all over the Mediterranean region, in southern Asia (where it may have originated), and in the Horn of Africa. Fenugreek is cultivated from Morocco to Tunisia as forage exclusively for horses; it cannot be used for feeding milk cattle because the scent of the hay passes into the milk itself. It is an annual, with a much-branched stem up to 20 in (50 cm) tall, and leaves like those of the medicinal herb. The flowers, in the leaf axils, are ½–1 in (1–2 cm), sessile, with a papilionate yellow-violet corolla. The fruit is a berry of about 4 in (10 cm) which contains ten large, rough, light brown seeds, rhomboidal in shape. They are very coriaceous, but since they contain a high quantity of pectin they swell up in water; they give out an aromatic odor and have a bitter flavor. The legumes are harvested before the full ripening of the seeds, which contain the alkaloid trigonellin and traces of ethereal oils. Extracts from the seeds have a typically sweet, spicy taste and are used in the United States for flavoring syrups and sauces; they also season pipe tobaccos. The seeds have galactogenic and anthelminthic properties; the ancients believed them to be aphrodisiac.

The leaves of *T. caerulea* (L.) Ser. (blue melilot) are used for flavoring fresh cheeses.

141 TROPAEOLUM MAJUS L.

Tropaeolaceae
Nasturtium, (G) Kapuzinerkresse, (F) capucine, (I) cappuccina, nasturzio, tropeolo

The shape of the leaves, round and glabrous, recall the shield on which the ancients placed the victors' trophies (*trópalon*) and accounts for the generic name. A plant of South American origin (Peru), it is commonly cultivated for ornament for the beauty of its flowers and leaves, and for its drooping habit. The "hooded" flowers bloom from spring to late autumn, with the calyx prolonged into a slender spur and a corolla whose separate petals each have a long claw, orange, flushed yellow or crimson. The plant is of creeping habit with fleshy, glaucous stems to which are attached umbels of alternate, erect leaves. The fruit has a spongy consistency and when ripe splits into its three formative carpels, thus releasing the three seeds.

These unripe fruits, together with the flower buds, can be used for preparing pickles; their sharp flavor is due to compounds similar to mustard-oils, gluctropeolin, which in the presence of the specific enzyme releases glucose and isothiocyanate of benzyl. The chopped leaves may garnish mixed vegetables and their taste is similar to that of rocket or cress. It has stimulant, antiseptic, diuretic, and antiscorbutic properties.

Commonly grown for ornament, nasturtium seeds are sown in spring in cool, fertile soil, in a position sheltered from wind and too much sun; they need regular and frequent watering.

142 TUBER MAGNATUM (Pico) Vitt.
Tuberaceae
Truffle, (G) Truffel, (F) truffe, (I) tartufo d'Alba

The genus *Tuber*, from the Latin name of the fungus, is probably associated etymologically with the Latin *tumidus*, swelling, because of the round shape of the carpophore. The truffles are the fruiting body of underground fungi, closely linked in mycorrhizal symbiosis with forest trees, especially deciduous species. Outwardly it resembles a tuber of a phanerogam; a cortical layer (peridium) encloses a streaked and variegated inner mass which, on microscopic examination, is shown to be the structure that bears the ascus and its sexual spores.

Of especial value among the representatives of the family Tuberaceae are the white truffle (*Tuber magnatum*) and the black truffle (*T. melanosporum* Vitt.). Both produce carpophores of considerable dimensions, the white with a smooth surface, the flesh pink veined with white, and the black with a rough surface, brown-fleshed veined with white. With their penetrating, peppery aroma, they are used grated or sliced for seasoning various dishes.

Species related to the black truffle are *T. brumale* Vit., *T. aestivum* Vitt., *T. mesentericum* Vitt. and *T. moschatum* De Ferry. Truffles, highly prized, are picked wild; and nowadays, as a result of farming and forestry practice, the most valued species are grown in reforested plantations. The white truffle lives in symbiosis with white and black poplars, pubescent oaks, lindens (limes), and willows; the black truffle with oaks, particularly the pubescent species, hazel, hornbeam, and pines.

---

143 TUSSILAGO FARFARA L.
Compositae
Coltsfoot, (G) Huflattich, (F) tussilage, (I) farfaraccio

The generic name reflects the properties this plant possesses in curing coughs; it has been called *farfara* since antiquity. Growing in all the temperate areas of Europe, it is found mainly on wet, compact, clay soil, in ditches, by roadsides, on embankments, dunes, and waste ground in general. It is a perennial rhizomatous plant which flowers very early, almost before winter is over. The showy golden-yellow flower heads, formed of ligulate ray florets and tubular central florets, are borne on a reddish stem, covered only by scales. The leaves, which sprout after flowering, have a long, sturdy stalk, a kidney-shaped base and a rounded blade with irregularly toothed margins; they are white and downy below, gray-green above, and eventually grow to a considerable size, up to 12 in (30 in) across. The fruits are achenes furnished with a pappus. The plant is not cultivated and if need be is harvested wild. The flower heads, some of them still closed to avoid fruiting, are picked at the end of February; the leaves are collected in May–June.

These parts are used for their expectorant, bechic and emollient properties to cure bronchial disorders. They contain mucilage, tannins, inulin, and resin. The young leaves are edible raw; the adult leaves, dried, burned and reduced to ashes can be utilized as a salt substitute.

The species of the genus *Petasites* have similar properties and uses.

144 VANILLA PLANIFOLIA Andr.

Vanilla fragrans Ames
Orchidaceae
Vanilla, (G) echte Vanille, (F) vanille, (I) vaniglia

Vanilla comes originally from Central America, where it grows wild on the fringes of the Mexican tropical forests; nowadays, however, it is cultivated mainly in Indonesia, the Comoro Islands and Réunion. This region produces about 80 percent of the world output (2,200 tons of commercial product, known as Bourbon vanilla, in 1978) and the three countries have been joined in the so-called "vanilla alliance" since 1964. Other less important producing countries are China, Uganda, and Mexico.

Vanilla is a liana, furnished with voluble, thick, fleshy green stems, and long elliptical, sessile, leathery leaves. The small greenish flowers appear in clusters at the leaf axils. They open for only a few hours in the morning and are then visited by hummingbirds for pollination; the birds carry the pollen, which sticks to their beaks, from one flower to another. If fertilization fails to occur, the flowers drop; but if it takes place, fruits develop within four weeks. The fruits are yellow-green pods, incorrectly called berries, up to 12 in (30 cm) long, that contain vast numbers of tiny seeds (up to 90,000); they ripen six months after fertilization.

When the plant is cultivated, the lianas are supported by poles or stakes, and pollination is done by hand (in Asia there are no hummingbirds). The pods are harvested before they are fully ripe. Commercial vanilla is obtained by special treatment of the fruits; they are immersed in hot steam at 160°F (70°C) so as to stop the vital activity of the tissues. A period of fermentation then follows which may last for up to four weeks, as a result of which the surface of the fruit is covered with crystals, glucose, and vanillin (up to 3 percent for each fruit), which are derived from glucovanillin. The fruits are black, due to the oxidizations from the fermentation process, but remain soft and flexible.

Vanilla was monopolized by Mexico until 1800; and from English herbal collections it would appear that some specimens were brought first to Antwerp and then to Paris in 1817. The Dutch, in 1819, established the first vanilla plantation in Java, and the French, three years later, in Réunion; but because no usable fruits were produced for lack of pollinators, in 1841 manual pollination was introduced, ending the Mexican monopoly.

The aroma of natural vanilla is more full than that of synthetic vanilla (obtained chemically from lignin and other products), inasmuch as the aromatic compounds include more than 35 components. Vanilla is widely used in the food industry and is the principal flavoring agent of chocolate; vanilla sugar is used in the kitchen for flavoring sweets. In the liquor trade it is an ingredient for aromatic drinks, and in cosmetics it is used in the manufacture of certain scents and face powders.

Other species of vanilla are *V. pompona* Scheide, from the West Indies and Mexico, and *V. tahitiensis*, from Polynesia, sought mainly by the North American perfumery trade for its particular scent of heliotrope (piperonal). A preparation known as salep is obtained, in western Asia, eastern and central-northern Europe, from the tubers of certain wild orchids, especially of the genus *Orchis*. The tubers, dried and powdered, boiled in water and honey, are used for a drink with reputed energetic, aphrodisiac, and medicinal properties.

145 VERONICA OFFICINALIS L.

Scrophulariaceae

Speedwell, (G) Ehrenpreis, (F) thé d'Europe, (I) tè svizzero

The generic name, from *verus-unicus*, means real and unique and alludes to the properties of this plant. The plant grows on acid soil in mountain regions of eastern North America, Asia, and Europe. It is a perennial, with stems that creep along the ground, climbing where necessary, and hairy all over. The leaves are entire, sessile, opposite, and elliptical, with finely toothed margins. The flowers, in spikes, are blue or pink. The zygomorphous corolla forms a short tube that bears four deeply divided lobes. The fruit is a heart-shaped capsule. The plant, useful as ornamental ground cover in gardens, is cultivated for its medicinal and aromatic properties. It is sown in a seed bed in March, then transplanted in rows; because the seeds are very delicate, they are mixed with sand. It multiplies more easily by clump division in May. Organic feeding and hoeing for weed control are necessary.

The aerial parts are harvested during flowering and immediately dried to prevent blackening as a result of fermentation. Speedwell has sudorific properties and also counters inflammation in bronchial disorders; moreover, by reason of bitter principles, it is a stimulant and digestive. It is therefore also used in infusions, known variously as Swiss tea or European tea.

146 VETIVERIA ZIZANIOIDES Stapf.

Andropogon muricatus Tetz.

Gramineae

Vetiver, (G) Vetiver, (F) vétiver, (I) vetiver

This grass from the tropical lands of Asia (India, Indonesia, Sri Lanka, and the Philippines), East Africa, and Central America, grows wild but is widely cultivated for its long rhizomatous roots, which contain odorous principles and are interwoven in matting to perfume rooms.

Vetiver is grown mainly in Java, on Réunion, in the Seychelles, and Haiti which has become a major producer of the essence. Réunion produces more than 35 tons annually of essential oil, known as Bourbon vetiver. Other producing countries are Angola, Zaire, India, New Guinea, and Brazil.

The roots are harvested from June to November, washed and partially dried in the sun; extraction is then carried out by steam.

The essence is frequently used for cosmetics, perfumes, and soaps, the Java variety in particular for oriental-type, musky, woody compositions; its qualities also make it an effective fixative.

147 VIOLA ODORATA L.

Violaceae

Sweet violet, (G) Veilchen, (F) violette, (I) violetta

The scientific name refers to the visual and olfactory elements associated with the plant. It is a perennial species that grows wild in hedgerows and thickets, putting out lateral rooting stolons. The leaves, in rosettes, are petiolate and heart-shaped. The flowers, with a characteristic scent, are borne separately on delicate stems; the corollas are bilaterally symmetrical, formed of five dark violet petals with a nectar-bearing spur. The fruits are capsules.

There are numerous varieties of violet but the essence is extracted from the Parma and Victoria varieties, chiefly from the leaves, which are picked by hand to obtain the concrete and the absolute. The flowers can be crystallized and used to decorate confectionery. The absolute of the leaves is used in perfumery for delicate compositions. The liquid extracts from the flowers and roots have expectorant and emollient properties.

Cultivated as an ornamental, the pansy (*V. tricolor* L. var. *arvensis* Murro) is an annual species with pinnatisect leaves and corollas in yellow, white, and violet. It is sown outside in spring, the tiny seeds mixed with sand; the whole plants are harvested when in flower; they contain saponin, mucilage, tannins, and flavones, used mainly for herbal purposes.

148 ZINGIBER OFFICINALE Rosc.

Zingiberaceae

Ginger, (G) Ingwer, (F) gingembre, (I) zenzero

The name of the genus is derived from the term used in India. The plant is a monocotyledonous perennial herb, originally from southern Asia, where it has been cultivated from time immemorial and is no longer found in the wild state. It is a rhizomatous species that produces an aerial part of shrubby appearance, with lanceolate leaves and spikes of yellow flowers with purple claws, borne on stems covered only by bracts, shorter than the leaves. It is propagated easily by chopping up the branched, gnarled rhizomes, which are harvested after the flowering period; the roots are boiled in water and dried in the sun to prevent fermentation.

The rhizomes, if they still have the outer covering, constitute black ginger; if peeled or decorticated and often calcinated, they constitute white ginger. They both contain many constituents that give out a perfume which is sweet (zingiberol) with a sharp, penetrating and refreshing taste (zingiberene, zingerone, and gingerol). The powdered rhizomes are used in foods and to flavor jams, sweets, and ginger ale, and as ingredients for curry. The immature and thus less pungent rhizomes can also be made into crystallized ginger.

Ginger oil, obtained by distilling fresh ginger, is utilized in the liquor industry; and in the cosmetics trade it is used in the preparation of oriental and floral scents.

GLOSSARY

absolute   Raw material from which perfumes are made, obtained by melting the concrete (q.v.) in ethyl alcohol and then by distillation.

achene   Dry indehiscent fruit containing a single seed.

alternate   Arrangement of leaves or branches that are attached at different heights on either side of the stem.

anthelmintic   Expelling intestinal worms.

antiseptic   Destroying micro-organisms that cause septic disease.

aperient   Acting as a mild laxative.

aril   Fleshy involucre covering the seed.

axil   The point at which a branch or leaf stalk diverges from the stem.

balsamic   Aromatic, curing lung, skin, and mucous inflammations.

bechic   Soothing coughs and throat irritations.

bilobate   Plant organ divided into two lobes.

bipinnate   Doubly pinnate, as of a leaf with a central axis and lateral axes with leaflets attached.

bract   Modified leaf, usually with a protective function.

carminative   Stimulating the expulsion of intestinal gases.

cauline   Pertaining to the stem.

choleretic   Inducing the flow of bile.

concrete   Product obtained by extraction of solvents from non-resinous plants and then by evaporation of the solvents themselves, producing a solid pasty mass.

cordate   Heart-shaped.

corolla   The petals collectively; they are usually conspicuously colored for attracting insects.

corymb   Flat-topped flower cluster.

cultivar   Horticulturally produced variety of a plant.

deciduous   A plant that loses parts such as leaves at the beginning of the cold season.

decoction   Product obtained by treating the dried or fresh vegetal parts with water and bringing it to boiling point for a determined time.

dehiscent   Opening spontaneously to release seeds or pollen.

dentate   Toothed, as of leaf margins.

depurative   Purifying or cleansing agent.

diaphoretic   Inducing perspiration.

dioecious   Plant in which the male and female elements are borne by different individuals of the same species.

distillate   Product obtained from the condensation of vapors in distillation.

diuretic   Increasing the flow of urine.

drupe   Pulpy fruit with hard internal shell or "stone," usually enclosing a seed; for example, a peach.

emetic   Provoking vomiting.

emmenagogic   Stimulating the menstrual flow.

emollient   Softens the skin.

enfleurage   Method of extracting odorous principles from plants, placing the parts to be used (petals, etc.) in a thin layer on fat.

eupeptic   Aiding digestion.

extract   Concentrated product, obtained by treating plant material with a solvent.

febrifugal   Dispelling or reducing fever.

fixative   Substance that limits evaporation of the volatile components of perfumes.

galactogenic   Promoting the production of milk.

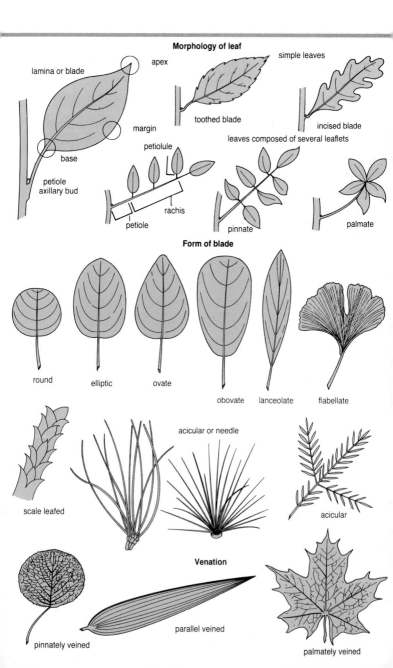

Morphology of leaf

lamina or blade

apex

simple leaves

toothed blade

incised blade

margin

base

petiolule

leaves composed of several leaflets

petiole
axillary bud

petiole

rachis

pinnate

palmate

Form of blade

round

elliptic

ovate

obovate

lanceolate

flabellate

scale leafed

acicular or needle

acicular

Venation

pinnately veined

parallel veined

palmately veined

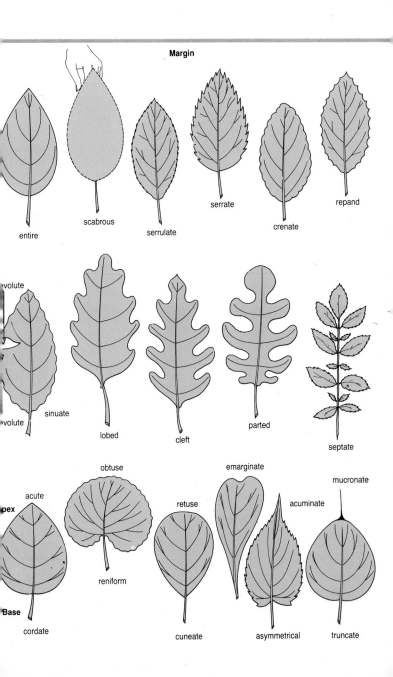

Margin

entire

scabrous

serrulate

serrate

crenate

repand

volute

volute

sinuate

lobed

cleft

parted

septate

pex

acute

obtuse

reniform

retuse

emarginate

acuminate

mucronate

Base

cordate

cuneate

asymmetrical

truncate

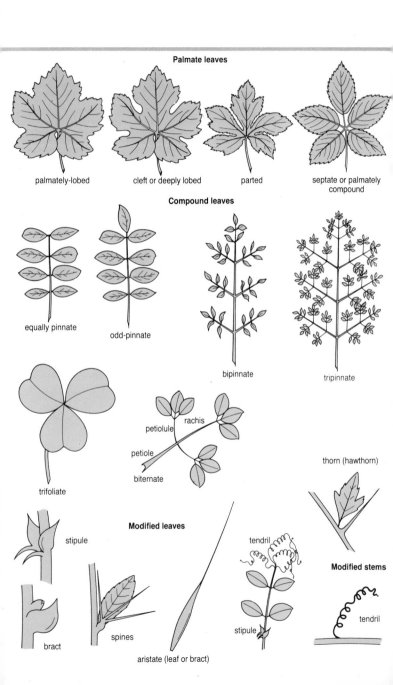

Palmate leaves

palmately-lobed

cleft or deeply lobed

parted

septate or palmately compound

Compound leaves

equally pinnate

odd-pinnate

bipinnate

tripinnate

trifoliate

petiolule

rachis

petiole

biternate

thorn (hawthorn)

Modified leaves

stipule

bract

spines

aristate (leaf or bract)

tendril

stipule

Modified stems

tendril

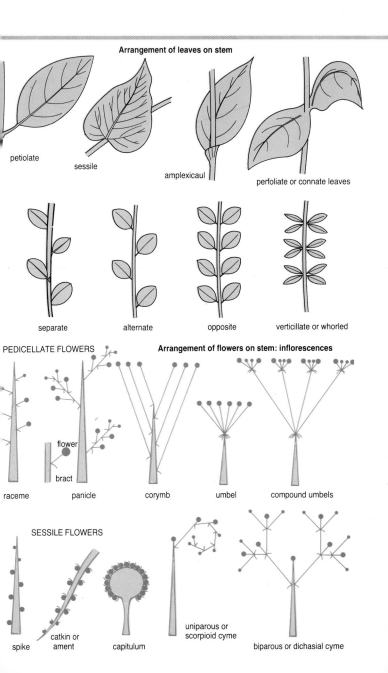

Arrangement of leaves on stem

petiolate

sessile

amplexicaul

perfoliate or connate leaves

separate

alternate

opposite

verticillate or whorled

PEDICELLATE FLOWERS

Arrangement of flowers on stem: inflorescences

flower

bract

raceme

panicle

corymb

umbel

compound umbels

SESSILE FLOWERS

spike

catkin or ament

capitulum

uniparous or scorpioid cyme

biparous or dichasial cyme

Flower

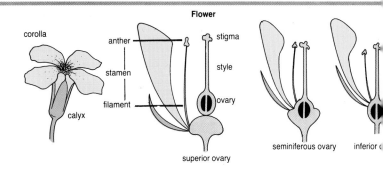

corolla

calyx

anther
stamen
filament

stigma
style
ovary

superior ovary

seminiferous ovary

inferior ovary

Floral symmetery

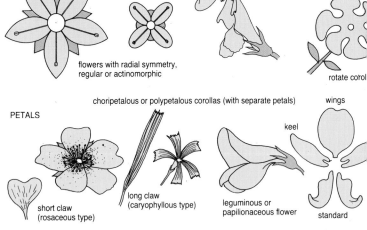

flowers with radial symmetry,
regular or actinomorphic

zygomorphic flowers, with only
one symmetrical plane

rotate corolla

choripetalous or polypetalous corollas (with separate petals)

PETALS

short claw
(rosaceous type)

long claw
(caryophyllous type)

leguminous or
papilionaceous flower

wings

keel

standard

sympetalous or gamopetalous corollas (with united petals)

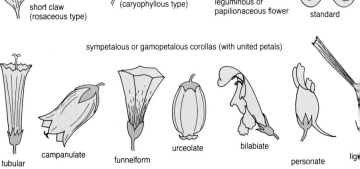

tubular

campanulate

funnelform

urceolate

bilabiate

personate

ligulate

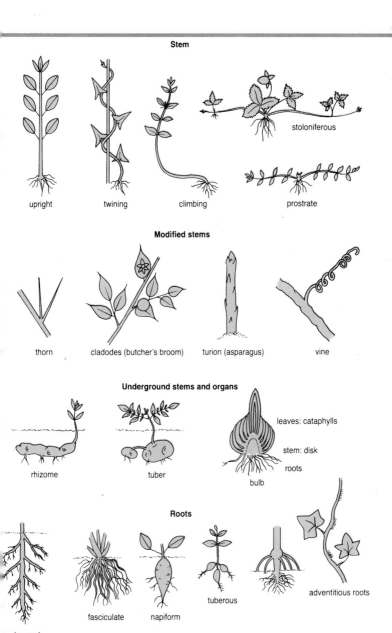

Stem

upright   twining   climbing   stoloniferous   prostrate

Modified stems

thorn   cladodes (butcher's broom)   turion (asparagus)   vine

Underground stems and organs

rhizome   tuber

leaves: cataphylls

stem: disk

roots

bulb

Roots

tap-root   fasciculate   napiform   tuberous   adventitious roots

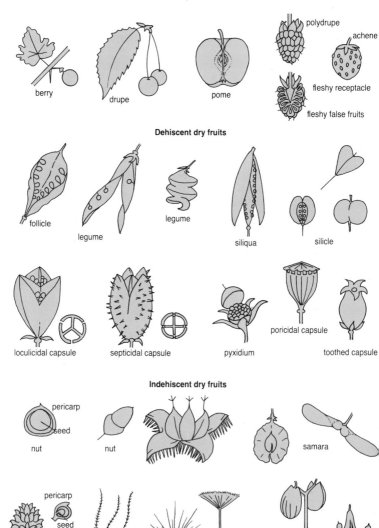

Fleshy fruits

berry

drupe

pome

polydrupe

achene

fleshy receptacle

fleshy false fruits

Dehiscent dry fruits

follicle

legume

legume

legume

siliqua

silicle

loculicidal capsule

septicidal capsule

pyxidium

poricidal capsule

toothed capsule

Indehiscent dry fruits

pericarp

seed

nut

nut

samara

pericarp

seed

achene

polyachene

achenes

achenes with pappus

schizocarps

fruits which split into
several parts

glucoside One of a group of compounds yielding glucose or other substance when treated with a dilute acid or when decomposed by an enzyme.

imparipinnate A pinnate leaf with a terminal leaflet.

inflorescence Flowering part of a plant, on which individual flowers are arranged in spikes, racemes, corymbs, panicles, etc.

infusion Solution obtained by pouring partly boiling water (or other solvent) over dried or fresh parts of a plant.

laciniate Cut into narrow, irregular lobes; jagged.

lanceolate Lance-shaped.

latex Opaque or milky liquid exuded by certain plants.

leaflet Part of a compound leaf.

ligulate Strap-shaped.

lobe Division of a leaf or petal.

lyrate Divided transversally into several lobes; lyre-shaped.

macerate Product obtained by contact between a solvent (water, alcohol, fat) and plant parts used, for a certain time and generally at room temperature.

melliferous Producing honey.

mericarp Partial fruit containing a single seed.

monoecious Plant that bears stamens and pistils on different flowers of same individual.

oleoresin Natural mixture of an essential oil and a resin.

opposite Arrangement of leaves or branches at the same level on opposite sides of the axis, sprouting from a single node.

panicle Compound inflorescence structure of many flowers on short stalks.

pericarp Part of fruit covering the seeds.

petiole Stalk supporting a leaf.

pinnate Compound leaf with leaflets on either side of the stalk; also a simple leaf with veins on either side of the leaf stalk.

pistil Female organ of reproduction in a flower. It consists of the ovary, style, and stigma (q.v.).

pomade Product obtained by enfleurage or maceration, not distillable by heating the components.

pubescent Covered with tiny hairs.

raceme Simple inflorescence bearing flowers on an elongated axis.

resinoid Product consisting of substances secreted or exuded by plants as balsams, gum resins, oleoresins, and resins.

rhizome Fleshy underground stem that develops horizontally; for example, an iris root stock.

rubefacient Provoking blushing.

schizocarp A fruit that splits into 1-seeded portions (mericarps).

spadix Inflorescence enfolded by a spathe (q.v.); for example, the "jack" in a jack-in-the-pulpit.

spasmolytic Relieving spasms or convulsions.

spathe Transformed leaf enclosing a spadix (q.v.); for example, the "pulpit" in a jack-in-the-pulpit.

spike Inflorescence consisting of an elongated main axis with sessile flowers.

stamen Male flower organ, consisting of filament and anther, that produces pollen.

stigma Enlarged terminal part of pistil (q.v.) on which pollen is deposited.

sudorific Inducing perspiration.

tannin Phenolic compounds present in wood, bark, leaves, and fruits, with astringent, tanning properties.

terminal Close to the tip, as of a leaf or branch.

tincture Product obtained by maceration or percolation of plant material with alcohol.

tunic Bract enfolding a bulb.

vermifugal Expelling intestinal worms or parasites.

vulnerary With scar-forming properties.

BIBLIOGRAPHY

APICIUS *The First Century AD Roman Cookery Book* (translated by B. Flower & E. Rosenbaum) Harrap, London, 1974

BOROS, G. *Unsere Küchen und Gewürzkraüter* Ulmer, Stuttgart, 1981

BOXER, A., BACK, P. *The Herb Book* Octopus, London, 1980

BREMNESS, L. *The Complete Book of Herbs* Dorling Kindersley, London, 1988

CATIZIONE, P., MAROTTI, M., TODERI, G., TÉTÉNYI, P. *Piante medicinali e aromatiche* Patron, Bologna, 1986

CLARKSON, R. E. *Herbs and Savoury Seeds* Constable, London, 1972

COUPLAN, F. *Le régal végétal I, II* Debard, Paris, 1983

ENCKE, F., BUCHHEIM, G., SEYBOLD, S. *Zander, Handwörterbuch der Pflanzennamen* Ulmer, Stuttgart, 1984

FENAROLI, G. *Sostanze aromatiche naturali* Hoepli, Milan, 1963

GARLAND, S. *The Herb and Spice Book* Windward, London, 1979

GERARD, J. *Gerard's Herbal* (1636) Minerva, London, 1974

GRIGSON, G. *A Herbal of All Sorts* Phoenix House, London, 1959

HALL, D. *The Book of Herbs* Angus & Robertson, London, 1972

INGLIS, B. *Natural Medicine* Collins, London, 1979

LAGENHEIM, J.H., THIMANN, K.V. *Botany* J. Wiley & Sons, New York, 1982

LUGANI, V. *Coltivazione delle piante officinali* CLESAV, Milan, 1985

MABEY, R. *Food For Free* Fontana, London, 1975

MABEY, R. *Plants with a Purpose* Collins, London, 1977

MACLEOD, D. *A Book of Herbs* Duckworth, London, 1968

MAGHAMI, P. *Culture et cueillette des plantes médicinales* Hachette, Paris, 1979

ROHDE, ELEANOUR SINCLAIR *Shakespeare's Wild Flowers, Fairy Lore, Gardens, Herbs, Gatherers of Simples & Bee Lore* Medici, London, 1935

SANEKI, K. *The Book of Herbs* Chartwell, Secaucus, New Jersey, 1987

SIMMONS, A.G. *Herb Gardens of Delight* Clinton Press, USA, 1974

SIMONETTI, G., WATSCHINGER, M. *Guida al riconiscimento delle erbe di campi e prati* Mondadori, Milan, 1986

STOBART, T. *Herbs, Spices and Flavourings* Penguin, London, 1977

STODOLA, J., VOLAK, J. *The Illustrated Book of Herbs* Octopus, London, 1984

WEINER, M.A. *Earth Medicine – Earth Foods* Collier Macmillan, London, 1972

ZIELINSKI, Q.B. *Modern Systematic Pomology* Pomona Books, Rokton, Ontario, 1977

INDEX